David Miller, chief sports writer for *The Times*, played football for Cambridge University, British Universities, Pegasus and FA Amateur XIs, and was a member of the 1956 Olympic training squad. That year he joined *The Times* as a sports sub-editor, later moved to the *Daily Telegraph*, and was the *Sunday Telegraph*'s first soccer correspondent when it began publication in 1961. In 1973 he joined the *Express* and returned to *The Times* in 1983. He has reported seven World Cups, over 120 World Cup matches, and more than 300 international matches in forty countries, and has seen all the FA Cup Finals since 1952. He has covered four Olympic Games, reporting on most sports. This is his sixth soccer book.

He is married, with a grown-up daughter and a son, and his hobby is cruiser-sailing.

D0773780

Also by David Miller

Father of Football: The Story of Sir Matt Busby
World Cup 1970
World Cup 1974
The Argentina Story: World Cup 1978
Cup Magic
Running Free (with Sebastian Coe)

The World To Play For

Trevor Francis
with David Miller

GRANADA
London Toronto Sydney New York

Published by Granada Publishing Limited in 1983

ISBN 0 586 05974 1

First published in Great Britain by
Sidgwick and Jackson Limited 1982
Copyright © Trevor Francis and David Miller 1982, 1983

Granada Publishing Limited
Frogmore, St Albans, Herts AL2 2NF
and
36 Golden Square, London W1R 4AH
515 Madison Avenue, New York, NY 10022, USA
117 York Street, Sydney, NSW 2000, Australia
60 International Blvd, Rexdale, Ontario, R9W 6J2, Canada
61 Beach Road, Auckland, New Zealand

Printed and bound in Great Britain by
Collins, Glasgow
Set in Times

Granada ®
Granada Publishing ®

Contents

Publisher's Note

To differentiate between the authors, text by Trevor Francis appears within quotation marks.

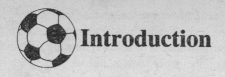 **Introduction**

The career of Trevor Francis has coincided with the era of greatest financial and tactical change in the history of the game. He was born in 1954, the year West Germany first won the World Cup, defeating Hungary against all expectation in Switzerland. By the time England won at Wembley in 1966 he was a schoolboy goal-scoring sensation in his home town of Plymouth, clearly destined to become one of the oustanding players of his generation. Yet, when he burst upon an unsuspecting public as a sixteen-year-old with Birmingham City, shortly after Brazil had triumphed for the third time in Mexico, the game was already a minefield in which there were fewer and fewer routes to fulfilment for brilliance such as his. The age of the star was in decline.

It says much for Francis's ability that he became, and remained, a star, in spite of defensive systems which intensified with every year. He was the most exciting player to emerge in England since Bobby Charlton was a boy; had he been born ten years ealier, his reflexes would probably have made him as prolific a scorer as Jimmy Greaves, but by the time he came to search for openings, the locks were as formidable as those at Alcatraz. There was not a manager who would not have bought him, nor a defence which did not fear him. It was a unanimous opinion that he would take his place as one of the most important England international players of the decade. Yet something went wrong.

It is difficult to pinpoint exactly what. There were

injuries, of course, at critical moments: the severing of a tendon behind the knee just after he had been selected for his first international senior squad in the autumn of 1974; the rupturing of an Achilles only weeks before the 1980 European Championship finals, when he seemed on the brink of fulfilling the highest expectations.

It did not help that England, going through a period of soul-searching mediocrity and twice failing to qualify for the finals of the World Cup, had a spell of four managers in three years. Most of all, perhaps, it was with hindsight unfortunate that the dice of life landed him at the start of his career with a club which, through the vagaries of management and directors, was unlikely ever to provide him with the most conspicuous stage for his talents. Because he was on the one hand by nature modest and undemonstrative, on the other the young hero of a big but essentially limited club, there was for some years neither the inclination nor the motive to leave. He was satisfied –and it is a virtue as well as a handicap – with less than he had the right to expect from his talent, so that by the time he finally sought to move, those precious years at the top were half run.

He reveals here, in our story of an eight-year span, almost by accident as it were, the most damning indictment of his time with Birmingham: that a mood pervaded the club in which losing did not seem to matter. Trevor is a sincere, thinking person, yet in an environment where he was constantly hailed as the hero, who could today criticize him for accepting in his early twenties the overall failure of the team, so long as he consistently delivered the goals? When you are already sitting above the clouds, why reach for the stars? Like George Best, though in a quite different way, he could have done with the advice of an older man. His father had no way of knowing that the club would ultimately fail his son. So for eight years his potential was being squandered, until he finally pushed

Birmingham into letting him go – and I say that as one who believes profoundly in the necessity of loyalty to the club. Yet Ron Greenwood knew the truth when he advised Trevor that, by his £1-million move to Nottingham Forest – the first such English fee – he would be bound to improve his game.

Of course, he was well paid, for Birmingham would not otherwise have been able to keep him; and by his moves to Forest, Manchester City and now Sampdoria in Italy, he has acquired money beyond the dreams of the son of a modest Gas Board employee. Therein lies the irony. The process of defensiveness and outright physical cheating which progressively made his job and that of other marksmen almost impossible, simultaneously raised the price on his head ever higher to almost absurd levels, such became the panic in the battle for success and, ultimately, survival among the clubs – a vicious circle of mutually destructive trends. By the time Trevor Francis and the £3-million Diego Maradona of Argentina reached the 1982 World Cup finals, there was now more space to manoeuvre inside the limousines they could each afford than there was when they played on the pitch! In football terms they were in danger of becoming, through no fault of their own, the richest men in the cemetery.

The pressures on everyone were intensified by television, to whom football had become a wanton harlot, selling itself voraciously, mindless of the consquences. We have attempted in this book not only to relate some of the events of the last few years and the influence upon them by leading personalities, within the range of Trevor's personal experience culminating with the World Cup in Spain, but to suggest ways in which the game can be saved from self-destruction. That this is a grave risk cannot be doubted after experiences both in England during recent years and in the World Cup of 1982.

As we sat writing after Italy's controversial victory, in

9

the soothing garden at the halcyon French Riviera retreat of Norman Gidney (Midlands businessman and friend of Trevor), we discussed among many things the usual 'World XI' beloved of armchair selectors after every tournament. I was momentarily snookered when another house guest asked me what Trevor would have to have done to be in my XI. The truth is, on reflection, that we will probably never know how good he might have been had he played for a sustained period in a successful team. If any of Bryan Robson's headers against West Germany in Madrid had gone in, and England had beaten France in the semi-final, might the quiet Devonian have been the hero of the final instead of Rossi, a man only recently reinstated after suspension for bribery? We shall never know.

What we do know is that throughout his career so far Francis has scored goals which electrified the crowds wherever he played; that he won a European Cup final and paved the way for another he then missed through injury; that he played with style and distinction and dignity and fairness; that what he has had to offer is what the crowds *really* want to see; that unless he and his like are protected in the future from the forces of violence and cynicism, this game of beauty and passions will not survive. I would always want men with the qualities that Trevor Francis has represented to be in my XI.

David Miller
September 1982

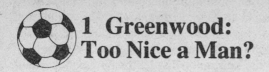

1 Greenwood: Too Nice a Man?

'The plane bringing us home from Budapest was flying smoothly at 30,000 feet over Belgium, about twenty minutes or half-an-hour out of Luton. We were all pretty happy. The 3-1 win over Hungary had put us back on course for the World Cup finals, following the disappointment a few days beforehand when we lost to Switzerland, and we were all relaxed, looking forward to the summer break at long last. I had not played the night before, but I was as thrilled as everyone with a result which had restored our morale, and we were all especially pleased for the manager, Ron Greenwood. We knew he had been under a lot of pressure, and there had been some speculation in the last few days in the Press about whether he might quit. The players had no idea exactly what the situation was, and before the match in Budapest we had a whip round and bought the manager some cut glass, as a presentation after the game. We were glad we had done it, and he was very touched, but none of us was sure if it might have been a departing gesture had we lost.

Now the champagne was flowing on the plane, when suddenly the manager stood up and faced us in the aisle in the front section, where we were separated from the Press and other passengers. The manager said: 'When I get to Luton, Dick Wragg, the chairman of the selectors, is going to be there to meet me and will announce to the Press' – and he paused – 'that I'm resigning. I had made up my mind whatever the result last night.' He sat down, and all around him there was a stunned silence. We could

11

not believe it. Geoff Hurst, his assistant who, as one of his players at West Ham, had scored a World Cup final hat trick and knew him better than most, came round the players and confirmed that it was a fact, that he had decided after the defeat by Switzerland that the result against Hungary would make no difference. Some of the players said to Hurst, 'He can't do it', and all he could say to us was, 'Well, it's up to you to do something.'

So three of the senior players, Kevin Keegan, Mick Mills and Ray Clemence, representing all of us, went to the manager and asked him seriously to change his mind. We were all on such a high: it didn't make sense. All the players agreed that when we arrived at Luton we would forget about the bags, and go straight to Mr Wragg and say that none of us wished the manager to go. Which is what we did. We tried to avoid the Press, but I never thought for a moment, with all the people there were on the plane, that the story would not break fairly quickly. I drove from Luton straight to Plymouth to see my parents, and I was expecting to hear the news at any time on the radio. But it never came . . . and the manager stayed.'

That was how Ron Greenwood still came to be in command of England's participation in the World Cup finals a year later, though not without further alarms. What it proved in human terms was that he was a deeply caring man – both in deciding to go, and then changing his mind. It would be easy to say that he was prepared to quit after the game in Basle because his nerve had gone, but as one who has known him professionally for almost thirty years, I like to think it was because he had genuinely come to the conclusion that a younger man might have more success.

When Don Revie disgracefully deserted the sinking ship midway through the abortive qualifying campaign of 1977,

I was one of those who advocated the appointment of Greenwood, on the grounds that he could be guaranteed to repair England's reputation for fair play, that the adventurous game which he had for so long nurtured at West Ham, to the obvious satisfaction of East London crowds, would bring colour back to England's cheeks. And so it did at first. But following the defeat in Basle, I had been moved to write in the *Daily Express*:

'This is my saddest day in football – to have to say that two respected friends must make way for replacements amid the debris of England's World Cup campaign. Ron Greenwood has failed to make the best of the inevitably bad job which Sir Harold Thompson, the FA chairman, handed him in good faith, but without specialist knowledge, four years ago. Between them, with Greenwood's indecision and Sir Harold's inaction, they have allowed England to drift to the brink of a third consecutive elimination from the finals . . . If England fail to get a point in Budapest, I believe the FA should invite Greenwood to remain as administrative chief, but should give the remainder of the qualifying programme on a temporary basis to one of our outstanding younger coaches such as Jack Charlton, Don Howe or Terry Venables.'

In the light of events throughout the remainder of Greenwood's tenure, I think this assessment of the situation in the summer of 1981 is seen to have been reasonably accurate.

'When Greenwood initially took the job, it was on a temporary basis, he was only helping out to the end of the season, officially. But I think he began to quite like the job, and the prestige that began to grow with it. With his early 4-2-4 formation he was getting a bit of success, and getting it playing entertaining football. But when things started to go not so well, that's when he began to think, I suspect, that he didn't need all the criticism, and that's when he decided he would opt out. No player or manager likes criticism, if he's honest about it, but some take it better than others. Ron Greenwood found it very difficult to accept, there were many times he would say how annoyed he was with comments in the Press, at times unnecessarily so, I thought. He was being over-sensitive. Ron Greenwood always had the respect of the players because he's essentially a nice man, although at times I've felt he was the type who was too nice to be in the job he was in. He would never blast players. What I liked about him particularly was that whenever England did well, he never wanted to take the credit, always giving it to the players, but when we didn't do well he always tried to shoulder the criticism, which is a tremendous attitude. In the Football League nowadays, quite a lot of the managers have become more famous than the players, and when the team plays well it's the manager who wants to take the credit. But when they play badly, it's the team's fault! This is increasingly the pattern with some First Division managers, to the point where youngsters are associating top teams not with the players but with the managers. I was especially pleased that Ron Greenwood never fell into this habit. As football managers go, he was very likeable, although it's not actually necessary for players to like the manager. What's important is that they should go out and play effectively, and I sometimes had to question Ron Greenwood's approach to selection.

There were games when he tried to accommodate players. He believed in loyalty to his players, which they appreciated, but at times I think he carried it too far, and that he only realized this towards the end. With a squad of twenty-two, he somehow wanted to play all twenty-two! He didn't find it easy telling players they were going to be left out, and in the early years he tried to give all the players a game. But it's so important what system a team plays, and if that means leaving out one or two skilful players because they don't fit in, so be it.

It was only gradually, after several poor results with much changed teams, for instance against Sweden in 1979 and Wales at Wrexham in 1980, that he began to realize it wasn't a sound policy. The reason players would always go out and play for him with spirit was that they *did* want to do well for him. But the team against Sweden, for example, could not possibly be right – three central strikers, Keegan, Woodcock and myself, plus Cunningham, in front of two midfield players, McDermott and Currie, who think almost solely about going forward and don't really relish the defensive side of the game. It was a team lacking balance and shape, although it *was* only a friendly. But for the World Cup qualifier against Norway in the autumn of 1981, we again had three central strikers, myself, Mariner and Keegan, with Hoddle out of his normal club position on the left of midfield. Instead of a natural replacement for Brooking, we tried to use Hoddle, which was not right either for him or for the team. It was clear early on that the team was lacking width, and as a result at half-time I was switched to a wide position on the right – where I would be trying to break into the same space as McDermott.'

It was in that tie in Oslo, which England critically lost 2-1, that doubts were once more raised about whether Ray Clemence was still entitled to be considered first-choice goalkeeper. He was, of course, immensely experienced, and had seemed up to that stage to be preferred by Greenwood, playing twenty-six times under his management to Peter Shilton's eleven. But the policy of constant switching was one which seemed quite illogical to many professional managers and players.

'It was certainly on the minds of quite a few of the squad. Ever since I've been involved with England, we've had these two outstanding 'keepers, and latterly Joe Corrigan as well, but I've always believed you pick your best team come what may. I believe this, even if it means leaving *me* out because I don't fit the system in use at the time: it's something a player has got to accept. A manager has got to name his No.1, I'm convinced, for he cannot be loyal to two men, and the goalkeeper is such a vitally important part of the team. He can instruct the players in front of him, the defence need to get to know what he wants, and although both Ray and Peter were excellent, there are no two 'keepers who are the same in the way they marshal a defence. Having spoken to Joe, I know by the finish he was a bit put out being regarded as No. 3, and on one occasion he went to see the manager about it. His argument, reasonably enough, was that if there was to be an equal opportunity between two, then why not between three?

Over the four-year period with Greenwood, Ray had seemed to be No.1, but as we approached the finals in Spain I sensed it was going to be tight; Peter was pushing him hard, and I've always regarded him as a great 'keeper from the days when I played against him at Forest for Birmingham. Strangely, the manager left it until the last possible moment to let the 'keepers know who was his choice in Spain – only the day before the opening match with France, as late as that. I'll never forget Ray's face, he was naturally very upset, and couldn't hide his feelings.'

In his twenty-seven games for England prior to the World Cup finals of 1982 Francis had only five times played in two consecutive matches and never in three, had only once had the same partner in consecutive games, and in all had partnered eight different central strikers: Stan Bowles, Mike Channon, Joe Royle and Stuart Pearson under Revie; Bob Latchford, Paul Mariner, Kevin Keegan and Tony Woodcock with Greenwood. It was hardly a pattern which might allow a player to become acclimatized, let alone confident.

'I always felt under Greenwood that I was an established member of the squad, but not the team. I felt I was good enough, but who wouldn't have done in my position? I'm sure others felt the same. But every time I played I seemed to be on trial, and after the Norway game in 1981, I had to wait six months before I played again. But if you looked at the situation, who *was* an England regular? As late as March before the World Cup, the only certs were Keegan and Bryan Robson, and after the Northern Ireland game even Keegan felt he was not sure.

In his first season (1977–8), Greenwood was playing to a system, 4-2-4, which was getting results, but I felt he was never sure whether to play Bob Latchford or me. I consider that with that system, with two wide players, you need a big man, and I remember Keegan at the time saying he preferred Bob. We kept the system through much of the following season – when I had injuries at Birmingham, moved to Forest, scored the winning goal in the European Cup final, and came back into the England squad on tour.

I knew it was up to me to convince the manager I was good enough. I came on as sub in the European qualifier against Bulgaria in Sofia, and everyone said how sharp I was, but then we had the Sweden match which wasn't so good, and against Austria in Vienna Bob got the nod. I was still not proving I was the man for the job. But against Austria the manager felt we were being outnumbered in midfield with 4-2-4, that we were being exposed. I remember we attacked a lot, but were vulnerable, and lost. That was just about the end of 4-2-4, and the following season we played 4-3-3 against Denmark at home, still with two wingers, and then Tony Woodcock and I played together against Ireland, scoring two each, and we felt we were a partnership for the future. We played again, against Bulgaria at home, then again in the spring when we beat Spain in Barcelona, but after that I snapped my Achilles and we were never really given another chance to see if we could settle.'

One of the reasons for this was that by the time Francis recovered, Woodcock had decided to leave Forest for Cologne, thus breaking a partnership which might have flourished for club and country. I was friendly with Woodcock, and told him that in my opinion he should wait until after the World Cup, that he was young enough to pick up Continental wages later, and that he would be advised to concentrate on his England career, which could be jeopardized by going to Germany. But he spoke to Greenwood, who assured him it would make no difference and might even improve his game, the way it had Keegan's at Hamburg. Woodcock did improve, yet Greenwood never went especially to watch him, and the inevitable conclusion is that Woodcock's chance declined abroad while Paul Mariner's rose at home.

'It was difficult to fathom things out. For example, I really enjoyed playing with Keegan up front against

Hungary in 1978, when we got four goals, yet the manager didn't seem happy about this. There was a time when he seemed to think Keegan was better in midfield, yet his best position *is* up front. He should have played there against Forest for Hamburg in the 1980 European Cup final, and I wish I'd been given the chance to play there with him more often. There was a four-year gap before we played together again, against Ireland – and again England got four.

People tend to say I should partner a big man, such as Latchford or Peter Withe, but I think the most important thing is that the manager should first and foremost select good technicians. It's all about playing, and if you can play, I believe you can play with *anyone*. I'm not boasting, but there's not a game goes by, at club or international level, when I don't do something, at least once in the game, that sets up a potential winner for me or another player. I said to Justin Fashanu, when he arrived at Forest, 'Whenever I get to the dead-ball line be ready, there's always a chance it'll land on your head, because I'll get balls back that you won't expect.' I was doing it in 1981–2 with Manchester City, and I've been doing it since I was sixteen, I don't know how. It was like that with England's second goal in 1981 against Ireland at Wembley, Chris Nicholl wasn't expecting the ball to come over when I pulled it back from near the flag for Keegan to score.'

The match-by-match fluctuation in selection was, by 1982, the most disturbing aspect of Greenwood's management, the more so when one had only to look at the post-war records to see that periods of international success, under Walter Winterbottom and then Alf Ramsey, had always coincided with stability of selection over a year or more.

19

Revie, a successful club manager, had totally misunderstood the difference between club and international management, believing that it was possible at international level to pick different teams to do different jobs in consecutive games. The truth is that an international team has so little time to play together, to achieve the kind of harmony established over months or years of daily training at club level, that continuity is vital. Miljan Miljanic, the widely respected Yugoslav who has had success at both levels with Red Star (Belgrade), Real Madrid and his national team, has always said:

'The two jobs are quite different. The club manager has a more or less fixed group of players and must find a system to suit their abilities. The international manager must work the other way round – decide upon a system, and then fit in the players who will make it work.'

This is what Ramsey had done in 1966 and 1970, but Greenwood had come to use the same profusion of players as Revie. Then, by one of those strange twists, and in this instance a most sad one, England's situation was influenced by events off the field. Greenwood's assistant Bill Taylor, a coach with notable achievements with Manchester City and Fulham, became seriously ill, and in the autumn of 1981 he died. To replace him, Greenwood promoted Don Howe, his B XI coach and the architect for many years of consistently efficient Arsenal teams.

Following the debacle in Oslo, and before England played their final qualifying tie at home to Hungary – having in the interval been rescued by Romania's home defeat by the Swiss – I interviewed Howe to discuss his thoughts on England's priorities if they reached the finals. One of the most significant things he said: 'I think we have to find out whether Keegan and Francis really can play together up front.' With Howe's influence, England were about to embark on their most successful spell – if measured by absence of defeat – for sixteen years.

'The most important factor in any team in the present era is organization. Don Howe obviously works on playing to a system, in which you become a very difficult team to beat, like Forest and Liverpool. Arsenal were such, and now suddenly here were England developing into a team which was hard to beat. Even being a forward, I'm in agreement with this approach. The manager let Don take a bigger and bigger part as the days went by, and by the time we came to the final preparation for Spain, he gave him *carte blanche* on set pieces, for and against. I'd heard a lot about Don being boring and defensive-minded, but I was very impressed with him. We trained incredibly hard under him before we left England for Spain, and the joke among the players was that it was the earliest they had ever started pre-season training! We were even more apprehensive one morning when we saw a stop-watch in his hand. Most players dread the stop-watch!

One of the main reasons Ron Greenwood eventually finished his career on eleven games without defeat was because he finally stuck to a settled system in a settled side. A great deal of the credit, I feel, must go to Don Howe. As a manager, Greenwood loves players to express themselves. What would have suited him more than anything, what he would have loved, would have been to manage the Brazilians. That was the way he wanted the game to be played. But unfortunately in England we don't have the players to play it that way! It was becoming apparent, even while Bill Taylor was still with us, that Don Howe was being groomed to take over. His gradual, increasing influence was always subtle, never

21

heavy-handed, it was always a joint effort with the manager, a discussion of ideas and tactics.

I had the feeling that the manager welcomed his assistance, was glad to lean on him, even if in a subconscious way. Don's contribution grew and grew as time went by, and his major contribution was in Spain, where he had more and more influence on training, setting up practice routines, with the manager glad for him to do so.

Ron Greenwood probably realized that history's final assessment of him would depend on whether we got through the first round in Spain, however unfair that might be. I've never seen him more on edge, more nervous than he was before the French game. We had a police escort, and when we approached the stadium, there was another coach blocking our route to the dressing-room area. The manager suddenly started letting off steam, 'What's going on, where's the escort when we need them?', then having a go at the driver and telling him to 'get through'. He was right in what he was saying, but it was totally out of character. Normally he would sit at the front of the coach and not say a word!

At Wembley, there are always people in and out of the dressing-room before the game, far too many for my liking, often more officials, tea-men, and attendants than players. In Bilbao the manager questioned everyone who came in, and not for security reasons. He was more relaxed after we'd won, and more back to normal for the next game against the Czechs, but after we beat Kuwait by only one goal he was very annoyed. Just when we were pleased with the overall achievement, even though we too were disappointed with the performance against Kuwait, he said: 'If we're honest, we were bloody awful, that was the worst of our nine unbeaten games. Let's start thinking about Madrid. I want everyone in bed by midnight!' That was not like him, he usually let us unwind a bit after a win.

With the approach of the second-round match against

Germany, he was not as tense as before France, yet he openly admitted to the Press that it was the biggest game of his career. It *was* a special game because of our rivalry with them over the years, rather like the Scots. There's nobody we'd rather beat than those two! After the Germany game he was relaxed, and arranged for us to go to watch the Germany-Spain game in the stadium, but then changed his mind, saying he thought there might be too much aggro with Spanish supporters. I would like to have been there, and so would some of the others. I think the pressure did affect his decisions. When we heard that one of the England supporters had been stabbed in Madrid by a gang of thugs and left for dead, I suggested we should go and see him in hospital, take some souvenirs. No photographers or anything. We were going into Madrid shopping anyway, and the manager said it was a great idea, so I left it with him, but I never heard another word. The World Cup may be big, but I felt a bloke's life was more important.'

Nobody can fully understand the pressures on managers during a World Cup. As Miljanic has said, it is a kind of war. Without Howe, I wonder whether Greenwood would have stood up to the pressure as well as he did. His press conferences were unfailingly friendly to journalists of all nationalities who wished to attend. He was the old urbane schoolmaster once more, sitting behind his desk at West Ham for the post-match talk-in we had attended so often down the years. Just occasionally a barb of sarcasm crept in, as when, asked by a foreigner after the France game whether he had recognized the dismally out-of-touch Platini, he had replied, 'He had the No.10 on his back, didn't he?', throwing the interpreters into a flurry of confusion. With Brian Clough, such a comment is standard aggressiveness, like his slanderous comment on television during the first round about his own player, John Robertson, having no intelligence. But with Greenwood, it is always a sign that he is feeling slightly cornered.

'I've said on many occasions that Brian Clough is the best manager in the country – and the best manager should be England manager. Clough's brand of abrasive, arrogant outspokenness often results in his upsetting people. He's not a bit interested in conformity and regulations, so that although I think he's the best, I realize there's hardly any chance of his ever becoming England manager.

With Clough and Peter Taylor, I think the England team would have become a settled side much earlier than we did. When I went to Forest, my £1-million fee didn't matter, what *did* was that I had to fit into their proved way and system for success. Had Clough and Taylor been offered the job, I think they would only have taken it if they could have insisted on having the players together for longer. They had a unique way of raising players' confidence. Most important of all they would send them out mentally right, so that they couldn't wait to start. Greenwood never did this from start to finish, it's not his style. We respected him, but he never roused us, it's not in his make-up to do so. People sometimes say there's no need to motivate international players, that if they need motivating they should not be there in the first place, but you could say that of club players, going out in front of a crowd of 40,000.

Clough and Taylor would not have been loved by the England players, though that would not have bothered them. Yet when any manager is helping you to win as regularly as they do, you get to like them. I think they could still have the *hold* on international players that they do at club level, even only meeting for a week every other month. But if Clough were going to be appointed, it should have been at the time of Greenwood's temporary appointment. Forest were then the best they've ever been, but subsequently they've gone down a bit, and Clough's chance went. Bobby Robson became the obvious candidate when Greenwood finally resigned after the World Cup.'

# 2 Clough Conundrum

In the spring of 1977 Nottingham Forest finished third in the Second Division to win promotion, an event which passed without much of a fanfare. Wolves and Chelsea had taken the first two places. Forest had finished their programme; Bolton needed five points out of their last six to overtake them, but could manage only three. Brian Clough was on holiday in the Mediterranean when he heard that, for the second time, he and Peter Taylor had taken a club almost derelict in the lower reaches of the Second Division back to the First. Two years later, in May 1979, in one of the most remarkable spells of management of all time, Forest had won the European Cup – for good measure defeating Liverpool, holders for the two previous years, in the first round. In between those two events, they had twice won the League Cup, defeating Liverpool and Southampton respectively; and, to qualify for the European Cup, had finished seven points clear of Liverpool in their first season back in the first Division.

On the way to the European final, Clough had at last persuaded Jim Smith, at the time Birmingham's manager, to part with Trevor Francis in the first million-pound deal in British football. Yet Francis was ineligible to play until the final itself in Munich against Malmo of Sweden. He would be one of the anxious spectators as Forest drew 3-3 in the first leg of the semi-final at home to Cologne – the *Daily Express* headline read, 'Ooh de Cologne!' – and then spectacularly won the second leg 1-0 with a sixty-fifth minute header by Ian Bowyer, the unsung deputy for the injured Archie Gemmill. That was a near perfect tactical performance, perhaps the most outstanding of all examples of the managerial ability of an exceptional pair. For the final on a sunny evening in the 1979 Olympic Stadium their hand would be strengthened by arguably Britain's best player – though he seemed almost superfluous against the little club of Swedish amateurs managed by Englishman Bob Houghton (even if they had disposed of Monaco, Dynamo Kiev, Wisla from Krakow, and FC Austria to get there).

Yet, after no more than a handful of inconsequential league games – Forest had this time finished second in the League, eight points behind Liverpool – it was still not clear what function Trevor would be given by his new masters, with all Europe studying him. Confronted by Malmo's obsessive off-side tactics, Clough chose to use him in a midfield role, saying: 'We like teams to come at us. Malmo, from what I have seen in two matches, will not. It will be imperative to break down their off-side tactics with supporting strikes from the midfield men, who are more difficult to mark.'

This contained the germ of a growing controversy. Clough and Taylor had paid a king's ransom for an acknowledged star player with the bare-faced intention of reshaping his approach to the game – typical of their nerve. They believed that only then would Trevor's natural brilliance, apparent since he played in the First Division at sixteen, be fully capitalized upon within Forest's remarkable team discipline. Trevor, to his immense credit, had totally accepted the way in which his new employers had doused any star treatment by the media and were attempting to recycle his skills. Trevor would say modestly on the eve of the final: 'Of course I have played most of my career up front and prefer playing there. But I have found more space in midfield in certain ways, and frankly the way Forest are going at the moment, I am delighted to be included anywhere.'

In a predominantly and depressingly cautious final, Trevor broke the deadlock of Malmo's soporific tactics with a perfectly timed blind-side run and lunging header in the forty-fifth minute. The new boy not only won the prize, but disclosed new dimensions in his game which made him a throbbing candidate for an England team about to go on tour against Bulgaria (a European qualifier), Sweden, and Austria. The wealth of this final was at the turnstiles, not on the pitch, Forest taking their share of a million-pound gross gate, with the prospect of two more plum games in the autumn in the intercontinental club final against Independiente of Buenos Aires, and the European Super-cup against Cup Winners holders Barcelona.

To Forest's credit they never failed from start to finish in their intention of sending John Robertson and Francis round the fringes of Malmo's rearguard, or pushing Francis through the middle from deep positions. It was fitting that they should take the Cup by these tactics, just as their frustration was reaching a peak at the end of the first half. In injury time, Ian Bowyer slung the ball out to Robertson who was hugging the left touch-line. With a side-step and a burst he accelerated round the outside of the two men who policed him all night, Prytz and Erlendsson. With precision he curled the ball round the back of the defence and beyond the groping hands of Malmo's massive goalkeeper Jan Moeller. There, on the far post in a blur of red, was Trevor, at the end of a thirty-yard run, hurling himself forward to head the ball into the roof of the net.

With half an hour to go, following a brilliant run by Trevor, Robertson hit the post. There had been only one possible result, but Helmut Schoen, former West Germany manager, led the indictment of a thousand critics when he said: 'Forest were the only justifiable winners, but wholly destructive football such as that played by Malmo can only destroy the game itself for the public. It is a pity that the people of Germany could not witness the true quality of Forest.'

Deep must have been the anguish in parts of Derby, where Clough and Taylor had quit six years before in a needless, acrimonious row with chairman Sam Longson, after taking Derby from the Second Division to a League title and a European semi-final, on a helter-skelter of expertise and publicity no less spectacular than their achievements with Forest. They had gone to Derby after fashioning their managerial partnership while making bricks without straw at Hartlepool. Following the Derby fracas, they moved to Brighton, splitting when Clough agreed to replace Don Revie at Leeds. He survived there only forty-four days. They were re-united back in obscurity in Nottingham. Just what sort of men were they?

'I always found it was particularly hard playing for Clough as a striker, because he had been so good at his job himself, scoring almost a goal a game as a centre-forward with Middlesbrough and Sunderland, even if it was in the Second Division. He was unlucky that a nasty injury put him out of the game prematurely when by all accounts he might have played in the 1962 World Cup for England. He demanded so much as a manager. I never saw him play, but he was always quick to tell me he was the best. Any Forest striker could always be sure he would be quick to be criticized – Peter Withe, Tony Woodcock, Garry Birtles, myself, we all got it, and later no doubt it was the turn of Justin Fashanu and Ian Wallace. I always got the impression that whenever you had any sort of chance in the box, Clough thought it was an easy chance.

29

It is often said that Clough and Taylor are dictators. Sure, I suspect they like to create that image, but they're not really like that. As players we had great respect for them, played our hearts out for them, and during the week it was no different. It would be good for every player in the country to play under them at some stage, just to find out what they can do for a team and for individual players – and it is remarkable – though of course I could not compare them from personal experience with the likes of Bob Paisley and Lawrie McMenemy.

The most impressive quality with Clough and Taylor was not in their coaching. They never took training! It lay in motivation, sending players out in the right frame of mind. They would make a point of doing it whether it was a testimonial match or a European Cup tie, they would never tolerate any sloppiness. It was a stark contrast with all my years at Birmingham. There, with several of the managers, nothing much happened before ten to three, and then the attitude was mostly, 'OK, go out and play the game.' But with Clough and Taylor, the most important ten minutes of the week began at two forty-five. I'd grown up to think the game was all about coaching and tactics, which you concentrated on during the week, and that if those were done properly it would all come right on Saturday. Yet at Forest, I suddenly discovered that the most important function of the manager, or in this case managers, was getting the players to produce a consistent level of performance week in week out by emphasis on mental attitude. It was very much a matter of man-management. It was easy for outsiders to ask, I am sure, how Forest could possibly have won the League with those players! Men like Frank Clark, Ian Bowyer, Martin O'Neill, Kenny Burns, Peter Withe, John O'Hare, Larry Lloyd, John McGovern and John Robertson, who had all come from lower divisions or who must have thought beforehand that their careers were on the decline. Yet brought together by Clough and Taylor, their attitude and commitment to the club were never less than total.

Frank Clark achieved more in the last eighteen months of his career than he could ever have dreamed possible. If there ever came a chance while I was still playing to rejoin Clough and Taylor, I would not hesitate. When I signed for Forest they said provocatively to the Press that they thought I had great potential! And they had just paid a million for me. I thought to myself, well, what can they get out of me that no one else has got? I thought, of course, that I was a good player, but they taught me a great deal more. All the while I was playing at Birmingham, it somehow didn't seem all that important if I didn't play well on any particular day. Subconsciously, I suppose I knew I was unlikely to be dropped. Yet at Forest, if I scored twice in the first half and then didn't play well in the second half, I'd get a roasting. It's only now that I fully realize how big a part management can play in a player's career. I think this point has been proved at Ipswich, where, in spite of all the skills and all the players the club had under Bobby Robson, they were not sufficient to win them the Championship. What Liverpool have had, though, is the same commitment and attitude as Forest had, as well as their skill. I think these qualities were responsible for Spurs doing so well in 1982, too. They'd discovered more of the will to win.

There was only one time that I ever thought Clough or Taylor went too far, and that was when I had a bust-up with Pete, as he was known to the players, after the Super-cup against Barcelona. (Clough we always referred to as 'Boss'.) In the second half Asensi had gone over the top badly, and gashed my shin. I tried jogging, but there was no way I would be able to continue, so I came off. Taylor snapped at me, 'It's not that bad, you haven't broken your leg.' Yet it was necessary for a Spanish doctor to insert six stitches. After the medal ceremony at the finish I must have been looking angry, and Taylor asked me: 'What's up?' I told him point blank: 'Don't ever have a go at me like that again.' We'd drawn 1-1 away to win 2-1 on aggregate.

People just won't believe how little conventional coaching there was with Forest. It was nearly all left to Jimmy Gordon, the trainer. We'd have a warm-up, do some stretching exercises, and then go straight into five-a-side. Occasionally we might do some shuttle runs. We trained far harder at Birmingham, but on reflection this often meant that when we went out to play on Saturday we were jaded. You will rarely find a fitter team than Forest. We seldom practised dead-ball situations during the season. Certain principles were established pre-season, and then left to us to operate consistently, so that you knew exactly what was expected of you. I remember once when we were going to play at Stoke, and Kenny Burns was worried that they had so many players who were effective in the air at corners, for example Doyle, Chapman and Dennis Smith. Clough retorted: 'Stoke? I don't want to talk about their players.' But Kenny wouldn't leave it alone. so Clough told him: 'Just go and play in their half of the field, and then there won't be any corners at our end.'

Simplicity, that's what they believed in. At free kicks they either wanted two big men to get up in front of goal, or for Frank Gray or myself to hit the target. Clough and Taylor were so confident in their ability to send players out mentally right, and it usually worked. It has often been said that Forest were defensive, but we played to a 4-4-2 system that was little different from many other teams, except that we played with five men across the middle whenever Liverpool were the opposition, and we did the same against Hamburg in the European Cup final in Madrid. People won't believe what I've said, that we practised so little yet seemed so organized. But the reason was firstly the regularity of the system so that all of us knew exactly what was expected, and secondly the motivation we were given by the management. We were not especially defensive. Clough and Taylor were always emphatic that our full backs, Anderson and Gray, must get forward as often as possible in the penalty area. They constantly stressed, 'Go all the way, or come off and have a bath.'

The incident with Taylor in Barcelona was in fact the second time I had an illustration of their attitude to injury. When you are injured and out of action you're no good to them, and no use to the club for the time being, so they don't bother with you. The first time was when I came back at the start of the 1979–80 season from playing in America in the summer, still suffering from a groin injury. Clough was annoyed and said he was going to stop my wages. I thought he was joking, but he wasn't. When they found out, the Professional Footballers' Association contacted the club to say they could not do this. But the fact was I didn't receive any wages for six weeks. The controversy dragged on. I wasn't desperately in need of money, but I was concerned about the principle. However, at the end of the season I was injured, having snapped my Achilles, and although it was in the contract that it was up to the manager's discretion whether to pay bonuses to a player who was not playing, in fact Clough paid up. So I forgot the wages dispute, but otherwise I would have fought it. I didn't want any scenes, any more than I did at Birmingham, that's not my style. But I would have held out for the principle if it hadn't been for what I felt was fair – or, indeed, generous – treatment over the bonus.'

Although, as the 1979–80 season progressed, Trevor had become an established favourite with the Forest crowd, with his electrifying acceleration and spectacular goals, the internal disagreement with the management about what was his most effective position rumbled on, and came to a head in mid-March with the League Cup final against Wolves, in which Forest began outright favourites, both as holders for the past two years, and having knocked out Liverpool in the semi-final. The match at Wembley appeared to be Forest's last gateway to Europe that season.

They were not going to win the League; Tony Woodcock had accepted the German jackpot and departed to Cologne; and ten days previously they had been defeated 1-0 at home in the first leg of the European Cup quarter final by Dynamo of East Berlin. Repeatedly, Clough had stressed that a continuing presence in Europe was fundamental to the club's playing and financial structure, but the League Cup proved to be an even bigger setback than the game with Dynamo. Wolves, the luckiest team at Wembley since England were held to a draw by Poland seven years before, won by a freak, only goal. Peter Shilton, attempting to catch a high ball out on the edge of the penalty area which he had no hope of reaching, collided with his centre-back Dave Needham, presenting Andy Gray with an open net. Wolves' managerial team of John Barnwell and Ritchie Barker had cleverly planned the switching in midfield of Kenny Hibbitt and Peter Daniel, putting Hibbitt central and using Daniel to smother Robertson. Daniel not only did an effective job, forcing Robertson to wander away from the wing, but it was his long, high cross which brought the decisive goal. As Barker said: 'The use of a high ball to Andy Gray was something we always thought would put pressure on Forest. We decided we were not too proud to use that kind of simple old-fashioned tactic at Wembley – and in the event it was that ball which won the match. Although by switching Daniel we lost his thrust through the middle, we knew he would have the stamina to put the brakes on Robertson and still be able to push forward.' Yet the clearly better team had lost, thanks to poor finishing and the luck of Wolves' 'keeper Paul Bradshaw. Referee David Richardson strangely failed to book Emlyn Hughes for a professional foul on Francis a yard outside the area. Trevor had had an undistinguished game, and there was now speculation that financially hard-pressed Forest might cash in their star player on the transfer market.

In the stunned silence outside the Forest dressing-room after the match, Clough gave weight to the speculation when he said: 'Francis was disappointing – but he has been playing that way all season. We put him in the middle, and he doesn't give the hustle and bustle needed from forwards if they are to create and score goals. So we put him out wide as we did today, and that doesn't work either. He seems caught between two stools. Not only that, but he doesn't last the pace very well.' The problems were self-evident with the team overall, for they had lost almost as many matches that season as in the previous three put together.

'In one of my first games for Forest I had played up front. It was at Old Trafford and very icy, and we were three down in fifteen minutes. At the Monday team meeting Taylor had said: 'We'll never have you playing with your back to goal again.' He obviously thought I would be better running at defenders. I never agreed with him, though we discussed it often and he'd always listen. Taylor had a great say in team selection. They were joint managers, in it together, and Peter always preferred me playing from midfield. I always made it clear I wanted to play in the central striking position. The result was that I was moved about a lot. Taylor felt that the team was at its best when I first arrived, with Robbo on the left, me on the right, and Woodcock and Birtles through the middle. This gave the craft of Robbo on one flank, and my pace and scoring ability on the other. This still enabled them to play 4-4-2 with two wide men, Robbo and me, tucking in defensively where required. With Birtles and Woodcock playing so well when I arrived, I was prepared to bide my time, but when Woodcock left for Cologne I wanted to move into the middle, and was not happy remaining in midfield.

At Wembley against Wolves (in the 1980 League Cup final), I started out on the right, then went up front, then went back wide again. Clough and Taylor were on the bench as usual, and I had the impression that it was Taylor making the changes. It wasn't a good performance, we'd been expected to win, and I felt I was made the scapegoat. I was slammed by both Clough and Taylor in the Press on Sunday, and again on Monday. I was angry, and told them so when I saw them at the airport on Monday as we set off for East Berlin and the second leg of the European Cup quarter final. I was particularly annoyed because nothing much had been said to me in the dressing-room afterwards at Wembley. With Clough around, you could always expect headlines, but there would often be a difference between what he said to me or the team and what he said to the Press.'

Geoffrey McPherson, chairman of the club, spelled out the realities as we sat in the smart new Swedish-built hotel dominating one of East Berlin's drab boulevards. Even with the £7,000,000 sale of Woodcock, Forest faced a deficit of at least half that sum the following season without European soccer. McPherson said:

'We will support the management as far as possible in every way. We are as ambitious as they are. If funds can be provided, they will be. But there has to be realism. Up to now Brian and Peter have a brilliant record in the transfer market, and Saturday's defeat at Wembley is the only thing which has gone wrong for this club in four fantastic seasons. But the fact is we are faced with declining attendances. If the people of Nottingham would support us, give us some capacity gates of 36,000, it would be much easier to provide money for transfers. We might possibly be able to increase our loan from the bank, because it is secured by the city council, but it is imperative that we tread carefully.'

The one obvious way to raise money was to sell Trevor, and before the game with Dynamo, Clough put the responsibility squarely on his seeming million-pound misfit. How much criticism was Francis prepared to take, the Press speculated, if the team failed as it seemed they must? Everything had been roses for him in the previous May when he scored the goal which won the European Cup in Munich. Ten months later he was neither settled with Forest nor established with England. Had he been happier as the star in a losing Birmingham side than he now was as merely one of a top team in trouble? Clough said: 'Trevor has to accept that he is under pressure. We had to score one goal in Cologne last year, we've got to get two here. If we get one, I think we will get another. It will be fascinating to see Dynamo's tactics. I'd like to see how they would react to conceding a goal at home. That's why Birtles and Francis are absolutely vital tomorrow.'

Trevor rose dramatically to answer the criticisms with two goals in the first half hour, to thrust Forest into the European Cup semi-final with a great escape through the Berlin wall. His second, smashed on the turn off the under-side of the cross-bar as Martin O'Neill squeezed the ball into the penalty area, was one of the sharpest he ever scored. His first had come after a quarter of an hour when Dave Needham headed on a free kick by Lloyd. Forest's third came when Robertson was sent flying and then scoredhimself from the penalty. Though Dynamo made it 3-1, Forest were through, having recaptured their old form and with Francis showing the touch which made him one of Europe's most dangerous forwards. Clough claimed: 'Our first half performance was absolutely superb. Francis made the important breakthrough, and went on to have a brilliant ninety minutes. I know I criticized him after Wembley, but he put his house in order. John McGovern was outstanding in the second half.'

'When we met at the airport on Monday, I felt low because of the doubts which I knew there were about me. I hadn't known at Wembley what position I was going to play until twenty minutes before the kick-off, and in Berlin I still hadn't been told an hour beforehand. Then Clough approached me: where did I want to play? 'Up front alongside Birtles' – 'OK, then play there – and stay there.'

It was just what I needed. I knew we had it all to do, and I was delighted by the way things went. I felt I'd cracked it, and that I would now get a long run in what I felt was my best position. Contrary to some of the reports, I was basically happy enough at the club, and I stayed in that front position until my Achilles injury, and when I recovered from that midway through the following season there was never any suggestion that I would not stay up front.'

In the European Cup semi-final against Ajax, Trevor was again at his most damaging, scoring the first in a two-goal win in the opening home leg – his fourth goal in four European appearances. Ajax were outplayed and, though they won the return 1-0, Forest were through to the final again, in which they would meet Hamburg – for whom Kevin Keegan was still the inspiration. Now, perhaps at the pinnacle of his career and about to fulfil all those expectations, Trevor was in superb form, partnering Cologne colleague Woodcock as England trounced Spain in a friendly in Barcelona. Then misfortune struck.

'Clough was away watching Hamburg when my Achilles snapped ten minutes from the end of a game with Crystal Palace. I'd scored two. Suddenly, accelerating, I felt as if a stone had been thrown from the crowd, or as if I'd been shot. I was running at the last defender and just collapsed.

As Jimmy Gordon ran onto the field, I sensed it was my Achilles, but I was clutching at straws and asked: 'Did somebody kick me?' With Jimmy's help I got up and tried to walk, but I couldn't move, and, with the crowd clapping, was taken off behind the goal in a wheel chair which was so old I fell out of it. Peter Jackson, the club surgeon, confirmed the worst. I would miss the European final and also the Nations finals in Italy with England. 'Will I be fit for the start of next season?' I asked anxiously. 'No chance,' said Jackson. I was particularly disappointed about missing the Hamburg game because, unlike the year before, I felt this time I had really earned my place. The home leg against Ajax had been my best game in Europe. Clough said he didn't want me in Madrid on crutches, I would be bad for morale, but I had already made up my own mind not to go. Some friends had invited me to Cannes and I watched the game on TV in a crowded room, unknown to almost everybody, sitting in the dark at the back. At the finish, everybody but me was able to leap in the air!

We'd won with the only goal from Robbo after twenty minutes, thanks mainly to a fantastic performance by

Peter Shilton in goal. The most emotional moment for me was watching them running around the wonderful Bernabeu Stadium with the cup, showing it to the fans, and my not being there. Hamburg, strangely, played to our strength, Kenny Burns and Larry Lloyd in the middle of defence. Hamburg brought on Hrubesch in the second half, but it didn't matter who it was with Larry and Kenny playing as they were then. As a neutral, certainly, I would have said it was a very poor game. When you're playing in a final all you care is that you win, but when I watch I want it to be the best game ever.

Until Aston Villa's exciting yet lucky win over Bayern Munich in Rotterdam, the recent European finals had all been poor spectacles – Liverpool's win over Bruges, Forest's against Malmo and Hamburg, and Liverpool's over Real Madrid gave little to spectators. We didn't play well as a team against Malmo. They were too well organized. But that's how we were against Hamburg, playing a 4-5-1 formation because I was injured, leaving Birtles on his own up front. That way you just hope you'll score early on and that they will keep hitting in high balls, which they did.

After my injury I didn't actually see Clough for seven weeks. He never came to see me in hospital. Then, when I was down in Cannes, I bought the English papers and found I was being sold to Barcelona! I couldn't believe it, it was a joke. Here I was in plaster and the clubs had agreed a £1.5 million transfer. I contacted Forest to find out what was happening, and agreed to go over to Barcelona for three days. When I got there, the Spaniards wanted to take the plaster off to assess the injury, but in the end did their tests with it on, using an electronic scanner. They viewed it from ten different positions, which all showed it was healing perfectly. Nothing materialized from this visit, and I never got to the bottom of what Clough and Taylor were up to. When I arrived back,

I saw Clough the day I came out of plaster, and asked whether he was selling me. All he would say was: 'I couldn't refuse that sort of money,' but I was still none the wiser. I didn't play in the First Division until December. Just before that, I made my return in the Super-cup in Valencia. I couldn't have had a tougher game, yet from that day I consider I played better than at any other time in my career. That's only what I think, of course. There's more determination in my play. I've twice been close to being finished and realize how important it is to play each game as if it's your last.

We finished the 1980–1 season only seventh in the League, having gone out of the European Cup in the first round to CSKA of Sofia, out of the FA Cup quarter final to Ipswich after a replay. I then went on tour with England for the World Cup qualifying games, played in the defeat by Switzerland, and then was left out of the team which recovered in Budapest. It was unsatisfactory from my point of view, though of course I was delighted when we beat Hungary. But back in pre-season training with Forest (1981–2), I found myself in midfield again! In the opening League game against Southampton I was played wide on the right. After twenty minutes, I switched with Robbo, and then scored twice in three minutes. During the summer Clough had signed Justin Fashanu from Norwich. On the pre-season tour in Spain, I shared a room with Justin, and he said he'd told Clough that the only reason he would sign was to be able to play together with me. Perhaps he felt it might increase his international chances. Anyway, Clough assured him I would be staying.'

were the motives of Clough and Taylor in signing the unproven Fashanu, and promising him that he would play with Francis, when all the indications were that they

41

must have known that they could not afford to keep them both? At roughly the same price, how could it make sense to buy Fashanu only to sell Francis, even allowing for the fact that Francis's contract and therefore his saleable value had only one season to run? Throughout the most inconspicuous and least successful season they had had in years, Clough and Taylor claimed to be team-building, yet they seemed more intent on selling than buying, with the departure of Frank Gray and Kenny Burns as well as Francis. It is clear that there was no pressure from the club committee to sell Francis, only to remain within clearly defined overall financial limits in the administration of the team regarding transfers and salaries.

Geoffrey McPherson, the chairman of the club, could throw no light on the sequence of events when he said:

'If any player's departure was a disappointment for the crowd, that of Francis was most of all. I didn't know at the time that Fashanu had been told he would be playing with Francis, I only heard later, but the management had already signed another striker, Wallace from Coventry. The committee has no influence on these matters. The reasons why Clough and Taylor sell are not necessarily available to us. They might explain it, though we know it is all part of a plan, though one part of a jig-saw when in place does not necessarily explain to you the position of others. Was it a puzzle that Francis departed after Fashanu arrived? Yes, I find it hard to explain some of the moves. Whatever the master plan was, I don't know, but on the evidence of the season it did not work particularly well. But players who have not performed up to their value have certainly upset Clough.'

'On the Monday after the opening Saturday, I played what was to be my last game with Forest. It was the same as at Old Trafford, where I played wide on the right. Clough and Taylor made it clear to me they wanted a million for me. I genuinely believe they put me on the wing in order to make it easier to get rid of me, knowing that I would object. They're not bothered about the public, they're too sure of their own judgement. They knew I was interested in playing for Forest and doing well, that I liked the club – but also that I wanted to play up front. If they played me on the wing, they knew I'd go. When Justin heard the rumours he begged me not to go. He said: 'The reason I've come here is to play with you. I'm off to see Peter Taylor, to find out what it's all about.'

Justin was deeply upset. Taylor thought that I'd sent him in to see him. Throughout our stay in Spain, I had been talking to Clough and Taylor. I told them I had a year's contract left, that I wanted to stay if they would play me up front. But they were worried about freedom of contract. So I said, make me an offer of a new contract. They never did. Within a week I was gone.

Later during the season I honestly thought Clough and Taylor might quit. Without the players they had released there was less strength in the squad than ever. Yet after they had won against Malmo back in 1979, I believe they thought they could do anything and get away with it. The side has slowly disintegrated since then. The year they beat Malmo they finished second in the League but they never looked like doing that again.

I thought Taylor's resignation towards the end of the 1981–2 season was a premature thing, that we would find he'd be back again soon, when he'd had time for a rest and a holiday and the excitement of a new season arrived. I spoke to Fashanu and Wallace when they were put on the transfer list by Taylor, during Clough's absence because of illness, and Taylor had told them that whatever happened to Clough there was no way he himself would be leaving. It wasn't surprising, to me, when Taylor returned to the game, at Derby. It was ironic they drew Forest in the Cup – and I think he did well to keep Derby up.'

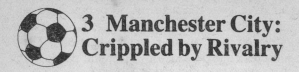

3 Manchester City: Crippled by Rivalry

'I joined Manchester City in 1981 full of fresh optimism, ambition and expectation – a big club, I thought, in a big city. The first time I had any doubts, and began to wonder whether I might have made a mistake, was when I discovered the club had not paid my wages for more than two months! That was the first indication I had that City were on the same slippery slope towards financial crisis as Bristol City, Hull and Wolves. Normally my wages were paid straight to my accountant, and that was why there was some delay before I realized that they were behind. It was just after Christmas, and I went to see the club secretary, Bernard Halford, to ask what was going on. I liked the club, and the last thing I wanted to do was rock the boat. They soon paid the overdue money, and I supposed it was just that they wanted to delay large payments as long as reasonably possible to keep down the interest on their overdraft. My salary of around £2,000 a week was obviously a large item, and I agreed that it should be paid monthly in future, instead of fortnightly.

Yet I had to chase them two or three times over the next six months when they were well behind with paying me, and when the crisis came to a head and I was transferred to Sampdoria at the beginning of August, they had still not paid me for June and July. I knew, too that Kevin Reeves was owed a loyalty bonus, though all these things were settled up in the end.

By degrees other signs began to show that all was not well, and the rest of the players also realized the club was heading for difficulties. There was a Christmas party for the players' children, and afterwards Joe Corrigan was sent round to collect £10 a head! Nothing much really, but it seemed petty. Telephones started to be removed from the treatment room and elsewhere. The physio Roy Bailey was most unhappy about this, I remember, and also about the fact that he was ordered to try to economize on elastic bandages for ankle strapping at training. He was supposed to make them keep for the next day, and you can imagine what it's like trying to use adhesive bandage a second time. The chief scout, Ken Barnes, was told not to make 'phone calls before the cheaper rate begins at 1.00 p.m., and a till was put in the players' lounge so that even visiting players had to buy their own drinks after a game. Something I've never experienced at any other First Division club.

There were cuts in staff, too . Two girls who used to clean the baths and showers were dismissed after Christmas, and from then on apprentices had to do it. And for the last three months of the season, we started cutting back on travelling expenses, midweek and Saturday. To go to Middlesbrough, say, we would travel the day of the game, instead of going away the night before and staying at a plush hotel.

Just how serious the situation had become was really brought home to me with something of a shock. I was having problems with a groin injury, and Roy Bailey rang the club's consultant surgeon to ask him to see me. He said 'No'! Apparently the club owed him money going back more than a year. He'd gone on seeing players without payment because he cared about their fitness, but now he said he had to make a stand, and I suppose I was as good a lever as he could use. A major club could hardly afford not to get advice on the fitness of its biggest investment. The matter immediately went to boardroom level via the manager, John Bond, and I think the money was paid, though I only saw the consultant later.

Now I began to fear that I could have no long-term future

with Manchester City. This was a genuine blow because I really loved the place: the people, the club, the atmosphere, everything about it except for the disturbing news, still not public then, that they were seemingly heading for the rocks. And *I* was a major part of the problem, the millstone round their necks. What an irony, when the intentions had been, on both sides, that I would help them climb towards success and eventually glory.

I think the word must have been getting around on the grapevine that City might be prepared to part with me, because two days before the transfer deadline, Southampton came in with an offer. Bond had spoken with Lawrie McMenemy, who wanted to do an exchange involving Steve Williams and me, but I understood later that it had been blocked at board level. Then in April, Bond made a bid for Gary Owen at West Bromwich, but Ronnie Allen, the Albion manager, said only if City were prepared to let me go. Bond called me in: Would I agree to go? I knew then that it was desperate.

I somehow hoped that it would work out OK, that I would be able to stay, that City would be able to find a way round. I didn't *want* to go. I was happy, we were just about to move into the new house we had had built. But I sensed that City were further away than ever from the success they so badly wanted, and that the longer I remained the more problems they would have. I knew in my heart that I would probably have to move on. But where?'

For almost twenty-five years Manchester City have been battling against not just another football team in the town but a legend created by an air crash – the tragedy at Munich which gave Matt Busby's brilliant young United team even greater fame in death than they would possibly have achieved had they lived. Before that dreadful afternoon in February 1958, there were merely two clubs in Manchester, earnest rivals each with their own character, traditions and history. City, if anything, were the more famous, had the larger following locally down the years until the arrival across town of Busby, ex-City wing-half, as manager at Old Trafford immediately after the war.

Out of the ashes of Munich climbed a youngster who was to become one of the world's most illustrious players, Bobby Charlton. And he would later be joined by another, Denis Law, who had quit City to go to Torino before returning to Manchester . . . and the 'other' club. City swallowed their pride, and swallowed even harder as the mid-Sixties were illuminated by a still brighter talent at Old Trafford, George Best. But City's moment was to come again.

Joe Mercer would arrive, when there seemed no hope left, and together with the flamboyant Malcolm Allison would lift them back to equality with United, rekindling the fires of Maine Road with a brand of football which had the pulse racing and the heart singing. Francis Lee, Mike Summerbee and Colin Bell would bring back the glory, and within a few short years City were again a force, their followers could once more walk tall; and the Old Trafford candle burned low.

Throughout the Seventies, with Leeds, Liverpool, Arsenal and then Nottingham Forest the major forces in English soccer, City and United remained locked in a rivalry which was in danger of being more destructive than it was creative. The lust for supremacy encouraged both clubs to overreach themselves financially, a trend reflected throughout the game.

Busby (now Sir Matt) retired. After less than satisfactory spells under Wilf McGuinness and Frank O'Farrell, both over-shadowed by Busby presence, United enjoyed transitory success in cup competitions with the deplorable Tommy Docherty, and then Dave Sexton, whom they sacked controversially to replace him with the bejewelled Ron Atkinson from West Bromwich. City meanwhile had been going through an equally frenetic period: sacking Allison, replacing him with the disciplinarian Ron Saunders and regretting it; trying out Allison's ex-skipper Tony Brook; then recalling Allison, who brought them to the brink of bankruptcy by transfer extravagance; and finally hiring John Bond from Norwich. The Maine Road loyalists stoically endured all these traumas, and were gratified when Bond, rationalizing a team he inherited from Allison with three centre-halves but no defence, reached the 1981 Cup final, losing to Spurs after a replay. It was into this turmoil of Lancashire rivalry, and hair-raising financial instability, that Trevor Francis found himself unexpectedly transferred in the autumn of 1981 – a £1-million counter-attraction to Frank Stapleton and the imminent arrival of Bryan Robson at Old Trafford.

'When I knew that I would be leaving Forest, I wanted to be absolutely sure I was making the right move. It would probably, I thought, be my last. I was twenty-seven. I had nothing from the game, in terms of medals, except a European Cup medal for beating Malmo – though I did get one when we beat Hamburg even though I was injured – and a League Cup loser's medal. No championships, no FA Cup. If I was going to move from Forest, it had to be to a club with at least as much chance of winning trophies, because I was still ambitious to be part of something important, especially as I might not have that many more years at the top.

Almost inevitably, I suppose, Manchester United were interested in me, and Ron Atkinson came over to talk to me. He said he wanted me to play alongside Frank Stapleton, and I understood that part of the deal was that

Garry Birtles would return to Forest. Atkinson said he had already spoken to Clough, and when I mentioned it, Clough told me: 'It's all agreed, you'll be at Old Trafford in forty-eight hours.' But for some reason it fell through, and a week before the first match of the season, John Bond came to see me at the City ground. He was so enthusiastic. He was convinced City were on the way to big things. I can remember his saying: 'We've just had a great season, we could have won the FA Cup – but it's only just beginning!' It seemed an impressive set-up. Bond wanted me as partner for Kevin Reeves, and told me that if I signed, he could still go out and buy another million-pound player the next day. I'd been in two minds about City. At the back of my mind was the situation on Merseyside, where there was always huge rivalry between Everton and Liverpool, and Everton were always the one doing the chasing, Liverpool the one *winning* things. In Manchester, I felt instinctively that the club more likely to win things was United. When Bond said that he could go and buy another million-player besides me, that decided the matter. City were the club for me. Little did I realize then that I'd been completely deceived.

I only briefly spoke to Peter Swales, the City chairman, at the time of the transfer. In fact I only spoke to him a handful of times throughout my eleven months with the club. He never came to the dressing-room or in any way interfered with the day-to-day handling of the players. To complete the transfer, he did all the financial talking with my agent Dennis Roach. The contract Manchester United had offered me was really excellent. What City offered now was far in excess of United. I couldn't believe it. It was much too high. Over three years, which of course were never completed, it was worth £100,000 a year plus bonuses. Swales, it seems, had put me on a contract the club could not afford, I can see that now, but at the time who was I to complain? Obviously with hindsight, my contract was at the root of their problems. Swales could

49

have got me for much less, and if their finances were in the state we now know they were, why didn't City go for two or three players for the same overall total, and build a team properly? A million-pound player ought to be the *last* cog in a side which is already established and the one who will help make the final push to the summit – the way it was with Forest. But the million-pound player should never be part of the foundation in a side still needing two or three other basic players. That's operating back to front. If City really had had the money to go out and buy more players, it might have been different. The reality was the other way round – within a few months they had to start getting rid of players to reduce their wages bill, pushed through the roof by my transfer. Swales was like a man who goes out to buy a Jaguar, and comes home with a Rolls, at the risk of its being repossessed by the finance company.

The trouble had of course begun in Malcolm Allison's second spell with the club, when he had spent millions on players such as Daley, McKenzie, Robinson, Deyna and others. Swales must have supported him in this, and I'm sure I now know why – he was always striving to keep pace with United. And it would always be difficult, because although City had put tremendous efforts into building up the Junior Blues and other aspects of care for the supporters, United had the bigger following, generating a much bigger income. In one sense, I have to blame Swales for allowing the club to overreach itself, but at the same time I sympathize. I, too, used to dream about what City might achieve. It *ought* to be a great club, and it was a wrench when I had to leave only seven months after we had been sitting on top of the League table, with expectation sky-high.

The irony was that I might so easily have gone to United. I felt in 1981–2 that United did not score enough goals to maintain a championship challenge. Maybe if I could have been there with Stapleton it would have been different. I'm sure we could have won the League. I never really felt that Stapleton and Birtles went together. Stapleton needs someone like Tony Woodcock, or myself, or Alan Brazil. With any one of those, United would have won the Championship, I reckon. But the blend was not right, even though the basic squad was good enough to have won. Ray Wilkins and Bryan Robson are two of the players I admire most in the First Division, yet even though they play together for England, I'm not sure whether they give United the right balance. All teams need goals from midfield these days. Look at Liverpool – McDermott, Lee, Souness and Whelan were all capable of scoring, but Coppell, Wilkins, Robson and Moses didn't get enough goals between them. The addition of Muhren improved the balance.

Part of the excitement in Manchester is that the supporters of both clubs have a hunger to win with style, and the rivalry is as great between the players as the supporters. I never got caught up in it the way the local players are. Paul Power would never dream of going to Old Trafford unless he was playing there; Joe Corrigan was the same! But as an 'outsider' I still couldn't help liking United.

Coming to Manchester from Nottingham, there was such an enormous difference, the town was so much more football orientated. In Nottingham, it's a take-it-or-leave-it attitude. In Manchester they care, everyone is either Red or Blue. As a boy in Plymouth, I suppose I was a United fan. I immediately found at Maine Road that the City supporters are tremendously loyal. In some respects the support is bigger than United's, but it's all within the city, while United draws support from all over the country.

In a strange way I found there was not so much pressure on me as at Nottingham: a second £1-million fee was not the burden the first had been. The people have a greater expectation yet are more friendly. It's only through having been elsewhere that I realized what a good club it was.

Players like Nicky Reid could only realize *how* good after leaving. If there was a fault, it was that it was too good. Players got the best of everything, kit, treatment room, travelling, until eventually they took it for granted. Compared to Birmingham or Nottingham City, City is such a big club, it was like walking into a hotel. Everything was done the right way before the cuts.

You could not help being conscious of the past, of the former stars, and there was still talk within the club of the Sixties, of the days of Mercer and Allison. You knew that a great deal was expected of you, that you had so much to live up to. I really wanted to play well for the club, because they appreciated so much what I did on the field. The public were far more aware than at Forest. You could actually hear a reaction from the terraces when you did something spectacular, whereas at Forest there was often no reaction.

Not that I ever wanted to be thought of as a free-loader, but in Manchester as a player you are a welcome guest at so many places, whereas in Nottingham you would always be charged, not that I minded for a moment. The difference is that in Manchester they're delighted to see you, and want you to feel wanted. It's a bigger city, but with the friendliness and hospitality of a much smaller town.

In Nottingham, maybe one journalist would turn up from the Press at the ground each day, perhaps not that. In Manchester, there was a press conference with the two managers almost every day while the teams were in town. When I first arrived, I would give interviews, and feel I'd not said anything really important or significant, then pick up the paper the next day and find huge headlines. The life of the football clubs is so closely interwoven with the daily life of the people.

Whenever I went out in Manchester, I thought of George Best. In my opinion he was the finest player there has ever been in Britain, certainly that I have seen. He could do everything, the complete player. But I can imagine George getting tied up with some of the people, all that free champagne flowing! I loved going out to dinner in the evenings, and I could picture George, the single lad, with his pockets full of money and the town full of girls. I can see how easy it was for him to go off the rails, and I feel for him a lot, it was so sad the way it happened. I'm fortunate that I'm married, yet I think I could have turned away from things, that I could have coped, the way Kevin Keegan has. But if your character was at all suspect you would have no chance in a place like Manchester.'

One of the things which had distinguished United, during the prime of Busby's management, had been the hospitality of the club, a pervading mood of friendliness towards all, which I myself had experienced as a young journalist on *The Times* in the Fifties. Yet during the latter part of the Seventies, it seemed to me, this bonhomie began to evaporate, and City became the place where the doors were always open, where they made greater efforts to reach the young people of the town, to counteract the tide of violence and alienation which had soured the game. United were still a big club, but City were now the one with the family atmosphere which once had been the hallmark of United.

'What proved for me how marvellously friendly City are was the way the old players called in, men like Bell, Lee and Summerbee, jogged a few laps, had a sauna and a cup of tea, and talked about the old times and the new. Even Tony Book came back as youth team manager after being sacked from the first team, which says a great deal. Yet there were moments when I though the club was too friendly, when there was too much coming and going in the treatment room and dressing-room by people not directly involved with the club. Some of the players had their ambition blunted by the degree of luxury: this I particularly noticed having come from Nottingham. It's a great club, but for some of them it was too good. I remember coming back in 1981–2 after losing at Swansea, and on the Monday morning there were players in the team who clearly did not care that much about the result. It showed that they hadn't enough pride in themselves or the club. It is necessary for a club to strike the right balance between what it gives to the players and what it gets back from them. There were times last season when that balance wasn't there.

Yet it was still partly wretched bad luck that City fell away as much as they did in the second half or the season. In December 1981, we went to the top by beating Wolves at home, a match in which I scored one of the best goals in my life. But already we were getting one or two injuries, and you could see we lacked strength in depth. It was particularly severe blow losing Dennis Tueart, with an Achilles injury. At the time he was playing some of the best football of his career. Coming from deep positions, he was the top scorer at the time, and as I've said, it's so important to be getting goals from midfield if you are to be up among the leaders.

From the start of February, when we were still lying second, nothing went right. In no time we were coming apart at the seams – and of all things, at a time of trouble we were getting rid of players just when we needed them, and not replacing them. With two extra players at the start of February, we could still have won the Championship, or at the very least qualified for the UEFA Cup. Instead, Martin O'Neill and Gerry Gow were sold, and Tommy Hutchinson and Phil Boyer allowed out on loan. I could understand Boyer wanting to go, he was not in the team, but I knew we needed him in the squad. As for Hutchinson, he'd played almost every game up till then, but then we let him go to Hong Kong for £15,000! It was obvious we could no longer sustain a serious challenge, then or for some time. I'm sure it was the same for the others, but it was very depressing for me, after all the early hopes. Paul Power had an injury problem, and so did I. People were saying I was 'injury prone', and what had been a happy club on full throttle was now a place of pessimism.

The last straw, for the supporters, was when it was decided to let Nicky Reid go. I gather the club owed money to Seattle, for the transfer of Kevin Bond, the manager's son, and I think Reid went to pay off the debt. In the last match of the season at home to Coventry, Kevin Bond was booed at his first touch of the ball, and all the way through the game, and after the finish had to leave the club by a side exit to avoid an angry demonstration. It was a shame, and totally unfair, because he's a great lad. I think he would like to get away from the club, simply to get away from his Dad, and I think he's right, football-wise.

I played with a father-and-son set-up in Detroit, where Ken Furphy was the manager, and his son Keith was in the team as a striker. It's never a good situation. The supporters don't like it, and players are always looking for those little things to pick on. It weaken's the manager's position, and there's no way I would ever have a son of mine in the club if I became a manager, no matter how good he was.

I liked John Bond as a man from the start, and I still do, though like the rest of us he's got his faults! He was so frustrated by the financial situation at the club, being unable to buy players. The one thing I can't forgive him is for misleading me about the team-building prospects. Bond loved to wheel and deal but after signing Asa Hartford just after he got me, he never bought another player. He would chat openly about how hard he had tried, almost every day he reeled off players he would like to get.

He knew if he could have got his hands on the right player we could have won the League, and the thought was driving him mad.

He can be a bit excitable as a manager, but he's a very good coach. There's a lot of attention paid to coaching at City, and I learned a lot. If Clough and Taylor could have added this aspect of the game to Forest, the team would have been even better. Bond works a great deal on forward amd midfield play, on making the right kind of runs in certain situations, to get wide players to hit the near post with crosses. We concentrated a lot on individual skills within the movement of the game. At Forest we never did any of that. Bond does much of the coaching himself, and comes across as having a real coach's knowledge. He often referred to Ron Greenwood and his time with him at West Ham, for he has nothing but admiration for Greenwood as a coach.

Bond is the type of man who always wants to take part in everything; if things are not going right he wants to demonstrate personally how and why. He takes part in all the five-a-sides, and is a terrible loser and gets very moody! He wants the best from players all the time, and hands out unmerciful stick, it doesn't matter who the player is, even his son. He's always for perfection. But all players are not blessed with the same ability, and though I think he's an excellent coach, at times I think he expects too much.

He has a conspicuous habit of criticizing full-backs, probably because that was his position with West Ham. Two people who really got it in the neck all the time were Ray Ranson and Boby McDonald – and he tore them off a strip to the point where I felt it depressed their play. With some players, it doesn't matter how much you shout, it will never raise them. Some need a more gentle hand, but Bond would knock them so low they were reluctant to express themselves, to take on responsibility. He'd have Ray or Bob in his office and say he was going to find replacements, that they would never play for the first team again. But then he would make it up with them, because he knew, and they knew, that he couldn't afford to buy new players.

One of the few occasions when I nearly fell out with Bond was over my sending off – the first time ever – against Everton at Maine Road on 20 March. There was a loose ball, just before half-time, and I went in on the goalkeeper, and was judged by the referee to have fouled him, though I had thought it was a reasonable 50–50 ball. I fell, catching the 'keeper at the same time. While I was on the ground, someone kicked my heel, and as I got up I was pushed. To defend myself I shoved my head forward. It wasn't really a butt, there was no force, no intention to hurt Billy Wright. It was a gesture, to show I wasn't going to be intimidated. I was astonished when the ref sent me off, because I was in control of myself, but I don't disagree with him, it looked bad, and was silly.

I'd only had two previous bookings in my whole career – a foul on Bob Wilson, the Arsenal 'keeper, and for feigning injury, in the opinion of an officious ref called Burtenshaw, which just was not true. Now I was fined in excess of £1,000 by the club! And the manager said if it had been his son, he'd have taken him behind a hedge and given him a good hiding. I didn't think that was the right thing to say. I talked to Gordon Taylor, chairman of the Players' Union, and appealed against the fine. It annoyed me that there was no recognized code of conduct within the club, with consistent penalties. Nicky Reid and Asa Hartford had been sent off; Nicky had no fine, and Asa £200. Others were suspended on the totting-up process, but *not* fined by the club.

I had a hearing, at which John Smith of Liverpool and Sir Matt Busby were sitting. My excellent disciplinary record was put to them – and the fine was upheld! Immediately I applied for an independent hearing, and within two or three days Bond offered to halve the fine, which I accepted.

What pleased me was that he agreed that there should be a code of conduct for the next season, signed at the same time as bonus sheets.

I've been critical about my time with City. Yet Swales only wanted the best for City, and Bond was a great coach in many respects. And the supporters were tremendous – about whom I can't say enough. There are one or two who have told me they wish I'd never signed, because now they only feel even worse. I loved the club, and I was so sorry to leave, and I know the supporters deserve better. I can only hope the finances improve. If people blame star players like me, I can only say that I've never held anyone to ransom, it is not the likes of myself who have pushed transfer fees and wages sky-high, but the clubs competing for our services. Partly it's pride. When the discussions were going on about my leaving, Swales stated: 'Francis will never go to United while I'm alive!' I could understand his feelings. The rivalry in Manchester runs high, and it makes it a fantastic city in which to be a footballer. That's why I've kept my house, just outside, in Cheshire. I'd love to come back to Manchester one day, and that was one of the reasons why I insisted on a two-year contract when the Sampdoria president wanted me to sign for three years. But what surprised me was that City did not get the first option on me if I do come back. Although I felt City were not good enough to win anything, I never dreamed they would go down! They had enough players to keep them in the First Division. You have got to ask one or two questions about the players' application after John Bond left. I don't blame Swales. City had more ability than Birmingham, who survived because of their fighting qualities.'

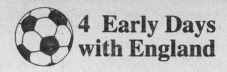

4 Early Days with England

While the World Cup finals of 1974 were in progress in West Germany, the FA appointed Don Revie as England manager in succession to Sir Alf Ramsey. England's elimination from the finals by Poland in the autumn had been in part the cause of Ramsey's dismissal the following spring. For seven matches the stand-in manager had been Uncle Joe Mercer, who had lost only to Scotland at Hampden, and had achieved three draws, with Argentina and, on tour, East Germany and Yugoslavia, all of whom would be competing in the finals. He had introduced touch players such as Dobson, Weller and Worthington, persistently addressed players by the wrong name, and presided over an interlude of cheerful informality. Revie, the tank commander from Leeds, would be something different.

From the outset, however, Revie made the fundamental error of using far too many players, of snatching at straws with incessant team changes, so that he played eight different central strikers in eight games in his first season. This reached thirteen by the end of his second season, in which England had been eliminated from the European Championship finals by Czechoslovakia. The only striker selected consistently was Mike Channon, first introduced by Ramsey in 1972, who, in his forty-six internationals over a six-season spell until abruptly discarded by Ron Greenwood, established himself as England's eighth highest post-war scorer with twenty-one goals, almost a goal every other game. Yet with Revie's constant fluctuation, the opportunity was seemingly there for a player with the flair of Francis to make the break-through.

'My first call-up for a senior international was for Revie's first match, the European qualifier at home to Czechoslovakia in 1974 when I was still twenty. But unfortunately I damaged my knee the week before, and was out of action for a long time, which was a big disappointment. Whatever Revie thought of me, he didn't send for me again until the spring of 1977, just when things were beginning to go really badly for him. We'd lost away to Italy in the World Cup qualifier in the autumn, and now we were playing Holland, a team which we knew would extend us. There were *seven* changes, yet Revie seemed calm enough beforehand, saying to me: 'Go out and play as you do for your club, if you can find seventy-five per cent of your club form, that will do for me.' But we went down 2-0, and the tide was really turning against him.

We had a lot of respect for him because of what he had won with Leeds. You have to respect records. He was very hard-working, though I never got close to him during the few months before he left. He took part in everything we did, the training, the massage sessions, he was always there, always concerned for his players. At the end of the season a year or two before, I'd gone up to him and said that I'd wanted to work at my game, and what aspect did he think I should concentrate on? He'd said 'heading' in a friendly way. It seemed clear to me however that he liked Kevin Keegan and Mike Channon, that he was very close to them and one or two of the other players, and that I was not amongst them. I played in the next game after Holland, when we put five past Luxembourg, and scored my first England goal. I missed the next two matches against Ireland and Wales, but came back against Scotland at Wembley when we lost 2-1, and the critics were really after him. The next day we set off for South America. Revie had gone to watch Finland, and Les Cocker was in charge of the side for the opening game against Brazil. I was surprised to be picked, though I thought I'd done well enough against Scotland. We held Brazil 0-0, and two days later Cocker told me not to play tennis in the sun. I felt sure from his manner this meant I would be in the next game against Argentina.

So I rang my wife Helen to tell her, but that evening Revie was back, and announced that there was one change – Channon for me. I have to admit I was close to packing my bags, put off only by the fact that it was a long way home! Jack Wiseman, the Birmingham chairman who was a member of the FA committee out there, sensibly advised me against it. I talked the situation over with Phil Neal and Ray Kennedy. It was the lowest point of my career. Revie hadn't even seen me, but he must have overruled Cocker. We drew in Buenos Aires with a goal by Stuart Pearson, Trevor Cherry being very unfairly sent off. And there were no changes for the third game against Uruguay, a goalless draw and the worst international match I have ever seen. I felt Revie must bring me on as sub, but he didn't. I felt disillusioned, and less than happy with his regimented routines, the carpet bowls and the bingo, when a lot of the time I and others just wanted to rest.'

What none of the players, officials or journalists knew, except almost certainly Cocker, was that Revie had already arranged to quit and take the Arab jackpot – a renegade action which brought him ignominy, and a ten-year ban by the FA, subsequently set aside in the High Court in a judgement which upheld his claims but even further destroyed his character and credibility. Once again England were virtually out of the World Cup, and managerless. After much speculation and the inevitable clamour for Clough, Ron Greenwood was invited to take over for the following season (1977–8), including the remainder of the qualifying programme against Luxembourg and Italy – a forlorn hope, with Italy able to lose at Wembley and still qualify by scoring more goals against Luxembourg.

'I was in Marbella when the news broke about Revie, and I was shocked. I'd felt he was the right man for the job, but my criticism was that he made far too many changes, it was never a settled team. All good teams become good sides precisely because they are a *team*. I was back in Ron Greenwood's first match against Switzerland. He had travelled round beforehand to every club with an international player, to have a talk. He said he wanted us to take on more individual responsibility, to express ourselves both on the field and in tactical discussions before matches. We drew 0-0 with the Swiss, and the crowd gave us a bit of stick, though the Swiss played well. It was obvious to me that while many people supposed we had a divine right to win at Wembley, this was no longer so – as results would prove.

Greenwood was disappointed, though he never said much. He was not like Clough or Bond, who give you a blasting, he's very reserved. There were many times later on when I thought he should have blasted people verbally, but it did not surprise me that he didn't, because of his character. As I have already said, I don't agree that international players don't require motivation, I think we all do.

In Luxembourg, where we needed a hatfull, the manager named a 3-4-3 formation, with Mariner, myself and Hill in front of McDermott, Callaghan, Wilkins and Kennedy. Keegan was unwell and was sent back to Hamburg, though my feeling was that he would have been left out anyway. Ian Callaghan was recalled because the manager wanted to pack the team with Liverpool players. But after the Swiss game I knew how much football had changed, that we were no longer one of the top countries, that the smaller countries had improved tactically and we hadn't. We'd stood still, our skill factor hadn't improved either. I knew even Luxembourg was going to be difficult, and we only got two goals, which wasn't enough.

There was much speculation before we played Italy at Wembley about whether Bob Latchford, now with Everton, and I would renew our Birmingham partnership. We were interviewed the previous Saturday, and I was fairly guarded. Bob said he hoped it would happen, but the manager decided to bring back Keegan alongside Bob in a 4-2-4 formation, so I sensed it must have been a choice between Kevin and me, a choice that would continue in the foreseeable future.

The line-up was Coppell, Latchford, Keegan, Barnes, with Wilkins and Brooking behind them, and me on the bench. We won 2-0, and it was one of England's best displays since I've been with the squad. I got on in the last ten minutes, but the game was already over. Afterwards I thought to myself how important it is to be part of a successful performance. There's luck, to some extent, to be in when the team is playing well. I wished I'd been playing.

I didn't expect to play in the next game in February against West Germany, but I would have loved to have been on that marvellous Olympic pitch in Munich, a superb playing surface. I little realized I'd be back there the following year in a European Cup final. The better player you are, the more advantage a good surface is. The only change in the front six was Pearson for Latchford, with me again on the bench. I thought England were unlucky to lose 2-1, but I was beginning to wonder how I could fit into the system, with Latchford the target man and Keegan playing off him. With Pearson replacing Latchford against Germany, it was clearly Keegan or me for the other position. West Germany won with a Bonhof free-kick, which we had discussed beforehand, so it was particularly disappointing to be caught out.

Against Brazil at Wembley, which was a World Cup warm-up for them, Greenwood had Keegan in midfield with Tony Currie, and me alongside Latchford. I had the feeling he wanted Kevin and me in the same team, but wasn't sure how to achieve it. Yet I knew that Keegan's best position was up front, so that in the long run it was going to be a question of whether Greenwood would change the system and play without a target-man. Brazil were very physical that night, very disappointing in their attitude. One or two were lucky to stay on the field. It was my first international with Bob; we drew 1-1, and we were together again in the next game against Wales, winning 3-1 in one of those end-of-season games which most of us would rather not play.

Tony Woodcock replaced me against Ireland, in a 4-3-3, but we reverted to 4-2-4 up at Hampden, with me playing alongside Mariner. We won by the only goal in Scotland's last match before going to Argentina for the World Cup finals. I challenged Rough, their 'keeper, for a cross from Barnes: he dropped it and Coppell scored. Their manager MacLeod was very bitter about the result. Greenwood was the most passionate I've ever seen him that day. He'd been spat upon beforehand, when entering the stadium, by the wildly nationalistic home supporters and he was incensed. Yet we didn't need any encouraging. It was the first time I had played with Paul Mariner. He's got a lot of ability, though I would not really call him a target-man.

Our last match of 77/78 was at home to Hungary, who were also just off to Argentina. Greenwood kept to 4-2-4, but used Keegan and me together for the first time up front. In training he devoted a lot of time to us, saying he wanted me to play forward and Keegan to play just off me behind: 'Let's keep it on the floor, make it flexible, you've got *carte blanche*, so go out and give an exhibition.' For the first time in an England squad, I felt I'd really arrived. We had a very clear-cut 4-1 win. I scored, and it was tremendously satisfying to have been part of a convincing performance.

I was very surprised when, in an interview around this time, Keegan said that he had never been able to get to know me, that I was very quiet and he wondered whether I would ever fulfil my potential. Certainly, I *am* fairly quiet, but those who know me would say I am easy enough to get on with – at least, I would like to think they would. He probably said what he did because he is the complete opposite to me. When we check in for a match, I tend to say 'hello' to everyone, and go off to my room. Kevin walks in and bounces around full of confidence. We're all different, and I was surprised he couldn't understand that.'

Just when he had achieved his most significant performance yet, Francis was kept out of England's autumn programme of three matches at the beginning of the 1978–9 season, and the start of the European qualifying group, with an injury which put his ankle in plaster. What had come to be regarded as Greenwood's 'normal' front six – Wilkins, Brooking, Coppell, Latchford, Keegan, Barnes – won a Copenhagen helter-skelter 4-3, then drew in Dublin 1-1, and with Woodcock in place of Latchford beat the Czechs 1-0 at Wembley.

'I went to the Czech game with Alberto Tarantini, Argentina's left-back, who had joined Birmingham after the World Cup. The pitch was very icy, and Peter Shilton was brilliant. We'd gone back to playing without a target-man, but you couldn't judge because of the conditions. Tony Woodcock came off with a bad gash and the sub was Latchford! This clearly revealed the extent of the manager's uncertainty about *how* he wanted to play. Latchford was back for the next game against Northern Ireland, whom we had to play twice in succession, European and Home Championship games. For the second, the formation was 4-3-3 but still with two wingers. If there was a time when I was out of the running, this was it.

My ankle was better and in February 1979 I was transferred to Forest. Playing down at Stamford Bridge for Birmingham not long before, I'd met Greenwood by chance and discussed my situation. He said he thought Forest would do me a lot of good. Also, that I'd not been considered because of injury, but that once I was fit I would be back in. I joined Forest, started as substitute(!) then played wide or in midfield – everywhere but in my best position, up front. I was fit, but how could I force my way back into the England team when the manager wanted me as a striker? Because of the European final against Malmo in Munich, there were no Forest players in the squad for the Scotland match, in which the 'normal'-front six played and England won 3-1.

I scored the winning goal in Munich, was back in the England squad for the tour, and was being tipped to play against Bulgaria in Sofia, the key game in the European qualifying group. The management told me beforehand I'd be playing some part of the match, and I came on as sub for Latchford in an emphatic 3-0 win. I was back in the running and included in the team against Sweden, in a 4-3-3 line-up with nine changes! We drew a bad game 0-0, and I felt it was another illustration of the element of luck in playing the right matches.

Of course it was wrong to make so many changes, and to include Keegan, who had gone back to play for Hamburg the day before, playing three games in five days. The decision was left to Kevin. You could understand Greenwood if he was selecting from twelve, but not when he had a squad of twenty-two. Keegan was obviously at the forefront of his thinking.

It was fairly evident that we would revert to 4-2-4 for the last match, a friendly against Austria, and that it would be between me and Bob, not me and Kevin, even though I had torn Bulgaria apart in the second half. Yet in the street in Vienna a day before the team was announced, I read an English paper quoting Keegan as saying he 'preferred to play with a big fellow up front'. That was a pretty clear indication to me that I would be out. I was! The manager again spoke to me before the game, saying there was a good chance I'd get on, so I knew it must have been pretty close between me and Bob. I came on earlier than I expected, Bob got injured, and I continued where I left off in Bulgaria. We lost an exciting match 4-3, and whether that decided the manager against 4-2-4 from then on, I don't know. At any rate, Bob Latchford never played again, and the manager obviously changed tack.

I came back from America in the summer of 1979 with a groin injury, which put me in trouble with Clough at Forest and out of the England squad against Denmark, for which the formation was 4-3-3. We'd played 4-2-4 against them away, and now the 4-3-3 at home revealed the manager was becoming concerned with the goals we were giving away, and wanted another man in midfield, although we still had two wingers.

For the next game against Northern Ireland, Barnes was out, and I played with Woodcock, who was then still at Forest. We both got two in a 5-1 win, the only time I've scored twice for England. The manager was very pleased, the papers said I must be certain for the team in the European finals in Italy. Keegan had played midfield, but I was more concerned that Tony and I had worked so well together. We should have continued unchanged for the home game with Bulgaria, but it was postponed for twenty-four hours because of fog. As a result Keegan went back to Hamburg allowing Kevin Reeves to get his first cap as a striker. The manager asked me to play deep behind the front two, just when I wanted to build my partnership with Tony.

Tony and I were together again for the friendly against Spain in Barcelona; we both scored in a 2-0 win, with an impressive performance by the whole team. After that game and Northern Ireland, Tony and I felt we had cracked it, that we would be the right combination for the future. The Press and television seemed to agree. I scored probably my best goal for England, with a long diagonal run from the left to take a pass from Steve Coppell, which I controlled in the air and struck second touch past Arconada. I felt very high, the best ever after an England game up till then.'

The euphoria created by that result, against a team not among the top six in Europe, generated a false optimism at home about England's prospects in the European finals – which was undiluted by the wretched misfortune of Francis snapping his Achilles tendon shortly afterwards, playing for Forest. For the next four games against Argentina (3-1), Wales (1-4), Northern Ireland (1-1), and Scotland (2-0), Greenwood alternated between Dave

Johnson and Paul Mariner as the central striker in a 4-3-3 formation.

For the opening match in the European finals against Belgium in Turin, Johnson was partnered by Woodcock, with Keegan playing out of position in the opinion of many, in midfield. England drew 1-1, Woodcock having an excellent winning goal disallowed for a hair-line off-side decision against left-back Kenny Sansom, a decision which was ultimately to cost us a chance of third place. In the next game against Italy, Greenwood took a colossal gamble by selecting Garry Birtles for his first cap, also inexplicably dropping Brooking from midfield, and recalling Kennedy. The choice of Birtles in such a game, whatever the theory, was in practical terms as irrational as Revie's selection of Stan Bowles against the Italians in Rome four years before. For the final match with Spain, Keegan reverted to attack, and Glen Hoddle played in midfield in Greenwoods first 4-4-2 formation. England won 2-1.

'When we played Belgium, I was having transfer discussions with Barcelona in Spain – with my leg in plaster! They took twenty X-rays, announced the injury was mending perfectly, but they never reached a deal with Clough. I watched the game on Spanish television. Ray Wilkins scored an excellent goal, then we gave away a bad one, but still played well enough to have won, even without Woodcock's disallowed goal. Italy was always going to be the toughest match, with a draw a good result. It was a hell of a baptism for Garry Birtles. Having played with him all season, I knew he'd been in brilliant form, but if he was under consideration then he should have been picked *earlier*. Quite honestly he was knackered, what he needed most of all was a rest.

European football is completely different from League football, because of the man-for-man marking. With Keegan's experience of this, twice European Footballer of the Year, we should have used him up front all the time, and this was proved by his effectiveness against Spain. Woodcock had by then gone to Cologne, and we could have played two men who were up against man-for-man every week in Germany.

The irony for me was that, from struggling for three years to get a regular place in the team, now everyone including the manager was saying that one of the reasons we didn't get through the first round was because of *my* absence. I made me feel good, it was some kind of compensation – but I knew everyone would expect even more of me when I got back.'

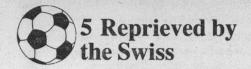

5 Reprieved by the Swiss

The 1980/82 World Cup campaign began smoothly enough when a side including the bustling little Ipswich striker Eric Gates put four goals past Norway at Wembley. Graham Rix, for some time a prominent youngster in the Arsenal side – his had been the missed penalty in the Cup Winners Cup final that summer which had sadly given victory to Valencia in Brussels – was introduced on the left of midfield, while Bryan Robson's growing reputation with West Bromwich assured his selection. However, the yo-yo sequence of results which was to be the despair of the manager, not to say his critics, began immediately following the Norway game, with a 2-1 defeat in Romania. Birtles, absent against Norway, was given his second game because Keegan, in addition to Francis and Wilkins, was injured. Yet the muddle which many of us had feared, and indeed some of us had predicted before the European finals, was now alarmingly upon us. Not for the first time Greenwood made a strange substitution, replacing Birtles with Real Madrid winger Laurie Cunningham and at a stage when the match was almost past saving.

The concern which I had expressed was that Greenwood had prepared and taken to the European finals a team which, because of age, could never survive all the way through to the World Cup. Why not therefore have made the European tournament the breeding ground for the World Cup, when the time available to gain experience with new and younger players is so short? Why, in a difficult cup-tie abroad, leave Coppell on the bench and experiment with the muscular but limited Gates? Why spend three seasons giving experience to Barnes, only then to discard him? Those who criticized the manager could not be accused of arguing from hindsight, because these points had been made long ago.

Although being critical of Greenwood made some of us feel as uncomfortable as being rude to Father Christmas, we were wondering if we could still believe in him, in his curate's egg of a team. All we asked was that he should remain true to the principles he established at West Ham – that win or lose, the team should be worth watching. Yet the idea that Greenwood might, with England, show the world how to play was fast disintegrating. He himself had been strangely hedging against failure, suggesting that if England flopped in the World Cup, it might be because some potential international player married the wrong woman or otherwise fell by the way, not because he got the tactics and selection wrong. This extraordinary suggestion, that it is not so much Saturday afternoon that counts as Saturday night, was another indication, I felt, that Greenwood was too philosophical, too ready to accept being blown off course by factors outside his control, instead of having a determination to mould them to his will. When I asked him how he had planned the development of the team for the European finals in relation to the World Cup, he asserted that an international manager cannot plan, that he is dependent on the production of players. Of course, there is an element of truth in that, but it is a fundamental aspect of the manager's job to discern in advance the character of players and to gauge whether they will develop or will ultimately let him down. Character as much as skill won the 1966 World Cup.

Yet his own inconsistencies were now as considerable as those of his players. How could Kennedy be preferred to Brooking against Italy and then, only five playing weeks later, not even find himself in the squad against Norway? And what of Paul Mariner? He played in Greenwood's second match in '77, yet after Francis's injury was still relegated behind Johnson and Birtles before being recalled against Norway. There was no difference in his potential over three years, except in the manager's opinion. Tactical stability was every bit as important as matrimonial stability.

Another development which was giving cause for concern was the way the FA were exposing themselves as being commercially over-zealous, with the high-priced marketing of England-style kit to school boys, and grossly inflated prices against Norway, fixed in advance in the expectation of profiting from a greater success in Italy. Public disenchantment reached a peak during the unsatisfactory 2-1 win over Switzerland; the team left the field to a volley of boos from a 70,000 crowd which expected rather more for its £365,000. The more you charge, the more people demand. Were the FA justified in winding the price up like a high street shop? The most depressing note of the evening was the commercialism of the message flashed up on the electronic score-board as the boos cascaded down the terraces, the cure for all ill: 'Good luck to the squad from Bird's Eye'. Whether a free poster of Terry McDermott would be sufficient for kids to persuade their mothers to go out and buy an extra dozen beefburgers, one could not be sure, but it was an inescapable fact that by selling out to Mammon – rip-off tickets, rip-off kit for kids – the FA were forfeiting the natural loyalty of the public which Matthews & Co. had enjoyed, when playing for England was glory first and the odd free lunch later.

Of course, the contemporary players care deeply about their performance, and deeply about England. But now that international soccer is mostly confined to scuffling for results against second-rate opponents in qualifying matches, instead of playing prestige friendlies against famous countries and individuals, the public wants either goals or quality for £12.50. I doubt whether many of the 70,000 could tell you a week before or afterwards the names of any two Swiss players. This means that in any home match against lesser teams, England are on a hiding to nothing: the satisfaction *has* to come from the home team.

'For most of that autumn I was injured, slowly recovering from the operation on my Achilles. The manager invited me to the home game with Switzerland, following the defeat with Romania: in this sort of way, as one always knew, he was a sensitive and caring kind of man. I travelled up to London with Raimondo Ponte, our Swiss midfield player, who had joined Forest from Zurich. He was disappointed to be left out of their squad, but he had found it difficult to adapt to the English game and lost his form.

I made my come-back for Forest in the Super-cup against Valencia, and returned to the England side for the home friendly against Spain. I fondly supposed I could pick up where I had left off six months before, but it did not work out and we were beaten 2-1. Glen Hoddle scored a marvellous goal in his first match. He has wonderful skills, and was hoping to establish himself in the team, but wasn't given the opportunity. He never played two consecutive games, and it makes it very difficult when you keep getting left out, you are under so much pressure the next time you are picked. He'd become a favourite with me, he could do things no one else could, and I remember thinking he had more skill than anyone in the squad in my time. We next played Romania at home, a goalless draw, and for the first time I seriously doubted if we would qualify for Spain. At the time we simply thought we would go and win in Switzerland!

The best chance of the game against Romania fell to me from a bad pass from a defender, which left me one-against-one with the 'keeper. It was half-way through the second half, the 'keeper came flying off his line, and I had the choice of shooting past him or going round him, and opted for the second. I went past him, and shot for the empty goal, but a defender managed to get back and clear. It was highlighted on TV and was considered a bad miss, and that's the name of the game. I remember the Romanians leaping about at the end, as if they had won the World Cup, just because they had taken three points off us. Tony Woodcock complained bitterly to me afterwards about the service from midfield being poor, that almost every ball was in the air. We both lost our places for the next match against Brazil.

Peter Withe had been impressive all season with Aston Villa, and now he was brought in for the next three games – Brazil, Wales and Scotland – in yet another new system, with one central striker and two wingers. I was delighted for Peter, I played with him at Birmingham, yet there were times then when he was fortunate to get into the reserves. He's improved immensely in recent years but the new system, with Barnes brought back on the left, was hardly ideal for Peter, who was used to having Gary Shaw alongside him at Villa, and now had nobody. But he had a more than adequate debut.

Brazil won 1-0 and were in a different class in the first half. They were superior in every department, though I tend to think this in every game we play – that we're second-class when it comes to *skill*, that almost every other national team is more skilful than we are in defence, midfield, and attack. I'm not saying they are better players all round, because there are other aspects such as aggression, running power, and competitiveness. But these days,

even lesser countries are matching us for skill. After a
goalless draw with Wales we lost 1-0 to Scotland, a
penalty by John Robertson. I came on in the second half
for Tony Woodcock, and there was a fair bit of national
gloom as we set off for the qualifier in Switzerland.'

Greenwood's continuing tenure was now in serious
doubt. The defeat by Brazil could have been worse, and it
was a reflection of the state of things that the public had
been pleased with a one-goal defeat. The FA were in bad
odour for cancelling at short notice the fixture with
Northern Ireland, and for not having the nerve to demand
from the Football League the preparation which would
give Greenwood a better chance. Cesar Menotti, manager
of World Champions Argentina, shook his head in amazement after watching the Brazil game, saying: 'What we
saw at Wembley was not representative of English football. If Liverpool or Ipswich meet the best club teams of
Argentina or Brazil they will probably be equal, but
England are not equal at international level.' Tele Santana, Brazil's manager, said that they should have attacked more and would probably have won by several
goals. The mood in the England squad was not improved
by Keegan's withdrawal from the Home Championships.
He was not the only one feeling tired, and some of the
players felt he should have stayed around to give encour-
agement, even at the end of a season in which he had had
a wretched run of injuries.

Greenwood was incensed when most of the newspapers
suggested, before the Scotland game, that Barnes was
being left out at the request of other players. This he hotly
denied, though there had undoubtedly been some general
discussion. In his decent, gentlemanly way, Greenwood
wanted to do what was best. Yet leaders must, of necess-

ity, be lonely men. Consultation by a manager with experienced players of the stature of Bobby Moore is one thing, but it should never be made public, and should certainly never be with players whose own positions are less than secure. The situation now was that within a year Greenwood had changed the tactical system no fewer than five times in a dozen matches, and against Scotland appeared to have done so at the request of the players. Against Switzerland, incredibly, there would be no fewer than *seven* changes, if one included the switching of Robson from centre-back to midfield.

'We felt we'd been unlucky against Scotland, that over the ninety minutes we'd been the better team, and we went to Switzerland with the object of winning. I wondered if it was the *right* thing to do. I knew, from playing with Clough, that away from home in cup-ties you should always keep it tight, go for a clean sheet, and I feel that should have been England's approach. I can hear people saying, 'If you can't beat Switzerland, what chance have you?', but that's where international football has changed. What looked an easy group before we started would have been so if we'd tackled the away games this way. There wouldn't have been the panic there was. Look at the kind of job Ian Bowyer did for Forest in away matches in midfield. But England were always liable to give away goals – two each in Romania, Switzerland and Norway, one in Hungary.

Included in the changes was the return of Keegan in midfield and Mariner and myself in attack, but I didn't do myself or England any favours, and was taken off at half-time when we were losing 2-0. Clough had obliged me to play in a friendly against Real Madrid when my Achilles was sore at the end of the season. I was sitting on the bench in the dressing-room at half-time thinking 'we've got to do it', when the manager came up and said: 'If you don't mind, I'm putting Terry McDermott on.' We were losing a World Cup tie, and still this nice man didn't want to hurt my feelings. I was left in the dressing-room to shower, feeling very low. Terry scored, but it was a terrible result, conceding two bad goals. Yet there was no reaction from the manager, no criticism. I wished we could have gone home in the week's interval before we played Hungary. Don Howe worked us hard, and by Wednesday we'd started to put Switzerland out of our heads, yet we knew another bad result would pitch us out of the World Cup.

It was no surprise when I was left out of the critical game in Budapest, and the manager decided to switch Keegan back into attack. What *was* a surprise was the dropping of Kenny Sansom, and the recall of Brooking. Greenwood obviously went for experience, preferring Mills, but Kenny was devastated, he'd played sixteen of the last twenty games and nine in a row. Many people had written off Trevor Brooking, and never thought he was in contention.

I came away from the Switzerland game feeling how much *they* wanted to beat us, whereas we hadn't shown we wanted to win enough. In Budapest it was the reverse, you could sense how much we wanted to win, and as I've said, mental preparation is so important: it was right against Hungary, wrong against Switzerland. Yet there was a time, when Hungary equalized just before half-time, when it didn't look too good for us. Brooking had put us in front. Yet I wasn't looking forward to the second half. Ray Clemence was to blame for the equalizer, and he spent most of half-time in the shower area, he was feeling so low. But it all came right, Brooking silencing the crowd with a fantastic left-foot shot, the best he has ever hit, to put us in front again, and it was all over when Keegan scored from a penalty eighteen minutes from the end. I have no doubt it was an immense satisfaction and relief for Greenwood, especially against Hungary, the country which for so long had been his inspiration.

I've already described events on the way home from Budapest, and when we gathered in September for the next game Greenwood said with a smile: 'I'm still here, thanks for the vote of confidence, now let's get down to beating Norway.' He wanted to play the same team, which had been 4-3-3, the front six having been McDermott, Robson, Brooking, Coppell, Mariner, Keegan. I certainly didn't expect to be in, but Coppell was injured, and the manager asked me to play just behind the front two, with Hoddle replacing Brooking. For twenty minutes it was going well, we were a goal in front through Robson, but for some reason this goal had an adverse effect. We became slack. The two goals we conceded were Sunday morning park affairs. Ray let in the first. Terry miskicked to set up the second. You just cannot give away goals like that at this level. At half-time the manager wanted a bit more width, and asked me to play on the wing, so in one match I played in two positions where I don't usually play for my club.

This was a prime example of a team selected to try to accommodate certain players, when on the day it would have been better to have played to a rigid formation. If it was better to have left Hoddle or me out of the team, then it should have been done, rather than play us out of our normal positions. We all like to pick teams, to think of the eleven best players and put them in. But that way you don't get a *team*. The system you play at international level, with so little time to practise, is as important if not more important than the players you play.

Certainly we thought we were out of the World Cup at the time. We sat in silence in the dressing-room, heads down, everyone dreading going back to England. We felt it more than any other defeat. 'Worst in thirty years!' was one headline. When I got home on the Thursday, everywhere I went in Manchester, shops and petrol stations, people asked, 'How could you lose to Norway?' There were plenty of insults – million-pound stars who couldn't beat a bunch of Eskimos, and so on. If I could have left the country for a week I would have. Southampton were due to play at Maine Road, and the next day I saw Keegan in our hotel in Cheshire, and we agreed they were the worst two days we had ever known.

It was an unbelievable relief when Switzerland let us off the hook by winning in Romania: the news was so good I had to check that it was true. So we were still in a position to qualify, merely by getting a point at home to Hungary, who were already through. I was having one or two injury problems and was left out, Steve Coppell returned, and Mariner gave us a one-goal win. I didn't surprise me the way the Hungarians played, without any heart.

We'd been reprieved, and I just hoped that we would be able to play in the finals in a way which would help people to forget how lucky we had been. I felt some of the criticism, about our commercial activity off the field, was unfair. There was no defence from criticism for what happened on the pitch, but we have so much spare time in between that I think it is quite reasonable to be involved in some commercial promotions. If you look at the Dutch, Italians, Germans or Spanish, they are even more commercial. People say the money means too much, but if it did we would go out and beat Norway by ten goals. People who criticized us for losing overlooked how important the result was to *us*.

We were left with the Home Internationals in which to get into shape, plus friendlies with Holland and Finland. We started off by beating Northern Ireland – with another change of system, playing Wilkins as sweeper behind Dave Watson and Steve Foster. Because of my form with Manchester City, I was back in the side, playing with Keegan up front after a four-year gap, and as on the previous occasion we won 4-1. Yet after all this time, I still felt on trial. Mariner was out of action with tendon trouble. Hoddle was in, on his club form he had to be, and in training the whole of the planning was around him. All the moves in practice began with Glen in possession. The manager explained that he was including Morley, Villa's left winger, to provide Hoddle with the same formation he had with Spurs, Morley representing Galvin, as it were.'

Shortly before England played Wales in Cardiff, Keegan got stuck in the bath with a back injury, returned home, and Withe partnered Francis, with Morley still on the wing and Wilkins reverting to a normal midfield role. England were severely criticized as a team beforehand by the Wales manager Mike England, but though Wales gave Thompson and Butcher some anxious moments, a fiercely struck shot by Francis following a free kick gave England victory.

'It was never going to be a classic because of the pitch. Terry Venables had warned Greenwood, and it was the worst I had ever played on except for Oslo. It seems extraordinary that an international can be played on a pitch used all season for Rugby League. We created enough chances for several goals, the kind of chances you have to be able to take if you're going to win competitions. I was pleased with the free-kick. We'd been practising all that morning, with Glen taking the kicks. But when it was awarded, Glen had gone off and I realized it was in a scoring position and immediately said to Wilkins that I'd have a go. He touched it to Robson who stopped it, leaving me with a dead ball. It changed the angle just enough.

I was surprised by Greenwood getting into a slanging match beforehand with Mike England, it was not his style. I felt he should have gone afterwards and talked to the Press about our victory, instead of refusing to speak. We had done in Wales what the Russians and Czechs had failed to do, we had won. Maybe Wales were unlucky to be the only British team not to qualify. Yet although we'd won, where did we stand? It was obvious the manager was *still* trying to find out what his best team was. What would have been the front three if Keegan had been fit? I don't think I would have played.

At this stage, we could have no idea what the team would be in the opening World Cup match against France. You would have perhaps bet on Robson and Keegan, and besides them probably only Coppell, which almost certainly meant that Hoddle would not play. For Holland at Wembley, I had a groin injury and wasn't considered. I trained alone with Coppell, who had a knee problem, hoping we would be fit for Scotland. We beat a disappointing Dutch team, and Greenwood laid into the players at half-time, unusually for him, saying he was very dissatisfied. When we started tactical work up at Troon for the game against Scotland, it at first appeared I was going to play, but the manager settled for Keegan and Mariner up front, in what had now become a clear 4-4-2 formation with Coppell, Wilkins, Robson and Brooking across the middle. It began to seem that the World Cup place for which I had been fighting for so long had disappeared, the more so when the team played very well in the first half against the Scots. Even as a sub on the bench, and hoping to get on, I could sense it would be a pity if the team had to be changed. But Mariner took himself off at half-time, and five minutes into the second half McDermott replaced

Keegan. Robertson came on for Scotland in place of Hartford and immediately they looked better balanced and we had less scope.

For the final preparation in Finland, Greenwood wanted to play his World Cup team, and with no changes in the front six from the side that started against Scotland. I was convinced that if I saw action in Spain it would be as a substitute unless either of the front players had an injury.

There was press talk that Keegan might be left out, that he was not playing to his maximum, but there was never any doubt in my mind that he would play against France. He'd had possibly his best English season ever with Southampton, was rightly named PFA Player of the Year and in my opinion could consider himself unlucky not to win the Football Writers' award. Having Kevin in the team, a big star, did lift the players, added to which he had a good goal-scoring record. Yet having said all that, had it been anyone else, I think his position in the England team *would* have been in doubt. We easily beat Finland who were the weakest international team we've played. I was on the bench, and was surprised when Greenwood asked, 'How do you fancy a run out on the right?' It's not my favourite position, but I said yes, fine. After the match, I said to him that he seemed reluctant to play me on the right, but that I felt I could do a job there if he really wanted, just as I had done for a year at Forest.'

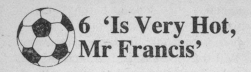 ## 6 'Is Very Hot, Mr Francis'

'We had been apprehensive about the hotel in Bilbao from some of the pictures that had been published in the Press, yet when we arrived we found it was basic but excellent. The staff all went out of their way to be obliging, the food was first-class, there was a good games-room and video-room, and everyone was happy. Preparation is important and ours was good. The training camp, a coach ride away, was absolutely first-class, and I just wish we could have stayed in Bilbao for the whole of the World Cup. The only thing that put us out was the rain in the first week, for we'd planned to train in the evening to avoid the heat, and it rained so much we switched to ordinary hours.

Five days before the opening game, Kevin Keegan hurt his back at the training ground. He carried on, but by the end it was troubling him. I didn't think too much about it, but twenty-four hours later he was obviously in real difficulty, with it affecting his walking and movement. I suddenly realized I had a chance of playing, that he was doubtful; and Kevin himself told one or two of the others that he was pessimistic. It's very difficult to put words to my feelings. Having had injuries in the past which cost me caps, I could imagine how *he* must be feeling. It could not have come at a worse time, yet on the other hand I was delighted now to have a chance of playing. I am sure any professional would tell you the same.'

In addition there had been doubt for some time about Trevor Brooking, who had been battling against a groin strain since before the squad left London, and two things gradually became apparent during the public training sessions and the press conferences which followed them: that Don Howe was having an increasingly influential hand in affairs, and that Graham Rix, one of his players at Arsenal, and not Glen Hoddle, was the imminent replacement for Brooking. Certainly Rix was a natural left-sided player, a quality essential in every team at this level. The day before the team was announced, Howe said significantly: 'We have been trying to get Graham to play a similar kind of game to Brooking at Arsenal this season.'

The doubt about Keegan engaged the attention of the world's Press more than almost any other item of team news among the twenty-four squads in the countdown to the start. Countless camera crews flocked to the England camp. The day before the game against France, with everyone thankful that Argentina had surrendered in the Falklands – the crisis which had totally overshadowed the World Cup back home – Greenwood announced a team including Rix and Francis . . . and Peter Shilton. Everyone present at training that morning had sensed the poignancy of the moment, as the manager stepped to one side and broke the news of his decision, five years in the making, to a dejected Ray Clemence – room-mate and rival of the man who had now got the job. Clemence said magnanimously: 'I'm bitterly disappointed, but only one of us can play, and so long as the one who plays does well, then that is the important thing.' Keegan, whose ambition had been to lead England into the finals for the first time in twelve years, said: 'The back feels worse today than it did yesterday, though I'm still hoping for a quick recovery. I think I have a chance of playing against Czechoslovakia on Sunday. Trevor Brooking and I, who are rooming together, know that those who have replaced us are good enough to give us a chance of taking part later in the tournament. Meanwhile we have decided to put a red cross on our bedroom door.'

'I was interviewed by a bevy of TV crews, Spanish, Mexican, French as well as English, all wanting to know how it felt to play instead of Keegan. I was under more pressure before this game than any I've ever played, even more than before the European Cup final. The tension was tremendous for everyone, there were several asking the doctor for sleeping tablets, and the FA had to provide FIFA with a careful list of any of the drugs which the doctor had given us.

The inclusion of Rix meant that someone who two months before must have had doubts about even being in the squad was now in the team. He was very much a Don Howe type of player, whereas Brooking is the definitive Greenwood player. None of the lads were despondent about the loss, the replacements were there on merit. There were even suggestions in the Press that Graham and I might strengthen the team. Time would tell. After announcing the team the manager pulled Mills and Thompson aside, and said he was making Micky the captain in place of Keegan because he was the more experienced. Micky did really well, it was an honour for him and he is one of the really nice guys in the game. It was all a bit unexpected for him, too, because earlier in the season he'd nearly left Ipswich to go as player-coach at Sunderland. And Paul Mariner must have been thrilled to have made it after all his tendon trouble.

As we walked off the training pitch the morning of the

match, I had been thinking that McDermott, Neal, Keegan and Hoddle, the recognized penalty men, were not in the team, so I said to the manager: 'We've practised set pieces but we don't have a penalty taker!' 'We do', he said, 'You.' He asked if I was happy about it and I said yes, and was left with the responsibility for the rest of the tournament, though the situation never arose.

An hour before the kick-off we went out to inspect the pitch at the stadium. You hear so much about the World Cup, yet when you are involved it's more special than you ever imagined. Walking out on that pitch at 4.15 p.m. to see what studs we would need, and the whole few hours beforehand, will live in my memory for ever, every minute of it. The atmosphere was electric. The stadium was very enclosed like an English ground, the temperature was well over 100°F, and the French and English supporters were making a hell of a din. Different players have different routines. Some like to go out and warm up quite hard, like Wilkins and Robson, and then have a cold shower. Shilton never does, he goes through a long series of stretching exercises and then has to have a cup of tea, wherever we are playing. The Spaniards had to make it specially for him. I like to be quiet and let Fred Street give me stretching exercises, and then a massage from the doctor. Coppell and Sansom are like me, you never hear a word from them.

Phil Thompson is more vociferous, and so is Terry Butcher. It became something we all respected Terry for; with twenty minutes to go when the tension was really building, he would suddenly come to life, start shouting at people, releasing his own tension and motivating others. We liked it, it got everybody going. The most nail-biting time is when you have just left the dressing-room and line up in the tunnel with the opposition. To have a fellow who is six foot four shouting out instructions is intimidating for the opposition and good psychological value. Ten minutes before we go out Wilkins would go round to every player to shake hands, it's something I think he relished. He'd taken over from Martin Buchan at United and I'd always felt he would eventually be the England captain.

Greenwood wished us luck as we left the dressing-room and we went out silently, conscious of the millions watching back home. We didn't need telling how important it was. When the National Anthem was played, you felt enormously proud to be there. The referee kept us waiting two minutes for the kick-off, but I was pleased, my legs were like jelly and it gave me time to knock the ball about and ease the tension. The heat was ferocious. When you're sun-bathing on holiday in 100°F you want to be in the swimming pool every five minutes. The prospect of ninety minutes of World Cup football was daunting.'

As the dour little Mills tossed in the centre circle with the sauve Platini, the chants of 'Allez la France' tumbling out of the packed stands drowned even the thousands of English supporters, who had been roaming the bars of the Basque city for more than a week like an invasion force, happily largely without incident.

England could not have dreamed of such a start as they now enjoyed. In Mar del Plata four years before, Lacombe of France had opened the scoring in the 1978 World Cup with a goal in thirty-one seconds against Italy, a record for the tournament. Now Bryan Robson reduced this to twenty-seven seconds. Wilkins sent Coppell free on the right, and he forced a throw near the flag, which he took himself. It was back-headed on the near post by Butcher, and Robson, completely unmarked on the far post, hooked the ball first bounce past a bemused Ettori. For ten minutes or so France were as mute as the patient in the dentist's chair who has had the anaesthetic and awaits the extraction. England's bustling, determined, physical approach to the game, not without its skill, non-plussed the French for whom Platini was playing so far back he might have been a defender. A chip by Butcher nearly put Francis away as England probed tellingly. Giresse, who was to become one of the truly entertaining players of these finals, beavered away in midfield for France without results. Wilkins lectured Mills and Butcher for their square passing and for almost being caught napping.

In the sixteenth minute Francis, going clear on the left, cut in to the near post and rapped the ball into the side-netting, with Robson yelling for the ball as he arrived a fraction late on a long run to the penalty spot. England were calling the tune in attack, covering and tackling diligently in defence. The urgency was theirs, with the threat of Platini, Rocheteau and Soler evident but constrained. Platini, tackled by Robson, wilted to the ground like a dying swan, and with twenty minutes gone the French still lacked the inspiration needed to set their adrenalin flowing. But England's impetus began to slow and in the twenty-fifth minute France equalized. Francis went off on a run but his pass was intercepted by Larios, whose quick ball to Giresse had England wrong-footed. A long pass down the right of England's defence caught them square and found Soler sprinting clear of Butcher, who may have been looking to catch him off-side. Soler slid by and beat Shilton with a cross-shot which crept just inside the left post. Between now and half-time France blossomed; Soler shot over the bar, Butcher was booked for a heavy tackle and it would have been no surprise had France been in front at the interval.

England reasserted themselves at the start of the second half. Francis nearly caught Ettori off guard with a left foot shot on the turn, and, from the parried ball, Wilkins shot over the bar. France had ceased to run directly at England's defenders, a move which had looked so profitable towards the end of the first half, and on the hour, from a pass by Rix, Francis had a drive turned over the bar. With twenty minutes to go England were in front again. Robson, pushing purposefully forward more than in any match he had yet played for England, was there to meet a cross from Francis with a powerful header. Three minutes later Butcher brought down Platini heavily ten yards outside the area and technically might well have been given the red card – but stayed – and Mariner was back to help head clear the free-kick. France rallied; Rix worked feverishly to help bolster the defence on the left, and it was the English stamina which finally proved too much for the French. With the humidity exhausting even the spectators, England put the result beyond doubt with seven minutes to go. A long cross by Rix was touched by Wilkins to Francis, whose deflected drive dropped in Mariner's lap for a gift he could hardly miss.

'Because we had been practising set pieces in the morning, you can imagine how satisfying it was when we went into the lead so quickly with Robson's goal – the perfect start. I could remember hearing the last thing said by someone as we left the dressing-room, 'Let's get an early goal.' It's always said, and doesn't often happen. Yet we were very quickly aware of the skills of the French. We knew there was a long way to go, and we would be in trouble if we gave them time to dwell on the ball. When I got through to the dead-ball line in the sixteenth minute, I knew I ought to pull it back, but when I glanced up there was no one there who was obvious for the ball, just a collection of shirts. When I looked back at the ball, I suddenly realized the 'keeper had left a space on the near post, so I went for it, but my execution was poor. I knew it must have looked bad, rightly so, and the manager pulled me up about it at half-time. I explained that I couldn't see anyone, but he wasn't happy.

What happened on their equalizer was that I went past Tresor, their sweeper, and played a forward ball to Mariner, but a defender read the pass and got in front of Paul. I never thought at that moment I would be the last English player to touch the ball before it went into our net! Again, I know I was in the wrong, but it was seventy yards from our goal and you don't think about conceding a goal in that situation. Maybe there should be one or two questions about the defence. The one player who was sure it was not off-side was Butcher. Coppell had a shot just on half-time which was very close, but the French had a good patch, nearly overrunning us for ten minutes, so 1-1 at half-time was fair.

After two early efforts in the second half I should have put us ahead on the hour. A throw from Coppell found Rix in acres of room, and he turned the ball back into my path. I ran onto it and if I'd kept it down I think I would have scored. Garrido, the Portuguese referee, gave a corner, but looking at the video I think the ball touched the bar, not the 'keeper's hand. I should have scored, but eight minutes later made amends when I set up the second for Robson. The ball was played through and I took it wide away from Tresor towards Mills, who called 'Leave it.' But out of the corner of my eye I saw Robson making a run over on the left, leaving his marker. I knew there was a chance if I could place the ball exactly right – and I managed to pick him off. Mills joked afterwards that he had called for the ball because he thought I was trying to do too much. It was a vital break. The sense of pressure on the pitch was still enormous, but I thought we'd be okay. When the ball was crossed for the third goal from the *right* by Rix, he was probably howled at by Howe for being there! Wilkins could have volleyed the ball, but I had checked my run deliberately and he touched the ball to me. Yet it ran fractionally too far. I was stretching and couldn't get any power, and really only helped it on its way and was lucky the deflection went straight to Paul.'

The next day in Valladolid, England's chances of reaching the second round were helpfully boosted when Czechoslovakia were held to a draw by Kuwait – a result which was in no way a surprise to me. I had witnessed some of the Arabs' preparation and was well aware that they would be among the most able of the outsiders admitted to the finals by the expansion to twenty-four teams. I had seen them match the Dutch club Go Ahead, and outplay Manchester City. They were Gulf and Asian Champions, Olympic quarter-finalists and had lost only twice in over thirty matches in three years.

   Indeed, they might well have won but for one of the more bizarre refereeing decisions in a badly refereed tournament. After twenty-six minutes Kuwait's centre-back Mayoof obstructed the Czech striker Vizek. The foul was, firstly, a yard outside the area, and secondly obstruction. FIFA had instructed all referees to give a penalty where obstruction involved physical contact, and Dwomoh from Ghana pointed to the spot, from which Panenka scored. From then, almost without interrruption until the end of the match, Kuwait had the 1976 European Champions under pressure. Their centre-forward Faisal unleashed a barrage of shots, often struck first time and from any range and angle, and he equalized with half an hour to go. Yacoub and Anbari also dazzled the phlegmatic Czechs; skipper Saed Al-Houti was everywhere in midfield; and Sheikh Fahad, the Kuwait president, had been rewarded in his belief that his tiny country could come to the World Cup as serious competitors. They had revealed all the positive qualities of their Brazilian coaches, Alberto and Chirol. Afterwards, though dismayed by the penalty decision, Alberto told me how he had spent half the match shouting at his men to exhibit some caution and to get back as they poured forward, leaving a weak defence. As I parked outside their hotel even their mascot camel, quietly chewing the cud, seemed to give a wink of confidence.

'For the second match, my wife Helen and sister Carolyn came out to Bilbao. My inclusion in the team for the first match had been announced too late for them to travel. Sansom, Hoddle and Rix all had their wives out there, too. The manager was very willing for them to come to the hotel in the afternoons when we were free, to bring children and have a coffee, or to come back for dinner after a game. It was a very relaxed scene, yet still totally committed: it was a great squad to be in. The manager wanted it to be as near as possible the same as life back in England. There were only three bachelors in the squad – McDermott, Foster and Anderson – though I don't think Viv Anderson's that far from the altar.

The contribution throughout our time in Spain of those not in the team, such as McDermott, Corrigan and Foster, was tremendous. It's so easy, over two or three weeks, for players who are not having the satisfaction and release of playing in matches to get discontented, but they never did.

The security continued throughout to be extremely tight, much more so than in our tour of Argentina in '77, when I had expected it to be severe. We had the second floor of the hotel, and to get there you had to go past four or five security men. Plain clothes men followed us onto the beach, and it was the same for the wives when they visited us.'

For the first time in three years, Ron Greenwood named an unchanged team for England's second match against Czechoslovakia. Keegan had broken down again the day after victory over France, and Greenwood was at great pains to deny reports that there was any rift between him and the team's regular captain. It was unfortunate for Greenwood that when he talked of hanging a reporter 'from the nearest tree' for suggesting as much, he had named the wrong journalist. The relationships between the Press and the squad were strained in the days before the second game, highlighted by Thompson's quite unreasonable resentment of mild criticism of England's defence in the always thoughtful columns of *The Guardian*. Such tensions, exhibited by both manager and certain of his players, were no more than normal in the crucible of a World Cup in which every nuance is intensified by those to whom it applies.

'The manager had been with Howe to watch the Czechs against Kuwait, and said it was a wasted journey. He did not want to talk about it 'because the Czechs could not possibly play as badly again', so to study them on video we looked at their recent match against West Germany in Cologne. Obviously we hoped to carry on where we left off against the French, but the Czechs were very cautious from the start and it was going to be up to us to make the break. Robson had two chances in the first half, I think he would feel he should have scored. But speaking as a forward, it was a great help to have him coming through in support so often. At half-time we were a bit annoyed we hadn't scored, yet fairly pleased with the way we'd played. Just before half-time Robson felt his groin go, and after tests in the dressing-room it was decided he wasn't fit to carry on. So Hoddle took over.

Our first goal again owed something to our work on set pieces in practice. At every corner it was my job to stand with their 'keeper, looking for any flick on from the near post. When Wilkins's kick came over beyond the near post to the 'keeper, he seemed to have it cleanly, but to my amazement let it go through his hands. The ball dropped behind him to give me the easiest international goal I've scored. It was not the sort of thing I'd ever expect to get in a league match, but it was a great relief, and we sensed we were on our way to the second round. Four minutes later, from a long ball down the middle, I chested it square to Mariner and set off for the return, but a defender checked me with his arm. Mariner had a defender between him and the goal, tried to force the ball into the box for me, and it was deflected by another defender into his own net – a goal which Paul tried to claim!'

It was much cooler, and overcast, for this game. The Spaniards, amicably disposed towards the English, flashed up a picture of Big Ben on the electronic board during 'God Save the Queen', only to be rewarded by moronic chants of 'What's it like to lose a war?' from the mindless hordes from East Ham and Stretford. The opening phases of the game were unbearably cautious, the Czechs incessantly passing back to the 'keeper. Wilkins had a drive parried, but the first real cheer came with the news on the big screen that Rummenigge had scored against Chile. England were playing some slick interpassing football, and in the sixteenth and twenty-sixth minutes Robson went close. His best chance came ten minutes before half-time. Francis centred from the right and the ball was partially cleared. Wilkins switched it to the left, Rix went round one man and crossed perfectly about eight yards out. Robson came thundering in, but his powerful header failed to hit the target, and it was as he fell under his own impetus that he was hurt. The Czechs were whistled off at half-time by the Spanish supporters, and rightly so. They offered little either before or after the two goals which sealed their fate. As Greenwood said: 'All we have done is qualify for the beginning of the World Cup.'

'The day afterwards, Keegan's back was now so bad that he was confined to his room, and the manager asked one or two of us to pop in and have a chat as 'he's feeling very low'. He was having to have his food taken in. He had been to see a local orthopaedic specialist without success. When I went to see him he was clearly in a lot of pain. The talk of a rift with the manager was totally untrue, and irritatingly led to photographers almost camping outside the hotel. Two days before we played Kuwait, Kevin went missing. It was a well-kept secret for none of the players knew where he was. We thought perhaps he was in a clinic in Bilbao, but the night before the Kuwait match, the manager told us he was in Hamburg.

The next we saw of Kevin was the following day at the training ground. He told me to keep secret the fact that he had driven to Madrid, a seven-hour journey, to avoid the Press and had flown from there to Hamburg to see a specialist he had consulted before. By the next day he said he felt good enough to play.'

Kuwait, in the interim, had been involved in extraordinary scenes in their game with France, when they had refused for seven minutes to restart after Giresse had made the score 4-1 late in the second half. As he was running through, a whistle had been blown in the crowd and many of the players, including the French, hesitated. The Russian referee Stupar allowed the goal, but after intervention by Sheikh Fahad on the touch line, and counter-protests by French manager Michel Hidalgo, Stupar annulled the goal and restarted the game with a dropped ball from where Giresse had made his run. FIFA subsequently suspended Stupar and fined Kuwait £7,000. Sheikh Fahad, dubbed 'His Highness the Royal Hooligan' in one English paper, categorically denied that his gesture from the main tribune had been a signal for his team to leave the pitch, only that he wished to speak with them to tell them to continue the game. Part of the Kuwaitis' resentment stemmed from the fact that one, if not two, of France's goals had been arguably off-side, and they were convinced, not without reason, that FIFA were trying to 'arrange' the second round. I had sympathy with their sentiments, but such behaviour could only put them in bad odour with the authorities in times to come. Yet in spite of this emotional trauma, they proceeded to restrict England to a single goal, while France, needing only to draw with the Czechs to go through, did just that.

'We had one or two injury problems before the Kuwait match besides Keegan and Brooking. Sansom could have played at a pinch but Neal took over; Robson was still unfit so Hoddle continued; and Foster replaced Butcher, who had one booking and was not risked so as to ensure he was available against West Germany in the second round. There was talk among the players about whether, because we had already qualified, the manager would try to give everyone a game. He'd done it in the past, trying to be loyal. But as Brazil had shown the night before, when they quite rightly kept an unchanged team for the formality of their third match against New Zealand, the World Cup is not a time for being loyal to substitutes. When Greenwood announced the team, he said he wanted to keep it as near as possible to what had become the regular side. The match was like the First Division against the Fourth, and I just haven't got the answer about how to deal with the problems you often get in this situation. We knew we ought to win; that they didn't play with a sweeper; that they used off-side tactics very effectively. We knew what to expect, but were caught repeatedly, though there were times when we genuinely beat the trap but were let down by bad decisions on the line.

The goal against Kuwait came from a long clearance by Shilton, which I flicked on to Mariner and then kept on running for the return. Paul back-heeled the ball back into my path, which left me about forty yards from goal, blocked by one defender, Mahboub. It's the kind of situation I like to be in, going head-on at a defender at speed. I knocked the ball past him and shot from the edge of the area. At half-time the manager stressed how important it was to score as many goals as possible in the second half, because of their value in the event of a points tie between two teams in the *second* round – which actually turned out to be completely wrong because the competition wasn't organized on those lines.

I had more chances at goal in that one game than at any other time in my international career. I was pleased with the goal, but it should have been a hat-trick. At the end of that game Rummenigge was already the competition's top scorer with four goals, but it should have been me. Why did I miss two or three? Physically and mentally I was tired, more so than ever before during a similar spell of competition. Because of the off-side trap, Mariner and I had to make so many runs, up and back, to try to beat it. Once again it was unbelievably hot. After ten minutes, a Kuwait defender came up to me and said: 'Is very hot, Mr Francis.' And I thought, 'Blimey, if he thinks it's hot after the kind of heat they get in the Middle East, then it must be.''

7 Scotland: A Social Victory

'Scotland had been the most impressive of the three British qualifiers, and they must have been dismayed by the draw for the finals, being drawn with Brazil and Russia. I was very dissatisfied personally with the way the teams were arranged in the different groups, and particularly with regard to, say, New Zealand, as well as Scotland. New Zealand had not only had to play more teams than almost anyone to qualify but had to travel further, and it was a great achievement for them, together with the other five 'minnows'. Yet they were all shoved into groups in a way that suggested the organizers were trying to get rid of them as quickly as possible. This was a poor reward for what they had done. I think the World Cup should to some extent be on the same principle as the FA Cup, where the highlights are so often provided not only by the small non-League club being drawn against one of the giants on its own ground – of course, not possible in the World Cup finals – but by small clubs getting through to the later rounds after a favourable draw. If two small teams get drawn together, then one of them is certain to go through; if two big clubs clash, well, that is bad luck, it's part of the fun, like Arsenal and Spurs or Swansea and Liverpool in 1981–2. It adds to the drama. And if you look back, the North Korea result in 1966, when they beat Italy, is remembered almost as much as the final between England and West Germany that year. I think it was wrong for six minnows all to go out in the first round, and for England to be seeded just because we were past winners. Normally I would say the Scots should just have to accept their luck, but in a draw which was so blatantly 'arranged', they got the short straw. I would like to have seen one of the minnows get to the semi-final. Look at the interest generated by Northern Ireland.'

Scotland's group opened in Seville on a day so hot that it made Guadalajara and Leon in 1970 seem like a picnic. At four in the afternoon it was nosing above 120°F, at which point I still had some 200 miles of the 400-mile journey from Madrid to drive. The rush of air coming into the car through the open windows was like the blast from an open oven. To slow down to go through the imposing, ancient city of Cordoba was almost to fry in the seat, and I arrived in Seville with barely an hour to spare. Three crazy American bachelors – by descent Columbian, Prussian and Iranian – who were still recovering from an all-night party the day before and were in Spain to see 'the Games', mercifully allowed me to have a quick shower in their hotel room, just around the corner from the stadium, and through the open window the steady beat of the samba drums of Brazil was making the hair on the back of one's neck stand up in expectation.

And justifiably. Not only did Brazil and Russia set the tournament alight after the leaden opening games in Barcelona (see Chapter 8) and Vigo, they gave back to football the skill, adventure, spectacle and sportsmanship which has been disappearing progressively since 1958. Here was the best Soviet team yet to come to the finals, a superb amalgam of the Dynamo clubs of Tbilisi and Kiev, heirs to the fame of Moscow Dynamo of 1946. But by the end the humid night air throbbed with an incessant samba beat as Brazil's supporters, themselves a unique spectacle wherever they gather, like a huge green and yellow moss, celebrated one of the great World Cup goals. Socrates, their elegant, strolling captain, had side-stepped two desperate Russian defenders to strike home a soaring, fearsome. unstoppable shot from over twenty yards. That seventy-fifth-minute goal had rescued the three-times champions from impending defeat, and had detonated a final, dazzling onslaught which culminated with left-winger Eder's winner twelve minutes later.

If I live to be eighty, I would not hope to see a more memorable game, a match which contained more action than almost the whole of the 1978 finals put together. What an array of talent we now knew Scotland must overcome; a daunting sight for Jock Stein. For in the final analysis one had to pay tribute as much to the noble contribution of the Russians. How our hearts went out to this disciplined, imaginative team as, bare-chested, they dragged their cramp-ridden bodies off the pitch at the end. The Spanish referee, Lamo Castillo, had made three of the most extraordinary decisions through neglect. He was another penalty-shy official who ignored what appeared to be three brazen fouls, the two most blatant by panicking Brazilians.

Yet Russia never resorted to pettiness, never for a stride deserted their exhilarating attempt to overthrow the world's premier football nation with the cross-bow thrusts of their wingers Shengelia and Blokhin. A roar from the crowd like breaking surf greeted the first electrifying run by Zico at the heart of Russian defence, where their skipper Chivadze played the ninety minutes with an iron will, and it was no time before the calm accuracy in midfield of Bessanov and Bal of Kiev and Daraselia of Tbilisi threatened the supremacy of the Brazilians. Indeed, they went in front with a freak goal after thirty-four minutes when Waldir Peres, always a suspect 'keeper, allowed a long-range shot from Bal to squeeze through his arms. Two minutes later Chivadze, struggling for a high ball with centre-forward Serginho, clearly handled the ball shoulder high, and astonishingly the referee gave an indirect free-kick. At half-time Brazil replaced Dirceu, star of the '78 finals, with Paulo Isidoro in midfield.

As the second half progressed, it looked as though Russia might hold out, and there was an element of anxiety in the Brazilian play – until Socrates produced his pearl. Thereafter the anxiety switched ends, though with the score still level with seven minutes remaining, Brazil's centre-back Luizinho handled in the penalty area. The referee looked hard at his Spanish linesman for confirmation of what he himself suspected, but did not receive it; and with three minutes to go, Eder ran at the defence and unleashed the winner.

'Russia played really well, we could all see that from the television, which is not always a guide, and it was never sure that Brazil would win. The heat must have been fantastic, and my feeling was that it contributed to Russia's conceding the late goals. Yet the one by Socrates was something special. After watching the game, I reckoned Scotland would struggle to qualify.'

As the inevitable jam of people and traffic developed round the Brazil team's hotel near the stadium, I set off through the sweltering night with Norman Fox of *The Times* on the 180-mile haul to Malaga, and the next night's start to Scotland's expedition. We passed almost as many ancient British black cabs with tartan streamers as you would see down Argyle Street, Glasgow, on a Saturday night after victory over England. But the streak of self-destruction which had stalked six previous World Cup managers had not been dispelled by Stein. Scotland were to thrash New Zealand 5-2, and the two goals conceded would prove their undoing.

What, for an hour, was a walkover against raw, inexperienced but athletic opponents, was for ten minutes in the second half suddenly turned into a crisis as Sumner and Wooddin of New Zealand pulled the score back from 3-0 to 3-2 to turn the game on its head. They were the kind of goals on which the legend of Scottish vulnerability has grown. The banner which beforehand proclaimed, 'Don't worry lads, Ally MacLeod's in Blackpool' – a reference to the kamikaze manager who had been in charge in Argentina – had too clearly tempted fate, and the delirious chanting of the Scottish fans at the eventual five-goal tally contained elements that reminded one of the orchestra which played as the *Titanic* went down.

There were moments when New Zealand looked as if they were going through a physical training routine, rather than playing a World Cup tie. Between the seventeenth and thirty-first minutes, Dalglish and Wark, twice, piled in the goals with unintentional assistance from 'keeper Van Hattum, which erased all memories of the 1978 disasters against Peru and Iran. It was not a matter of how, so much as how many?

Yet nine minutes into the second half skipper Danny McGrain and his 'keeper Alan Rough played through one of those slow-motion nightmares, allowing Sumner to burst past between them and score. McGrain was the more to blame, but worse was to follow as Wooddin ran half the length of the field through a static defence for a second New Zealand goal. Robertson stopped the rot with a clever free-kick over the defensive wall and Archibald, substitute for a heat-exhausted Alan Brazil, got a fifth with a header. It was a bizarre game, and the realistic Stein said: 'I'm not too dissatisfied, but we made bad defensive errors and gave them two bad goals. We'll be assassinated by Brazil and Russia if we make mistakes like that.'

'New Zealand, I would say, were the weakest team in the tournament. I just could not believe it when Scotland, three up against such opposition, and never in any danger previously, then got in such a mess. With New Zealand three down, they had not even looked like getting close enough to have a shot at goal, but after grabbing two it looked for a while as if they might even equalize. This was where Scotland lost the first round (goal difference decided the qualifiers in the event of equal points in the first and second rounds). Nevertheless I was surprised at the team which Stein picked for the next match against Brazil; it seemed that he virtually accepted Scotland would lose before the start and I couldn't understand his thinking, playing with only one forward, Archibald – it's not Scotland's game to play containing football. In fact they scored first, proving what I'd often felt about Brazil: that they, too, were always liable to give away a goal. I though the final score of 4-1 was slightly false, that the Scots had deserved better, yet it was the cause of the feeling that Brazil were all set to be champions again.'

The scene before the start in Malaga's blue-and-white painted stadium restored some of one's faith in human nature as well as football. For almost two hours before the kick-off, Scottish and Brazilian fans stood shoulder to shoulder on the terraces, unsegregated, slogging out the rivalry with a good-natured vocal vehemence which had an almost therapeutic value, a simultaneous appeal to

Providence and acceptance of Fate. There was not a punch thrown, as far as one could tell, between these huge terrestrial choirs. *This* was how the World Cup should be.

Cerezo returned to the Brazil side after suspension, but against every expectation it was Scotland who scored first. Three times at least Brazil had already threatened to go in front, when the most improbable figure, Dundee defender David Narey, stepped up to ignite the flames of real conflict. Souness hit a perfect long ball from left to right, Wark touched it square, and there was Narey, belting through on a run, to crash the ball into the roof of the net from the edge of the penalty area.

Although none should query the ultimate degree of Brazil's superiority, the game, like so many – like Brazil's against Russia – turned on a refereeing decision. In the thirty-third minute Cerezo, going for a return ball which it was by no means certain he would reach, a yard or two outside the penalty area collided with a static Hansen, who in no way had moved across his path. At the very most it was obstruction and an indirect free-kick, but the Costa Rican referee Siles Calderon awarded a direct kick. Zico, with great aplomb, curled the ball over the Scots' wall and past a motionless Rough to put Brazil level. Their former manager Joao Saldanha, now a television commentator, was emphatic: 'It was without doubt an indirect offence – but why did Scotland, setting out to play a defensive game, give so much room in the second half to our left-winger Eder?'

After half-time Scotland were swamped. Once centre-back Oscar had headed them in front from Junior's corner after five minutes, Brazil were in full flood. Eder beat Rough with a fiendish chip, and although Stein sent out Dalglish and McLeish for Miller and Hartford, Falcao hammered a fourth. Stein's early prediction that all would hinge on the game with Russia was now uncomfortably true. It was little consolation that Tele Santana, Brazil's

106

manager, said: 'We cannot play better than we did in the second half.'

'After Russia had done the necessary the next day, getting the three goals they needed against New Zealand to make sure that Scotland would then have to beat them to go through, all of us in the England squad were interested to see what Stein's selection would be against Russia, and whether he would include Dalglish. There was talk that Kenny might be left out, and when he was not even on the bench, we wondered if there had been some kind of rift. Instead, Stein brought in Jordan, who scored a good goal. Scotland played excellently in the first half, but I had the feeling that they were not going to win, that the Russians were improving. Rough might have made a better last-ditch effort at stopping Shengelia for the second goal, but the fault lay with Miller and Hansen, who will always have nightmares about it. Ever since I've been involved with England, we've had several goalkeepers such as Corrigan good enough to be in the team who have never got a chance to play because there were even better men, yet they would have been permanent fixtures in the Scotland team. When you're up against it, you're looking for something extra from the 'keeper. Whereas Rough actually helped Shengelia to make up his mind what he would do, someone like Shilton would have made the goal seem so small that Shengelia would have had doubts.

Scotland certainly brought a lot of enjoyment to spectators and viewers, but as always they seemed vulnerable by doing the occasional daft thing. In any tournament the name of the game is getting results, not entertaining, the ideal being to find a combination of the two, while cutting out the kind of errors they often made.

Graeme Souness had a good tournament. I've become an admirer of his in the last two years, he's one of the outstanding midfield players in Britain, a superb passer of the ball with a powerful shot who hits the target consistently. I just wish he would do what he did in the last quarter of an hour against Russia more often, go forward more, take defenders on as he did for the 2-2 goal. It's what stands between his remaining a good international player and becoming a great player. Gordon Strachan was very refreshing: he wanted to go at people all through the first round, and he was good to watch. Frank Gray and John Robertson combined well on the left. They'd both had a difficult season with their clubs, and in Spain they recaptured their old form.

Dalglish has had a fine career, and I was certain he'd be back. He's been written off, but I think we'll find he's still around on the international scene in a couple of years, because he's such a class player, and that kind of touch lasts longer than physical attributes. After a tremendous season for Ipswich, a lot was expected of Alan Brazil, and I was delighted he broke through. I know him because in '78 we played together in Detroit. He'll be disappointed he only had seventy minutes' playing time, fifty against New Zealand and twenty as a sub against Russia, but he's still twenty-four with more World Cups to come.

I remember reading in the newspapers up at Troon that Stein was upset with Steve Archibald when he arrived back with the squad late after the FA Cup replay; and he wasn't even in the sixteen against England, so he must have gone to Spain happy just to be in the squad. Yet he played in all three matches, though he won't have liked playing up front on his own against the Brazilians. It's a thankless task, and you have to rely so much on midfield players getting forward in support.

Usually John Wark manages this, for he's been scoring a lot the last two seasons, and he could have had a hat-

trick against New Zealand. There are not many international midfield players who get into the box as often as he
does. But someone like Wark, making those runs, would
suffer from the team changes. It's so important to keep
the team together the way Northern Ireland and England
did. Scotland never really gelled, you never knew what
their best team was, and you wondered whether Jock
Stein did. It's all very well to have outstanding players but
you have to concentrate on shaping a team, and after
playing us at Hampden, Scotland were still experimenting
against New Zealand. Against England, Stein tried to fit
Dalglish, Jordan and Brazil into the same attack! Certainly with Stein, unlike the past, you could be sure that
the squad would be prepared right, that he would stand
no messing. He'd been so successful with Celtic, and
nobody knew the ropes better than he did.'

So the higher realms of the World Cup tournament once
again eluded Scotland's burning hunger and great natural
talent for the game. As a lone piper played a last lament in
the steamy, emptying Malaga stadium, we knew the
competition was the poorer for their going. They had
played with fire and style and finally with brimming
hearts, but the draw with the able Russians was not
enough. There was a defiant pride in the standing ovation
their supporters gave them at the finish, as though to say
they had had value for money and they would be there
behind them the next time. There was many a grown man
with tears on his face all along the Costa del Sol that night,
as it began to sink in that Scotland had given more than
had been expected yet for the third time consecutively had
gone out of the first round on goal difference.

What promise there had been in the first quarter of an
hour as Jordan, from a cross by Robertson, brought a

marvellous save out of the agile Dasaev, then six minutes later raced through on Archibald's pass to score a fine goal. 'Here we go,' sang the tartan hordes, who had faithfully trailed back and forth over the gruelling hills between Seville and Malaga in transport which may once have passed an MOT but was now at times hard pressed on the hills to pass a bicycle. Then on the hour, that superb defender Chivadze had come bursting through to equalize, and all was in the balance again. Unquestionably there should have been a penalty for Scotland when, with fourteen minutes to go, Wark was pushed off the ball blatantly from behind, coming in on the far post to meet a cross from Robertson – a replica of the ball to Francis in the European Cup final. But the Romanian referee Rainea was hardly likely to give a penalty against Russia for an off-the-ball offence at that stage; and eight minutes later, in the tension of the moment, Miller and Hansen had their aberration which allowed Shengelia to score. Souness got one back, but it was not enough.

Yet there was one battle that had been won. Four years before, Stein had set out single-handed to rationalize a small nation's mistaken sense of herioc destiny. Of course he believed in pride, but not in the self-destructive streak of extrovert manhood which so often ended as public exhibition of immaturity. In the past two weeks Scotland had discovered honour, dignity and admiration, while still injecting their own special character into the competition. The sabre-rattling lust for heroism had been replaced by the intelligent, controlled approach to the international arena. One man alone was responsible for this. This time, both the team and their supporters had got it right. In temperatures of over 100°F, the Scottish clans had grown up side by side, on and off the field.

There had not been a single arrest for violence or drunkenness in Seville or Malaga throughout the Scottish presence. Even if Stein had not won the competition yet, he could take some of the credit for the social victory. He had tamed the wild animal in the collective soul of Scottish football. He knew that many other countries were playing a brand of football which was superior – but the important thing was that he *did* know. There had been Scottish managers in the past who, one has to say, were not sure where the sun rises.

Finally and tantalizingly, there was the thought of what Scotland might have done had they possessed a 'keeper of even average international competence. Stein was sensitive enough not to spell it out, but most people recognize that Scotland has had no one reliable between the posts since Bill Brown twenty years ago.

# 8 Cynicism Rules, OK?

In a Barcelona stadium ringed with more police than we had seen in either the 1978 World Cup in Argentina or the Moscow Olympics, a small boy released a dove to signify the opening of the 1982 finals. As he walked the forty yards from the touchline to the centre circle with a billion eyes upon him, the as yet unseen dove was contained in the football he was clasping. For fully a minute the manufacturers of that ball had the most priceless free advertisement. Amid such contradictions, it was difficult to take seriously the intended message of peace and sportmanship in Spain's opening ceremony before Argentina and Belgium got down to the serious business. And business is what it has most certainly become.

Football's most expensive player, the £3-million Diego Maradona, was about to make his debut in the World Cup for Argentina, but would we be allowed to see him play, by Belgium or anyone else? We did not have long to wait for an answer. After only twenty seconds Guy Vandersmissen, a twenty-five-year-old from Standard Liege specially picked for the job, lunged at Maradona and missed. After two minutes and fifteen seconds, Coeck lunged and the robust little Argentina rode the foul with the skill of a surf-boarder cresting a Malibu roller. After three and a half minutes Coeck lunged again and brought Maradona down. The pattern of the World Cup had been set irrevocably. It was further clarified when, for a free-kick for Argentina in the centre-circle,

Belgium, who were laughably said to have selected an 'attacking' team, had all eleven men behind the ball.

Belgium's 'attacking' team had the two full-backs, Gerets and Baecke, marking Argentina's wingers Diaz and Bertoni; two centre-backs, Millecamps and De Schriver, marking no one; and two midfield men, Coeck and Vandersmissen, marking Maradona. If he got past *them*, then Millecamps and De Schriver were waiting for him. The security was to be as total and tiresome a feature of the tournament on the pitch as outside the stadia.

Yet Belgium's utterly negative approach to the first half, and the victory by Vandenbergh's goal seventeen minutes into the second half, did not disguise the truth – that the World Champions of '78 were finished. Though Maradona hit the bar a quarter of an hour from the end, it was a galling experience for him in the Nou Camp Stadium where he would start the following season for FC Barcelona. Cesar Menotti, who had controversially left Maradona out of the team four years before, had now fallen into the trap of so many successful managers – keeping a winning team together when it has passed its zenith. There were nine of the '78 team still there, yet on this evidence Bertoni, Kempes, Gallego, Olguin and Tarantini were barely worth their places. Most extraordinary of all, in view of Argentina's long preparations for the defence of their title, they looked less than fit against Belgium's large, powerful and fast side.

'Belgium's win didn't surprise me as I didn't really give much to Argentina's chance of retaining the Cup. Yet, having said that, although he didn't have the best of finals, Maradona is still in my opinion the outstanding player in the game, with his strength and control, and the incredible changes of direction which his low centre of gravity allows him. Argentina were fortunate in having excellent players in all the central positions – Fillol in goal, Passarella as sweeper, Ardiles in midfield and Maradona up front, but without any of those four, they would have been really ordinary.

I was interested to see how Alberto Tarantini would play. He was a good friend of mine from Birmingham days, and I was godfather to his daugher. But I was very disappointed with his performances. I felt he should have got much more involved in the game than he did. The only time he did so was against Brazil. Kempes had a fantastic World Cup in Argentina, but when I played against him in the Super-cup in Valencia for Forest he didn't play well, and when you suddenly find a recognized striker playing in midfield it raises immediate doubts about his form, as it did now.

Belgium proved in the opening game they would be difficult to beat, though I never went along with Pele's assessment after that first match, that they were capable of winning the Cup. They probably worked harder than any other team in the tournament, apart from Italy, at closing down opposing players, at working in groups of two and three to get the ball back. They were built on a strong defence, and deliberately allowed Argentina to come at them; but the real test, in a way, was when they played El Salvador. They had to go *at* them, and when the obligation was on them to play, they were not as good. That game told me a lot; although I could see them doing well, I never thought they would go past the semi-final. I was most impressed with their right-back, Gerets, and it must have been a blow when he had to return home with concussion before the second round. He looked the best right-back in the competition.

Hungary I only saw in their second game, against Argentina, after they had put ten past El Salvador in their first game, and I felt they threw in the towel.'

Hungary became the first team in World Cup history to reach double figures in a single match when they beat El Salvador 10-1, with Kiss, fifty-sixth-minute substitute for Torocsik, scoring one of the fastest ever hat-tricks in an eight-minute spell. The euphoria soon vanished against Argentina, when Maradona showed his real form with two goals as Hungary went down 4-1. Argentina then, like Belgium, scored a narrow and tedious win over El Salvador to reach the second round.

'Italy and Poland were always favourites to qualify in their group, which was decidedly unimpressive, though the team which caught our eye on television was Cameroon. They didn't lose a game, and though they only scored one goal they only conceded one, and I thought they might well have won all three games. You would never have supposed at *that* stage that the group would produce two semi-finalists.'

The goalless opening draw between Italy and Poland was wholly predictable, and there was even talk of an 'arrangement', similar to the subsequent alleged one between West Germany and Austria which caused such an outcry. Dino Zoff, celebrating his one hundredth appearance, had to make only one save. Rossi, his three-year suspension for bribery lifted a year early to allow his return, was so indifferent that his continuation in the team was loudly questioned by the Italian Press. Italy might have won when Tardelli hit the bar in the eightieth minute after Antognoni had had a header cleared off the line by Lato.

Cameroon then held Peru – who in turn kept the group open by drawing 1-1 with Italy. Diaz, Peru's captain, deservedly equalized six minutes from time with a deflected shot. Showing some of the style which had so troubled Scotland four years before, Peru might have won but for some fine saves by Zoff. They were denied what seemed a clear penalty when one of their players was brought down by a fearsome tackle across the thighs in the second half, but West German referee Eschweiler ignored the incident.

A brilliant performance by Cameroon's skipper and goalkeeper N'Kono earned them yet another draw, this time with Poland – who eventually exhibited some real style when they put five past Peru. Lastly, Italy ground their way laboriously into second place with a draw with Cameroon, having scored a miserable two goals in three games to Cameroon's one. The five drawn games out of the group's total of six had produced only four goals, and the inhabitants of Vigo and Corunna must have wondered whether this really could have been the World Cup there had been so much talk about for the last four years.

In Gijon they soon had something to shout about when, on the same afternoon that England were beating France, Algeria toppled Germany 2-1 – a result to compare with the famous victory of the United States over England in 1950 and with North Korea's against Italy in 1966. The size of the upset could be measured by the fact that Germany were 9-1 on with the London bookmakers: and whereas Germany had lost only two games since the last World Cup, Algeria had finished fourth in the Africa Cup three months before. Yet now, on the admission of Germany's manager Jupp Derwall, his team was beaten by intelligence and clever counter-attacking. After a goal-less first half, Belloumi, Africa's Footballer of the Year, made the opening goal for Madjer, one of the outstanding newcomers to the world stage; and although Rummenigge equalized, Algeria grabbed the winner a minute afterwards with a superb goal from Belloumi.

The next day Austria beat Chile, with a header by Schachner, and now had to face Algeria, the competition's most exciting outsiders, I travelled to Oviedo from Bilbao, having watched England's defeat of the Czechs, along a road which for much of its 170 miles is little more than a spiral staircase, either going up or down, along the beautiful northern coast. When I arrived, Bobby Robson, there as a spy for Greenwood, confirmed that Algeria's win had been no fluke – a fact which I soon saw for myself when they outplayed Austria for much of the game, and they should have gone top of the group ahead of Germany, who had just beaten Chile 4-1 with a hat-trick from Rummenigge. But Algeria squandered their chances, and a two-goal win for Austria (Schachner and Krankl the scorers) was a travesty considering their caution.

Algerian supporters, several hundred in number, had threatened to pull down the perimeter fence before the start when one of their group, caught joyfully but illegally entering the field, was removed with gratuitous force by the police. Inside, Assad, Zadané, Madjer and Belloumi at times ran rings round the Austrians; Koncilia made several full-length saves and Belloumi hit the bar, but Algeria could not capitalize on their moral superiority. In one of the most cynical and symbolic gestures of the whole tournament, with Algeria pressing five minutes from the end, Austria's centre-back Obermayer chopped down Madjer, then laughingly held out a hand to help him back to his feet. The Australian referee Boskovic might as well have been blowing his whistle back home for all the influence he had.

Still attacking more persistently than almost any team in the finals, Algeria subsequently scored after only seven minutes against Chile, and re-emphasized their ability by winning 3-2 after leading 3-0 at half-time. Now Germany had to beat Austria to qualify. The game in Gijon was to prove one of the most deplorable in the World Cup history. Hrubesch scored for Germany after ten minutes, and both teams then went through the pretence of playing for the remaining eighty – a one-goal defeat still allowing Austria through ahead of Algeria on goal difference. With brazen contempt for the public, Germany avoided pressing home any move which might have led to another goal; and Austria politely returned the corrupt compliment. Algerian supporters, and indeed Spaniards, howled abuse in vain. Even Austria's manager admitted afterwards that it was shameful, but the thick-skinned Germans denied all accusations of a fix, the loudest voice among them being that of their president Hermann Neuberger, who was also chairman of the World Cup organizing committee.

It was said that Scottish referee Bob Valentine should have warned both teams for not trying, but that was beyond his power, and FIFA would only answer the public clamour for action with feeble expressions of 'regret'. The fact was that had the Algeria-Chile game kicked off on the same day at the same time, as always used to be the case twenty years ago, then the news that Algeria were three up at half-time would have had Germany and Austria battling tooth and nail. But television wants staggered kick-offs, and staggered kick-offs it must have, never mind the sport or sad, cheated Algeria.

9 'Irish Reserve Runs Wild in Spanish China Shop'

'I was very disappointed with Spain from the start. You expect the hosts to emerge as a strong team, especially when it's a country with the footballing traditions of Spain, and with the clubs they have produced in European competition over the years. But they never looked good from the first game against Honduras, which was suspected by many when the draw was made to be intended to set them up for the second round. The best team in the group, looking at the early matches, was certainly Yugoslavia, who had some excellent players but were too cautious in the opening game against Ireland, and were then, against Spain, on the receiving end of a terrible penalty decision.

Ireland's performance in qualifying was superb, it thrilled millions of people, and not just in Britain. Everyone was talking about the Irish. Whereas Scotland for the most part played open attacking football, Ireland played it very tight. They were less pretty to watch, but they were making the most of a squad which in theory was much weaker – only five First Division players from the Football League, two of them goalkeepers, plus a collection of men from the Second, Third and Fourth, the Irish League and the North American League. It was an enormous credit to Billy Bingham, the manager, and the players under skipper Martin O'Neill that they achieved what they did, getting the absolute maximum with careful planning and fantastic collective effort and spirit. (I'd first met Bingham when he was manager at Plymouth. I was fourteen and he had tried to get me to sign.)

Gerry Armstrong was a revelation for his side, he was so positive. It was obvious from the start of the competition that there were few players willing fully to go at defenders and take them on, but Gerry's asset is his speed and strength and he really used them. He looked very effective and it wasn't surprising that he soon had people from all countries sitting up and taking notice. Ireland's last game of the qualifying group, needing to win against Spain, was a tall order; I must confess the best I thought they could do was draw. Yet again, it was essentially a collective performance, and they deserved a win, particularly after some of the fouling by the Spanish, and the ludicrous sending off of Mal Donaghy. The goal which won the match was one of the highlights of the whole of the finals – Billy Hamilton's run on the right and the low cross, palmed out by Arconada and thumped home by Armstrong. That really lifted us all out of our seats, a great moment.'

Bidding to become the sixth host nation to win the World Cup, and with King Juan Carlos welcomed by a rapturous 50,000 crowd in Valencia, Spain found themselves a goal behind after only seven minutes against Honduras – a team who had been together under military supervised training for over two years. A clever move by Maradiaga, the Honduras play-maker, carried on by Figueroa, was swept into the net by Zelaya at the end of a run from midfield. Spain had much more of the ball, but Honduras successfully held out until Ufarte equalized from a penalty in the sixty-fifth minute when Satrustegui was brought down. Few had been in any doubt since before the competition began that the referees would certainly not be penalty-shy where the hosts were involved.

Yugoslavia came to the finals with one of the best records over two years of any team in Europe, having finished ahead of Italy in their qualifying group – a record in sharp contrast to Ireland, who had just gone through a wretched spring in which they had given away goals like a leaking boat lets in water. Yet the substantial question mark against Yugoslavia was whether their manager Miljan Miljanic had made a tactical error in playing no warm-up match of any kind immediately prior to the finals.

Bingham named the seventeen-year-old Manchester United reserve Norman Whiteside for his first cap, in a left-wing role shuttling between midfield and attack, in preference to Noel Brotherstone, and brought Glasgow Rangers reserve McClelland into the centre of defence alongside Chris Nicholl – part of the overall plan he had devised while on twelve days' training at Sussex University's grounds at Brighton. Jimmy Nicholl and David McCreery, who had returned from America, profited from that training period and would play some of their best football ever. The pace of the game against Yugoslavia, played in intense heat in Zaragoza, was slow and studied, with the Yugoslavs always the more threatening in their build-up from midfield, but several saves from the thirty-seven-year-old Jennings helped Ireland to a goalless draw.

With all four teams in the group now having a point, the pressure was on Spain in their next game, against the Yugoslavs. What resulted was one of the more deplorable games of a badly refereed tournament: the referee Lund Sorensen of Denmark allowed Spain to kick lumps out of the opposition without reprimand, and then gave the hosts the most outrageous penalty. Cynical fouls by Alonso, Camacho and Gordillo were not even given a yellow card. Once again Spain were desperate from early in the game; after eleven minutes, from a free-kick against Gordillo,

Petrovic curled the ball over the wall for Gudelj to head home.

Three minutes later, Yugoslavia's defender Zajec brought down Alonso fully two yards outside the penalty area – a fact plainly visible to the referee because Zajec made the tackle when going down on one knee and was still on the ground in that position when the referee arrived, pointing at the spot. Ufarte stepped up to take the kick and drove the ball wide. The referee ordered a retake, and Juanito scored. Still Yugoslavia were the more enterprising, coordinated and dangerous team, and this offered continued licence to the Spaniards to resort to excessive force. In the second half Yugoslavia lost heart, and in the sixty-sixth minute Juanito took a corner on the right, Quini miskicked in front of goal, and Saura on the far post scrambled the ball in.

Against Honduras, Ireland led after nine minutes; McIlroy's free-kick hitting the cross bar, Chris Nicholl headed square and Armstrong's header beat Arzu. Armstrong then hit a post and not long after half-time it seemed Ireland should have been awarded a penalty when Whiteside was brought down. But the kick was given just outside, and minutes later Honduras equalized through Laing. Jennings, in his ninety-third international, was again invaluable, and by the finish Ireland could not grumble at their point. It only began to look inadequate when Yugoslavia beat Honduras with a penalty by Petrovic, leaving Bingham's men needing to draw at the very least 2-2 against Spain . . . or win. There was talk of problems between Bingham and his captain O'Neill, whom he substituted with Healy after seventy-eight minutes against Honduras, but by the day of the momentous meeting with Spain, the Irish were in a collectively buoyant mood.

The noise in the Luis Casanova stadium in Valencia from the near hysterical crowd was deafening and unending. Just here and there on the terraces there were a few tiny pockets of Irish supporters, specks of emerald among the myriad of red and yellow. This was to be a night they would never forget. As the players stood during the national anthems, O'Neill and McIlroy gazed up tight-lipped at the engulfing wall of ear-splittting intimidation. They knew just what lay ahead. Beside them, Whiteside just grinned. Only the lollypop was missing. His youth was shielded by his naivety. When he first played, against Yugoslavia, he was the youngest player in World Cup history at seventeen years forty-one days (younger than Pele in 1958). He had been at school when Ireland played their first qualifying match in 1980, he had had one whole first team game for Manchester United, and now here he was on the world stage. Half an hour later, during mounting violence from Spain, he quietly thumped an opponent in the ribs off the ball, and Bingham on the bench muttered to himself: 'My, you're growing up fast.'

Ireland proceeded to play the game of their lives which will ring down the years, just as did their march to the quarter final in '58 with Blanchflower, McParland, Jimmy McIlroy, Greig, Peacock . . . and Bingham, a whip-lash little winger. Now as then, they gave a display of forti-tude, intelligence and no little skill, marvellously mar-shalling their limited resources in an epic victory which ranked with any I have seen in seven finals – a wonderful tonic for the people back home in beleaguered Ulster. Reduced to ten men when Donaghy was sent off with half an hour to go, they clung to Gerry Armstrong's goal not with panic but heroic calm. They made Spain look more mediocre and nervous than we already knew they were; a team almost certainly without hope of doing well in the second round, for which they now qualified. Ireland also qualified, ahead of Yugoslavia by only a single goal.

From the first minute Spain tackled and kicked with an abandon largely unchecked by the Paraguay referee

Hector Ortiz, who had not refereed a full international for two years and betrayed every sign of it. Again and again Ireland took cracks on the shins and the back of the legs as Spain threw themselves in like men possessed, yet utterly without cohesion. It was as calculated and disgraceful as the way Barcelona had kicked their way to success against Spurs that spring. Although Juanito was booked for punching McIlroy after twenty minutes, it was inevitable that Ireland would begin to retaliate, and McIlroy and Hamilton were booked before half-time, Hamilton for nothing discernible. McIlroy had merely made a gesture of anger when Saura's tackle left him with a huge gash down his shin.

Two minutes into the second half Hamilton dragged his marker, Tendillo, off on a long run on the right, from a pass by Jimmy Nicholl, and swung over a low, curling cross. Arconada – previously regarded as one of Europe's top goalkeepers but no longer so good – plunged forward but only succeeded in pushing the ball out towards the penalty spot. Armstrong, arriving at the end of a late run, rammed in the most beautiful gaol he will ever score. Soon the limping McIlroy was replaced by Tommy Cassidy, and after Donaghy had been sent off – for a mild push at Camacho when the two had collided on the touchline, and on the linesman's evidence – Sammy Nelson was sent out in place of Whiteside to help shore up the left. Jimmy Nicholl, Chris Nicholl, McClelland and O'Neill continued to resist the waves of Spanish attacks with style and confidence, and as the minutes ticked away one could hardly bear to look. With four minutes to go, Spain's sweeper Alesanco came up for a header which, with Jennings out of position, bounced two feet wide. Ireland had done it. An American news-agency headlined its story: 'Irish reserve runs wild in Spanish china shop', a slightly inaccurate reference to Armstrong. Because of a succession of injuries the previous season he had been

124

unable to command a regular place in the Watford Second Division team, which won promotion: hardly a reserve and now certainly the hero.

'Armstong's goal had us out of our chairs, and when the final whistle went we couldn't have been more pleased had it been our own victory. But having ourselves qualified for a second-round place with the hosts and European Champions, we couldn't help but envy the group which Ireland had now landed themselves in. Although they had deservedly gained a superb victory, if you looked at their next group you had to consider France as almost automatic qualifiers before a ball was kicked. That didn't seem right, indeed isn't right, when they had finished *second* in *our* group. We had beaten them, we had trounced Ireland earlier in the year, and now here we were with the far harder job of getting to the semi-final. We all took it for granted that if we could get past Spain and Germany, it would be France we would have to play in the semi. It followed, therefore, that we had a great chance of reaching the final, even though France had improved since we had beaten them, but ironically, we thought, it was going to be almost easier for France to get to the semis than it had been for them to get to the second round.'

The feelings of Francis and his colleagues were soon substantiated when France had an easy win over lacklustre, discredited Austria, who as in so many games in recent years often had nine or ten men behind the ball. In the intense heat of the Vicente Calderon stadium in Madrid, France's flair was always conspicuous, especially when Rocheteau came on for the injured Lacombe after fourteen minutes. The Paris St Germain striker led the dour Austrians a dance, and after several near misses it was he, after thirty-nine minutes, who forced the free-kick from which France scored the only goal. Genghini who had come into the team following the defeat by England, had shortly beforehand hit a post. Now, confronted by the Austrian wall, he struck a lovely shot into the angle between post and bar, way out of Koncilia's reach. In the second half France might even have had several more. What could Ireland do against them?

The answer was a lot – but not enough. In sauna-like humidity, they drew with Austria 2-2 in another, for them, epic encounter. Austria made five changes from the team beaten by France, including the dropping of the famed Krankl, but they were outrun and outplayed for the first half hour. After Hamilton and McIlroy – happily recovered from Saura's foul – had seen openings come and go, Ireland produced one of the most satisfying goals of the competition so far. Armstrong, who had been given by Bingham a role on the right, alternating forward runs with O'Neill, charged at the Austrian defence like a bull down the streets of Pamplona. His pace, and the unexpectedness of such boldness in this most defensive of World Cups, carried him past two Austrian defenders before they knew what was happening. When almost at the dead-ball line, Armstrong hooked the ball across and away from Koncilia. Hamilton, the big blond boy from Third Division Burnley, came hurtling in with perfect timing on the far post past two men to head home. And that was how it was at half-time. Five minutes into the second half, however, a corner from Prohaska was driven at goal by Baumeister and deflected into the net by centre-back Pezzey. Ireland still had it all to do, even more so when Austria took the lead after sixty-eight minutes with a free-kick by substitute Hintermaier.

McCreery, illegally breaking early from the wall in an attempt to block the kick, only succeeded in leaving the hole through which the ball went.

Back came Ireland to equalize within six minutes. Armstrong had a long-range shot deflected. Jimmy Nicholl, going in a seemingly impossible pursuit of the ball over forty yards, somehow beat Pezzey to it, lobbed the ball over the goal-mouth and there was Hamilton on the far post to score with a tremendous header from twelve yards. With twelve minutes to go, Armstrong made another exhilarating run past three defenders, slipped the ball to Jimmy Nicholl who was supporting on the wing, and Hamilton's header was just wide. A goal there would have given Ireland the chance to reach the semi-final, needing only to draw with France – something that proved beyond them anyway.

They crashed 4-1 against France, just as they had done in the quarter-final twenty-four years before. The romance was over. The talents of Giresse, Tigana, Platini and Genghini in midfield were just too much.

'It was a brave show, based more than anything on tremendous spirit. The first goal against Austria had been a classic – a great run by Armstrong, a perfect cross and a brave header by Hamilton. These two both proved what it can do to the opposition if you go past defenders with the ball – they look brilliant so long as the ball is in front of them, but once you get behind them, it's another game. This daring was one of the things which was so lacking in the whole tournament. And for Hamilton to come from the Third Division and do what he did was remarkable, *and* to be involved in goals which were among the most memorable. His was one of the extraordinary achievements of the World Cup, and on the surface he had a far more successful tournament than Maradona. It is this kind of surprise which keeps the game alive.

It was equally incredible to think that Whiteside was playing in the World Cup at only seventeen, and he's obviously a great prospect. Yet it would be crazy to compare him with George Best. I don't think in my time as a player there will ever be anyone in Britain to compare with George. I'd just begun to hear of Whiteside in Manchester towards the end of the season and one or two people said he was impressive, but don't let's get carried away. He's the best attacking player of his age to appear on the scene at the moment, but he has a long way to go.

I was particularly pleased for Martin O'Neill because he lives for Northern Ireland. Everyone gets a kick out of playing for his country, but Martin does more than anyone I know. The finals came at the end of an emotionally difficult season for him, moving from Norwich to Manchester City and then back to Norwich. I'm sure he played a major part in getting Norwich promoted, and it will be interesting to see how he does back in the First Division again. Also part of the 'engine room' with O'Neill and McCreer was McIlroy. I used to look at him at times and think the amount of work he got through was amazing. That was what got Ireland success, their attitude. McIlroy, too, liked to run at people, and that helped to make a bit of space for Armstrong, Hamilton and Whiteside.

Some people were surprised at the form of McCreery and Jimmy Nicholl, coming as they did from football in the States, but they have the wrong impression about the quality of the game out there. Though it's not as tough as the First Division, David and Jimmy would tell you that they had to work as hard for Tulsa and Toronto as for Manchester United and QPR. I think they would say that there's not much difference in standard, excluding the very top layer of British players. To success in football there is no short cut – hard work is the formula at any level.

Chris Nicholl had a great tournament at the back, so dominating in the air. He's not exactly gifted on the ground, so he makes a point of giving the ball quickly and simply to someone else in midfield. That's a sign of a good player; there are so many in the game who won't accept their own limitations. For Pat Jennings, who has been such a great goalkeeper for so long, just to be there must have been very satisfying. It will have been his first and last finals, a wonderful climax at what could have been the end of his international career. But who can say, with someone like Pat who goes on and on!'

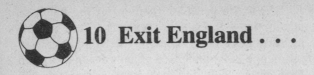

'When we arrived at Navacerrada, our headquarters thirty-five miles outside Madrid, the weather was very different from Bilbao. Every day the temperature was pushing up around 100°F, and it was fortunate that the training ground was right next door to the hotel. In Bilbao we had days off, were able to use the local golf club, play tennis, but at Navacerrada we were virtually camped in the hotel the whole time, and only had one day's relaxation. It's a beautiful little village in a green moutain valley, the place where Real Madrid often stay before big games, where Puskas and Gento and Di Stefano used to plan their triumphs! But because of security, we didn't have much chance to look around.

By the day before the game against Germany, everyone was fit. Joe Corrigan 'had returned from England. He'd been sent home by the doctor, who had diagnosed cartilage trouble, but the specialist in Manchester said there was no trace of anything! He came back completely OK. By now both Keegan and Brooking had recovered, so the squad was at full strength for the first time. But Kevin had not trained sufficiently to stake a serious claim for inclusion, and there was no surprise among the players when the manager named an unchanged team.'

Ever since Keegan first played for England almost ten years before, there had been no more industrious player, and only eighteen months previously he had seemed irreplaceable. On the morning the team was announced, he was as enthusiastic in training as ever, giving his all in the ten-a- side practice match; but at the finish he was off to the sanctuary of the hotel in a flash to avoid the cameras. To be yesterday's hero is sometimes tougher than attempting to be tomorrow's. The previous day he had talked about his sadness:

'Realistically, I have no chance of playing against Germany, and if the lads go out and win – and I hope they do – then there is no chance of the team being changed except through injury. Hopefully they will carry on winning, and that could mean I won't play in the tournament. I have always believed in the old maxim that you don't change a winning team. I have profited from it in the past, and now sadly I'm a victim of it. I am surprised how I have been able to accept the disappointment. I try to look as if I'm happy. I almost feel like an actor, the way I have to hide my feelings.'

'Franz Beckenbauer, Germany's skipper when they won the Cup in '74, came to one of our training mornings. He told us that Rummenigge was injured, was struggling to be fit in time, and from what Franz was saying it was clear that the Germans were very concerned about us. When we arrived at the stadium on the day, we were keen to know the German team, but it was nothing like we expected. Following Bobby Robson's report from the German's first-round games, we'd had a practice match with Tony Woodcock playing against us imitating Littbarski. We expected their front three to be Rummenigge, Hrubesch and Littbarski, but now Hrubesch was not even in the sixteen, and Littbarski was on the bench. It proved to us they really were worried.

Of course we wanted to get *forward* in the game, for

others to say we didn't was nonsense. But the way the Germans played prevented it. I was convinced within five minutes that they wanted to draw. Who could have imagined twelve months before, that the European Champions would have that kind of fear against England? I can understand what an awful match it must have been to watch. It was bad enough to *play* in! I felt trapped by their system – and also to some extent by ours.

We so nearly scored after nineteen minutes, with a header by Bryan Robson. Kenny Sansom crossed the ball, Mariner back-headed, and Robson got on to the end of it with another of his runs. It was a bit like the situation for one of Boniek's goals against Belgium, but Schumacher was not quite as far off his line as Custers of Belgium found himself, and stretching back in mid-air, he was just able to get a hand to the ball and turn it over. That was a vital opportunity in a match which was overall so negative. We came in at half-time reasonably pleased with the performance, even though we hadn't scored. We had attacked much more than the Germans and we felt that at least we were the team trying to play football. People say this is the game which cost us a place in the semi-final, but I feel we lost it when Germany beat Spain, and we didn't. Drawing with the Germans was not a bad result, even if it was a bad match. We'd have settled for that a year before, when we were losing in Basle!

The only incident of worth in the second half was Rummenigge's shot a few minutes from the end which hit the bar. You could sense a difference in feelings between the teams as they came off at the finish – Germany were pleased, while we were no more than satisfied. We may not have pleased the customers, which must always be a failing for professionals, but we had *tried* more than the Germans. Afterwards, I was drawn for the dope test with Ray Clemence, who was on the bench. Ray was quickly away, but it took me from 11.00 P.M. till 1.30 A.M. to produce a sample, after two orange juices, three beers, champagne which gave me a stomach ache, and water. I even went for a walk round the stadium. I'd lost 8lb in seventy-five minutes on the pitch, and now this was an added imposition. I had to get a taxi back to Nava-cerrada.'

Don Santiago Bernabeu, patron of some of the most spectacular teams the game has ever seen, must have turned in his grave. In the stadium which bears the name of Real Madrid's revered president, where Real have dazzled millions for thirty years, England and West Germany sent the World Cup to sleep. Worse than that, by such a display, football was taking money under false pretences, and the only winners were the advertisers with their boards around the perimeter of the pitch. In the middle there was nothing. Germany played like frightened sheep, and England had not the inventiveness to shear them as naked as they deserved to be. What a desperate plight for football when these two nations, three times winners of the tournament and traditionally the action-packed entertainers of Western Europe, play with such caution.

'A funeral', lamented the headline in *Extrabladet* of Copenhagen, where the Danes were avid supporters of the English game. 'A battle without combat,' protested *France Soir*. 'An empty stadium,' said *Le Figaro*. Greenwood, not unfairly, put the blame squarely on Germany, saying, 'If one side does not want to play, it's difficult. There was a feeling that Germany were a bit afraid of us, and that's the respect we have had for them in the past.' Nobody could have much respect for what had happened in this game. Dr Johnson, who did not miss much, once observed that a man would rather have a well-laid dinner table than a wife who spoke Greek. Similar thoughts were aroused by this arid draw.

'We all wanted the Germany-Spain game to end 0-0. But the day before we had a shock, when it was announced by FIFA that, in the event of two teams finishing level on points and goals in the second round, their first-round *placings*, not their points and goals, would be the means of deciding who went through to the semi-finals. As we and Germany had both finished top, we would be regarded as equal; and if we were equal in the second round, we would have to draw lots for the semi-final. When we had gained six points in the first round to Germany's four, this seemed grossly unfair. But what I found most incredible was that, in a tournament of this magnitude, when we were taking part for the first time for twelve years, someone had not read the rules properly even though they had been printed and circulated three years previously! We had been told that first-round goals would count, and we could not believe that we might now have to draw lots for the semi-final.

On the night, Spain were very poor, and from the start is was clear there could be only one eventual result, a win for Germany. It's a strange feeling, watching a game and actually wanting there to be no score. Arconada was badly at fault with Germany's opening goal after fifty minutes, parrying a shot from Dremmler straight to Littbarski. In the next few minutes we would have settled for the game stopping there. When Fischer scored again with a quarter of an hour to go, we were most concerned, because even with a score of 2-0 we would need three against Spain to avoid drawing lots. When Zamora scored with a header for Spain, with eight minutes left, the entire England squad leaped to their feet, and there were shouts of

'Espāna', which were much enjoyed by the waiters serving our dinner!

Because I'd come off late in the game against Germany, to be replaced by Tony Woodcock, the talk all week was whether I'd be left out against Spain. The assumption in most of the papers was that Keegan would play instead of me. I was constantly asked in TV interviews what I thought, and I had to be diplomatic. Because I had had a quiet game against Germany, I said that Keegan had to come into the reckoning, though I could have said more: that you don't judge a player on one game, for instance. It was only a month ago that people were saying that Keegan should be left out. Now, after I'd played reasonably well for four games, people were clamouring for him to come back, even though he'd not played in Spain or even been fit. I couldn't see the logic. But then I should have realized that Kevin Keegan is a very big name, and it was inevitable that people would speculate. Yet I was angry that the speculation was at my expense, and not, for example, Paul Mariner's, who had done no better or worse than I had. The competition for a place against Spain was growing, and my room-mate Woodcock felt that as he had been substitute all along, and had replaced me against Germany, he was ahead of Keegan in the queue to replace me, if that was to be the case. He felt annoyed that his claim was not being considered.

And would Brooking come back instead of Rix? The situation became even more complicated when Steve Coppell developed knee trouble after the Germany match, the knee suddenly swelling when he was out playing golf. Two days before we played Spain, the manager gave the first clue about the team, when we had a practice match and I played on the right in place of Steve, with Keegan up front with Mariner. That clearly seemed to be the plan if Steve was unfit, though we knew the manager had hoped to keep an unchanged team.

The next day Steve trained again, but Greenwood delayed announcing the team, telling the Press, and us: 'Tomorrow'. That afternoon we were watching the Wimbledon final, and I was sitting next to Steve. Jimmy Connors' victory was followed by the Poland-Russia match, and during that Steve complained he was in pain again, left at half-time, and went to bed. Greenwood then announced totally unexpectedly that there would be a team meeting at the end of the match on TV. When we gathered, he simply said: 'Stevie's not well, so Trevor will be on the right, and Tony Woodcock up front. Will Tony and Kevin Keegan stay behind, please.'

Over dinner, the whole squad was agog. Between 7.30 on Saturday night and the same time Sunday night, Greenwood had changed his mind dramatically, leaving Keegan out. After training on Sunday morning, he had admitted to the Press that it was the most difficult selection he had ever had to make. Could he have been influenced by Don Howe over dinner on Saturday night? It seemed the only explanation. Tony and I talked it over, and no one was more surprised than he was. Out of the blue, there was to be the renewal of our partnership against Spain two years before, when in Barcelona we had each scored one. Could we do it again tomorrow, even though I now had a slightly different role on the flank?

Although the British national anthem was booed for the first time in the tournament, the atmosphere in the stadium was strangely flat after our three electric games in Bilbao. We had so much of the game we were sure that if we could get one goal, others would follow. Mariner had a good chance just on half-time. I forced a corner, a defender sliding me over the line as I cut in; Rix took the kick, and Mariner on the near post headed past the angle of the posts.

In the dressing-room, Greenwood said: 'Keep going, if the goals don't come, I'll probably have to make changes,

Guidance for Trevor from Uncle Ron while training in Hertfordshire
for the European Championship in Italy, together with Emlyn Hughes
(Daily Express)

Sliding home a critical goal in the European Cup quarter-final second
leg in Berlin for Nottingham Forest against Dinamo *(Daily Express)*

Trevor looks serious and Peter Taylor, Forest assistant manager, looks impatient at a press conference called to deny rumours of a rift between Trevor and Brian Clough *(Daily Express)*

A jubilant Trevor carries aloft the European Cup after scoring the only goal for Forest in the 1979 final against Malmo in Munich *(Daily Express)*

All smiles as John Bond, Manchester City manager, welcomes Trevor to Maine Road upon his second £1 million transfer *(Daily Express)*

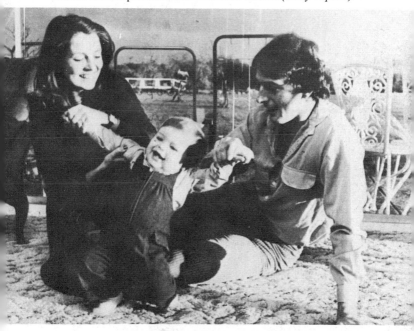

Helen and Trevor frolic with their son, Matthew, City's youngest fan *(Daily Express)*

Another injury. Trevor limps away from hospital in plaster; one of the setbacks which earned him the tag 'injury prone' *(Daily Express)*

Bryan Robson makes World Cup history with the fastest ever goal – scored in twenty-seven seconds against France *(Popperfoto)*

Trevor fires England in front against Czechoslovakia after goalkeeper
Seman has dropped the ball from a corner, with Terry Butcher (third
left) looking on *(Syndication International)*

Trevor again blasts at goal – against Kuwait *(Popperfoto)*

Trevor tussles with defender Mubarak as Kuwait, one of the exciting
new outsiders of the World Cup, restrict England to a one-goal victory
(Bob Thomas)

Brazilian referee Coelho over-reacts to a short-lived spasm of pain for
Breitner following a tackle by Robson while Rummenigge takes a breather *(Popperfoto)*

Schumacher (West Germany) tips a header by Bryan Robson over the
bar in England's most dangerous moment in their goalless second-
round draw *(Popperfoto)*

Trevor Francis and Liam Brady get down to business for their new
club, Sampdoria of Genoa *(Daily Express)*

try something different.' So it was no surprise when, after eighteen minutes of the second half, Brooking and Keegan replaced Rix and Woodcock. Five minutes after he came on, Keegan missed our best chance, right in front of goal, the sort of header he would normally tuck away – and that would have put us ahead with twenty minutes still to go.'

It was a galling night. England had eighteen goal attempts to four by Spain but, as against Poland in the qualifier in 1973, they could not put the ball in the net. Having prepared a base-line team, when they got to the net they found they could not volley. The weakest European team in the finals had been there for the taking, but Greenwood's delay in introducing the substitutes meant that by the time they got on the field, the game was already entering the desperation phase.

It had soon been evident that Robson was Spain's main target. First Tendillo and then Alonso brought him down, yet the first booking by Belgian referee Ponnet was Wilkins, for a foul on Camacho. For all the practice on set pieces, there was the bizarre sight in the twenty-second minute of Robson rolling a ball square to the left to Sansom – who was not even looking! Taking a swing, Sansom almost scored. The run of the game was almost wholly England's, with Sansom and Rix having a field day down Spain's right flank, but nothing came of the crosses. Two headers by Robson went close, so did another by Mariner, and a thirty-yard drive by Francis tested Arconada.

Within moments of Brooking's introduction, he began to penetrate behind the defence, and himself forced Arconada to save. A low cross by Francis flashed across the goal-mouth, but there was no one there to connect. It was Brooking who sent Robson to the line; but his centre was glanced wide of the far post from five yards by Keegan, when the ball needed a hard direct header.

'A few of the boys were in tears at the finish, but Greenwood kept stressing that we shouldn't feel ashamed, to get our heads up. Leaving the ground our coach was surrounded by a mob chanting, 'Malvinas Argentina', and 'Gibraltar España', and although the police were escorting us, a brick was thrown through one of the windows when the coach was a quarter of a mile from the stadium.

It had been another boiling evening, the temperature 111°F an hour before the kick-off. I lost 10 lb, more than in any game in my career. The average for most players was 7lb. After a bad stomach for a few days, I was lighter than normal and, in fact, I never put the weight back on after the Germany match, so by the finish of the tournament I was a stone lighter than at the start – which is a huge amount when you are at peak fitness. I know some people think I did not contribute much against Spain, because they tend to think of the end product, but I was a midfield player for that game, and by the end I was shattered. Tony Woodcock trains far harder in Germany than we do in England, and even he said what a huge difference there was out in Spain between training and actually playing in the matches. After only half an hour, he felt his legs were going, it was the hottest he'd ever known. It was suggested that Keegan and Brooking should have played from the start, but with the problems they had had, I honestly don't think they would have lasted beyond half-time at the most.'

11 Brazil: Too Good To Last

'Before the competition started, nobody particularly fancied Italy – difficult to beat, and all that, but not the team they were four years before. The first round did nothing to alter that view, if anything it confirmed it. Of the teams going into the last sixteen, there were six or seven you would have ranked ahead of the Italians, primarily because, like so many Italian teams, they were not scoring goals. All I really expected of the Italy-Argentina match was that it might be one of the dirtiest of the finals, and it was. It was surprising that no one was sent off until Gallego of Argentina in the last six minutes.

Gentile did an exceptional job, but he played to the limit of the laws. He gave Maradona a fearful time, both legally and illegally, so that you kept expecting Maradona to retaliate. Italy always make it difficult for anyone, with their relentless marking, but in my opinion the Romanian referee was far too lenient towards a lot of Italy's tackling and body-checking. The pity was that apart from this, it was a good game, and it immediately put a lot of pressure on Brazil, who had to play both teams and could not afford a single slip.'

There were thirty-nine fouls in the Italy-Argentina match, twenty-two of them by Italy. In a twenty-seven-minute spell in the first half, five men were booked – Rossi and

139

Gentile of Italy, Kempes, Maradona and Ardiles of Argentina, mostly for dissent concerning the fouls which had not been penalized by Rainea of Romania. Like so many of the referees in the competition, Rainea could plead in mitigation that it had become almost impossible to differentiate between the sham injury and the genuine.

The Italian players had been in no more benevolent mood off the pitch, having decided to boycott their own Press following reports that they had received £35,000 each for qualifying for the second round. The Italian Federation had denied this, saying that it was in fact £8,000, and the players maintained their silence all the way back to Rome, even in triumph. Zoff was appointed official spokesman, and a vote among the squad decided, by nineteen to three, to maintain the silence even after victory over Brazil, leaving the anguished journalists to fill whole columns unaided by the confidences of players, which is so much a part of their job.

The only team to have beaten Argentina in the 1978 World Cup, Italy now went ahead ten minutes into the second half with a goal from Tardelli, powerfully finishing off a subtle move between Conti and the elegant Antognoni, whose career would probably never have survived thus far without the conviction and support of his manager Bearzot. Argentina countered; Maradona hit a post and Passarella the bar, but in the sixty-seventh minute Rossi, put through by Graziani, had a shot blocked; from the rebound Conti contrived an opening for Cabrini – two goals: one each from a midfield marker and a full-back. Then Passarella scored for Argentina with a free-kick which caught Italy off-guard, disrupted by their own attempts at time-wasting, but the sending off of Gallego a minute later stifled any extended recovery. Argentina's title was gone, unless they could stage an exceptional reversal of form against Brazil.

'Brazil's performance against Argentina was one of the true exhibitions of football in the finals, a marvellous game, and a spectacle in some ways superior to their two earlier wins over Scotland and Russia. Argentina began really well, and should have scored once or twice; but Brazil were quite brilliant, and at this moment you could not imagine any team who could stop them from winning the Cup. Before the competition began, I had tipped West Germany, when most people fancied Brazil, though I expected the final to be Brazil-Germany if England did not get through. My reason for *not* tipping Brazil was that although they had so much skill I was never happy about their goalkeeper Waldir Peres, and if teams really got at them they were liable to give away goals. Visualizing a final between England and Brazil, and at that stage we felt we were entitled to do so with some seriousness, we considered we would at least have a chance – though we knew that chance had slightly diminished a few hours later when Germany had beaten Spain and increased our problems.

I'm certain Maradona should have had a penalty in the second half when Brazil were only one in front, but I wouldn't want to isolate that incident in a game where Brazil were by far the better team. Zico was quite breathtaking at times, and had a better tournament than Maradona, though I don't consider him a better player. Maradona has more instinct for where the goal is, he puts greater pressure on defenders. Junior at left back was incredible, too. How can you have so much skill as a defender? Falcao was even more impressive, one of the truly great players of the present time. He could do things that were stunning, with so little apparent effort. But what Brazil lacked, besides a 'keeper, was a centre-forward

– Serginho was poor, and a good central striker would have made all the difference by holding the line together. It was a pity they had lost Reinaldo through injury. Eder on the left wing was not quite in the same class as Falcao or Zico, even though he got a lot of publicity. He has an unbelievable left foot, hits ferocious free-kicks, and scored two great goals; but he rarely goes past defenders, he doesn't cause problems unless he's within shooting range, which admittedly is quite considerable. What stood out so much was that Serginho was in complete contrast to the rest of the team, he just didn't seem part of them.'

The competition came and went for sad Argentina – their sporting, military and political pride deflated in the same month – with Maradona leaving almost no mark but the imprint of his studs high on Brazilian substitute Batista's groin. It was the ultimate gesture of frustration from the ex-champions at the end of a match in which Brazil had systematically set out to belittle their traditional foe with one-touch, walking football. With alarming risks until they scored twice in seven minutes midway through the second half, Brazil clearly intended to defeat Argentina while giving the impression they were not really trying . . . in an effortless display of superiority.

Maradona was sent off by Mexican referee Rubio for his most childish foul five minutes from the end; and in that one absurd gesture of aimless retaliation was all the pent-up resentment of his own failure against the chloroform of Belgium, the barbarity of Italy in the person of Gentile, and the denial of that penalty when he had thrust past Junior and was fully a stride clear inside the area going straight at goal before Junior took his legs from behind. A saint would have faltered then. The same thwarted Argentinian machismo was the fuel of Passarella's equally vicious foul on Zico a few minutes earlier, when Zico had attempted an impossibly insolent piece of control on the touch-line with his back to the pitch, and had been kicked three feet in the air without so much as a yellow card showing as he was carried off.

Brazil had scored a sensational goal after only twelve minutes. Passarella conceded a free-kick, some thirty-five yards from goal. Eder, with his one slightly inward-bowed leg reminiscent of the incomparable Garrincha, ran at the ball, struck it over the Argentinian wall, and Fillol could only watch in dumb surrender as the ball swerved, lifted, then dipped and smashed against the bar. As it rebounded down behind Fillol, Zico stole in to touch it over the line. To the incessant samba rhythm from the terraces, Brazil embroidered bewildering patterns, little one-twos that left their opponents beating the air. Yet for the moment Argentina were not totally gone, and just before half-time Oscar had to move swiftly to shovel the ball away off Maradona for a corner.

For the second half Diaz replaced the ineffectual Kempes, and for twenty minutes Brazil had a real match on their hands, until two peerless passes by Zico settled it. First, he caressed the ball down the right for Falcao to drift clear and cross to the far post, where the lumbering Serginho headed down and in. Then a quicksilver move between Socrates, Eder and Falcao ended with Zico threading the ball diagonally across the back of the penalty area between three defenders for Junior to pounce cat-like and swat the ball with a lethal paw. Argentina, to their credit, tried to go out with a flourish. Passarella, as competitive as any player alive, forced a save from Peres, and Maradona shot over from sixteen yards. Then they started kicking flesh, though Diaz scored a fine goal.

'Brazil, needing only to draw against Italy, while Italy had to win, were thought to be certain semi-finalists by most. Zico had recovered from his blow on the calf; Klein of Israel was the referee, and he would surely control the game fairly if anyone could, checking any excess by Italy just as he had Argentina when Italy beat *them* in '78. Yet for the third time, Brazil went down at the start of a match. It was a good ball in from the left after five minutes by left-back Cabrini, which found Rossi unmarked close in. Brazil responded with a brilliant goal. Zico, who didn't get the treatment from Gentile which Maradona had, flicked a ball between his and Gentile's legs for Socrates to cut through on the right. I put Zoff at fault for allowing Socrates to beat him on the near post, though he did place the ball perfectly.

Italy led again, through a silly mistake by Cerezo who passed across his own goalmouth, putting Junior under pressure. Any other player would have whacked it, but Junior tried to control the ball, lost it to Rossi, and he put it away. Even then, at 2-1 down, I still fancied Brazil. Falcao scored half-way through the second half with a marvellous shot to make it 2-2. Some people said that at this point Brazil should have closed the game down. But first, they don't have the players to do so, so it's just not their style, and second they simply didn't have time. Rossi got his third a few minutes later; he was lucky when Tardelli, trying a shot from Conti's corner, got a rebound off Socrates which dropped at Rossi's feet. Like millions of others, I just couldn't believe Brazil were out. I didn't *want* to believe it. They'd given the tournament so much. Yet you had to hand it to Italy, they'd beaten the two big South American teams in successive matches, scoring five goals, more than twice what they had scored in three matches in the first round. They finally came out to play.'

Enzo Bearzot, holding court the following day to the international Press – the players would still discuss nothing more than the weather! – was fulsome in his praise of Brazil. 'They played the most beautiful football in the World Cup,' he said, ever willing to acknowledge the real values in the game. 'I am very sorry for them, but I believe Italy deserved to win.' For an hour and a half he talked, only finally breaking away when interrupted irritably by his president, Frederic Sordillo, to whom he snapped back: 'How many pieces of me do you think there are?' In spite of the vicious early criticism by his own Press, he has never doubted the communicating role of the media.

Zbigniew Boniek, an Italian by adoption, who was due to join Juventus at the end of the competition, had exerted an influence no less than Rossi's with his hat-trick for Poland in the opening game against Belgium, in the group including Russia. Rejected by several English clubs including the tottering Wolves, on account of his individualistic nature, he now shattered the Belgians, making a nonsense of their close marking and smothering defence. With the veteran Lato – survivor of the team which finished third in 1974 – and outside-left Smolarek, Boniek provided a feast for the hundreds of Polish supporters (many of whom in spite of careful political 'screening' would defect instead of returning home). Boniek's third goal against Belgium was a gem. Lato fooled three defenders, before releasing a diagonal pass which left Boniek with the perfect opening. Lato had also created the first, surging to the by-line before pulling the ball back into Boniek's path. With Russia also beating Belgium, by the only goal by Oganesian, the semifinal place was between the Poles, needing to draw, and their despised overlords, Russia, who had to win. The exit of the negative, physical Belgians was mourned by none.

There was no animosity from the Poles towards the Soviet players themselves, just a burning wish to give the subjugated people back home something to cheer. They gained the necessary draw, but at the price of a booking for Boniek, his second, which would keep him out of the semi-final with Italy. The Russians, playing their worst match, were strangely lack-lustre, as if they had no appetite for inflicting a victory which had such sombre overtones.

At the finish, knowing they had played without heart, seven of the Russians walked off without shaking hands with their jubilant opponents, who were not too concerned. Only two Russians moved to exchange shirts, while Chivadze, a captain of some dignity, made the round almost alone to offer the traditional thanks. A sea of red and white Polish flags swirled in happiness. There had not been a single hammer-and-sickle visible. What a strange anomaly it is that a nation which put the first man in space has such domestic and social tensions that it cannot allow its people to go abroad to watch a football tournament. As the celebrations continued on the pitch, a bearded sixteen-stone Polish trainer was weeping openly.

'Boniek's hat-trick was the best individual performance of the tournament in one match, not excluding Rossi's. Those were three superb goals. However, I rated the Russians highly after the first round, and expected them to beat the Poles, but when they *had* to win they were disappointing. Dasaev in goal was the best in the World Cup, apart from Shilton. His distribution was exceptional, catching and throwing sometimes within what seemed a couple of seconds. Blokhin failed badly to live up to his reputation. He has so much to offer, such pace and shooting power, but I was surprised at his attitude, spending so much of his time grumbling at the referee instead of getting on with the game. He is one of the quickest players in the game, but what did he produce? Russia had a tremendous captain in Chivadze, very composed and often getting into attack from the back. With the players they had, Russia should have reached the semi-final.'

12 Fouls and a Flourish in the Final

'I so much wanted France to win the semi-final and go on to win the Cup. I enjoyed their style. Like Brazil they were a joy to watch: they gave hope to the game and to the spectators. Not only that, but from a personal point of view there would have been some satisfaction in being able to say that we had beaten the World Champions. Their match with Germany in Seville was one of the best three or four of the finals, so exciting you didn't want it to end. I hoped all along that it would go to extra time, even though I knew how fierce that would be on the players, and what a strain they must be feeling. When Giresse made it 3-1 in the first half of extra time, it seemed that France were through, but I should have known better than to write off the Germans.

It was suggested that France was naive, that they should have brought an extra player back, but, like the Brazilians, I think they were simply incapable of changing their game. To do so was contrary to their nature, yet if they could have done it they would have been in the final. But what many people failed to see was that Germany showed a lot of character, as they have so often in the past. When Rummenigge scored within a few minutes of coming on as subsitute, you felt there was never any doubt that they would equalize. France were winning, yet they were suddenly so vulnerable all you could wonder was whether they would be able to avoid defeat. When Fischer equalized in the second half of extra time, there were still twelve minutes to go. When you have already played 108 minutes in the oven-like heat, and have just surrendered a 3-1 lead, another twelve minutes is a hell of a long time. I thought the French did well to hold out.

Yet having said all that, the foul by Schumacher, the German 'keeper, on Battiston early in the second half of normal time, was quite disgraceful – definitely a penalty, and certainly a sending-off offence. Against a team down to ten men, with a makeshift German goalkeeper, and in that tremendous heat with over half an hour still to go, that should have been a goal to put France 2-1 in front. It was a double irony that Schumacher was still on the field to save the penalty by Bossis in the shoot-out which decided the match – a terrible way to have to end a semi-final.

From the first game against England, Giresse had blossomed into one of the most gifted of all midfield players. He has such a lovely touch and feel for the ball, he is able to change direction in a split second without even a glance down at the ball, and he combined beautifully with Tigana, Genghini and Platini. That midfield line was comparable with Brazil's, and for me Giresse was France's key man. His finishing was questionable in the first round, but by the second round he was a force to be reckoned with, as well as a creator second to none. We will tend to remember his goal against Germany, but I thought his best was the second against Northern Ireland, a glorious flowing move which he started and finished.

It was strange that France, again like Brazil, should have had a suspect 'keeper. He didn't look the best against England. I always had the feeling that with him I might score in situations where against someone else there would be no chance. Yet in the last minute of extra time against Germany, he made one of the best saves of the tournament – a double save, and brave with it, when he looked stranded after the first one. With the score at 3-3, that took them into the penalties, and you just hoped so much that it would turn out to be his night, that the luck would turn France's way at the death.'

It had been the most dramatic semi-final since Germany went down 4-3 in extra time to Italy in 1970, but the excellence of the game was soured by the appalling foul by Schumacher, the heavyweight Cologne goalkeeper, on Battiston. In some sports he would have been suspended from international competition for life. It was deliberate, late, violent, off the ball, and possibly brought Battiston close to death. The French doctor says that for some seconds he had no pulse, he was unconscious for over three minutes, and required oxygen to assist his breathing. Not only did he lose three teeth from the blow with which Schumacher struck him, but it was subsequently discovered that he had a fractured vertebra in the neck, and would be out of action for the start of the season with St Etienne.

What had happened was that, with France now calling the tune in the second half, Platini split the German defence with a pass down the middle. Battiston, who had only moments before come on as substitute for the limping Genghini, raced through and shot from the edge of the area. His shot went wide, but Schumacher, advancing flat out, made no attempt to check his run and took off head on into the Frenchman, seeming to catch him in the face with his forearm. Battiston was out cold. Incredibly, the referee, Charles Corver from Holland, either did not see the incident – he could have been following the ball, though his line of vision should have been able to take in both the shot and the collision – or chose not to take any action. Neither did his linesman. The incident could not but mar the rest of the match, and whatever Germany might achieve in the final.

There were no surprises in the team selections, Germany having Rummenigge on the bench, with Fischer and Littbarski the front runners supported by Magath. France brought in Six for Soler on the left wing, but were otherwise as against Ireland. Germany quickly took the upper hand and went in front with a goal which did nothing for French confidence. Breitner sent Fischer through, Ettori raced out and dived at his feet, only for the ball to rebound conveniently to Littbarski, who scored easily. It took a penalty on the half hour to get France back in a match which Germany seemed unlikely to relinquish. Rocheteau was felled by Bernd Forster, Platini equalized.

After the injury to Battiston, who was replaced by Lopez, France had the better of things, and Rocheteau should have scored the winner from an opening made by full-back Amoros, who then crashed a shot against the bar in the last minute of normal time. When first the ambling yet perceptive Tresor, and then Giresse, put France two in front in the first half of extra time, France's hour of glory seemed assured – only for Rummenigge, from Littbarski's cross, and Fischer, with an overhead kick from Hrubesch's header, to deny them. The penalty drama was as follows:

Giresse scores, 1-0; Kaltz equalizes, 1-1; Amoros and then Breitner both score, 2-2; Rocheteau scores, 3-2; Ettori saves a feeble kick by Stielike, 3-2; Six fails to press home the advantage, Schumacher saving, 3-2; Littbarski scores, 3-3; Platini and Rummenigge score, 4-4. Now, after the first five kicks each, it is sudden death. Schumacher saves from Bossis, 4-4; Hrubesch beats Ettori low to his left, 4-5.

'After beating Argentina and Brazil, there was never any doubt in my mind that, in the other semi-final, Italy would beat Poland, who without Boniek through suspension, had little inspiration. His absence seemed to have a depressing effect on them. They offered almost no serious resistance, and I found myself asking if this could really be a World Cup semi-final. You expect something more at this stage of the competition, though we have to accept that the present form of the competition, with only two or three days to prepare for a semi-final, makes a crazy demand on players physically.

When Antognoni had to go off with an injury soon after Rossi had scored the first goal, I wondered if that might give Poland the edge. Antognoni is such a marvellously creative player, he's so composed on the ball, just like Souness, and I felt he was the one who made Italy tick. Yet they demonstrated emphatically that they can still play without him, and I thought this was one of the most impressive things about them in the last two matches.'

Bush fires raged in the hills above Barcelona the day before the match, clouding it in smoke and ash and producing unbearable temperatures of over 120°F. It was almost as hot the following day when Rossi, newly liberated by an expedient national federation from suspension for bribery, demonstrated that he had not forgotten how to accept a chance. With two goals to add to his three against Brazil, he buried Polish hopes and swept Italy to their fourth World Cup final. It was Antognoni, seven minutes before going off, who made the first, his free-kick being fractionally deflected into Rossi's path.

Marini replaced Antognoni after twenty-eight minutes, up to which point Poland had never threatened apart from one save by Zoff from Ciolek. Poland were limp, almost inert, but ten minutes before half time Ciolek rolled a free-kick through Lato's legs as a blind, and midfielder

Kupcewicz drove the ball against the outside of a post. Italy were doing enough but no more, a calculated performance. They were nearly caught out with just over half an hour to go, when Smolarek went past Collovati only to be brought down a yard inside the area. The Uruguayan referee Cardellino did nothing.

Soon we had a demonstration of one of the more absurd aspects of this often perverted World Cup. Conti, chasing a through ball, tripped over the advertising boards beyond the goal-line – and lay there feigning injury long enough for almost the entire Italian team to have a drink, and wash and brush up, from a trainer who galloped to his aid looking like a soft drinks vendor. Simultaneously a FIFA minion was going frantic on the half-way line, trying to prevent a Polish trainer giving the same succour to his players in the ferocious heat. *Water shall only be given to him that feigneth injury*. After seventy-two minutes Rossi scored his second, and Poland's expedition was stopped short of the summit. The Italian's repeated enactments of death suggested their next booking should be for La Scala opera house, Milan, rather than the Bernabeu, Madrid.

'You hope for so much from a World Cup final, even more than from an FA Cup final. It's the four-yearly climax to the game, and it ought to reflect all that's best, to set an example which we can all follow. Yet it was a desperate, dreadful first half. The only incident of note, apart from the endless succession of terrible fouls, was the penalty, taken by Cabrini almost as badly as some of the tackles. I couldn't believe the extent of the fouling, and the referee seemed to do almost nothing about it, the only booking was Conti after half an hour. It was impossible for either side to play football, though neither of them at that stage seemed particularly interested in doing so.

The second half was different, even before the opening goal, and eventually we had some really exciting action. I had expected Italy to win, though I was worried, as I have said, about the loss of Antognoni. They were further depleted when they lost Graziani from their attack after only six minutes. But his substitute Altobelli was competent, and eventually played a significant part in the match, so the team lost neither its balance nor its rhythm. I think it was a blunder by Jupp Derwall, the German manager, to play Rummenigge, because he clearly wasn't fit. I suspect Derwall played him because of his effect on the rest of the team against the French in the last twenty minutes of extra time in the semi-final. Yet you would have expected him to do well then, because the French were visibly flagging, and he didn't have to be one hundred per cent fit to be effective. Italy was going to be quite different, starting the game on equal terms.

When the ball went in for the first goal, after ten minutes or so of the second half, I wasn't sure initially who had scored, but I might have guessed. Rossi was in the middle of a phenomenal patch, and when you are scoring as he was, nothing seems to go wrong. It's difficult to describe how this kind of spell affects your confidence as a striker. The most difficult thing in the game suddenly becomes easy, the goal becomes bigger, you feel you are going to score every time. How do you explain confidence? It's just the same as for a cricketer, having a row of ducks or a string of centuries. I wouldn't say Rossi's was a brilliant header, but what was so superb was his professional sense, to be there at that moment. For once there were no boots flying, he could concentrate on the ball, and his judgement was better than that of all those around him.

Germany's substitute six minutes later totally played into Italy's hands. Germany took off a midfield player, Dremmler, and put on a striker, Hrubesch. The more they pushed forward, the more Italy caught them on the counter-punch. That's what Italy's league game is built on, week in, week out – the counter-attack. Germany didn't really have any alternative, and to be fair to them, the next two Italian goals were brilliant. Tardelli took his marvellously. He had a fantastic World Cup, I hadn't realized before how good a player he is. I'd regarded him, like a lot of people, I imagine, as simply one of the hard men of Italian football, which he was, but now he exhibited exceptional skills.

In this final we also saw the two most competent exponents of man-for-man marking in the world that I am aware of – Gentile and Karl-Heinz Forster. Up against this kind of player, as I was when we played Germany, the game is totally dependent on the ability of the referee to see that it remains fair, because there are always going to be fouls from the back on the man in possession. Gentile, who had already been suspended from the semi-final for two bookings, was totally let off for some of his clearly illegal challenges on Littbarski, and on others; yet in the end it was Littbarski who got booked! To win the World Cup, Italy had to overcome three key players they came up against – Maradona and Zico in the second round, and Littbarski in the final. Gentile was booked against both Maradona and Zico, but not Littbarski.'

The song which is locked away inside Italian football like a caged bird finally took wing, but only after an hour in which both teams, deadpan as undertakers, had seemed more intent on cremating the game than decorating it. It had been an insult to the TV audience of more than a billion. The crescendo of attack over the last half hour only served to emphasize the disgraceful cynicism of the first hour. And there was the very real danger that Italy's victory, however appealing the final flourish, would propagate this school of cynicism; that this shop window on the world would be judged by a million coaches and school-masters to have vindicated the darker side of the Italian game. Not that Italy were alone in the matter. In the first sixty-five minutes there were, by my count, no fewer than twenty fouls – ten by each side – which were bookable, fouls committed with no intention whatever of playing the ball, but only of stopping the man.

The affront to spectators did not stop there. Players of both teams simulated injury almost as often as they appealed for a free-kick or a throw-in which they knew was not due. We have grown accustomed to the latter, but the growth of the former is a new blight on the face of sportsmanship. The Germans, of course, have long been the most assiduous of the 'temporarily injured', a strange contradiction in a nation of such formidable competitors: but Oriali of Italy now out-acted everyone, sitting on the ground so often you though he was playing that children's party game where, when the whistle blows, the last one down is eliminated.

The referee only served to exacerbate matters. Arnaldo Coelho of Brazil was obviously a political choice, the first ever South American referee of the final, whose experience outside his own country was limited. In the first hour he booked only Conti and Dremmler. Stielike, Germany's sweeper, whose own behaviour was as cynical as any on the pitch, was lucky not to be sent off for arguing. Together with Oriali and Littbarski he was booked late in the game, and was bitter about what he regarded, un-justly, as Coelho's bias towards Italy; I thought the in-competence was evenly apportioned! Afterwards Stielike would say: 'Of course he should have sent me off, but that just shows he had no authority. I told him he was whistling for the Italians, and he would have done better to have put on a blue shirt from the beginning, and swallow his whistle.' The German's gave Coelho mock applause as he left the field at the finish: they would have done better to reserve some of their censure for their own conduct.

Strangely, in view of all the hacking and obstructing, the injury to Graziani after nine minutes, resulting from a tackle by Dremmler, was caused only by the way he fell on his shoulder, not by any violence of the impact. The chances of the first half hour, such as they were, belonged to Germany: Rummenigge spinning through three-quarters of a circle to shoot a foot wide; Fischer going close from a deep cross by Rummenigge. However, there was no doubt about the penalty after twenty-five minutes. A long cross by Altobelli was being met on the far post by Conti, when he was comprehensively demolished from behind by Briegel. Cabrini's penalty kick missed – but the fouling continued to find its mark.

The goal which would liberate the creative skills of Italy came in the fifty-sixth minute. Rummenigge fouled Oriali; a quick free-kick by Tardelli found Gentile in space on the right, and his low-driven cross to the far post was missed by Altobelli but met three feet off the ground by Rossi's head, for his sixth goal of the competition.

For another ten minutes or so the fouling continued until Tardelli smashed home a left foot shot, the culmination of a rapid move down the right involving Rossi, Bergomi and Scirea. Now Germany threw everything into a late bid to save the game – including caution. With nine minutes left, Briegel lost possession on the edge of Italy's penalty area, and within seconds Conti at the other end had given Altobelli the opening for the third. Breitner's late reply for Germany was one of his few discernible contributions to the game, his intelligence swamped by the early stupidities. At the finish, as Zoff went up to collect the trophy from King Carlos, the Madrid police, fresh from practice against innocent English supporters, took up the theme of violence established on the pitch by cheerfully clubbing the photographers as they attempted to record the celebrations.

While I mourned for the game I knew as a young man, which I had seen again here in short snatches from Brazil and France, I was pleased indirectly for Enzo Bearzot, a sincere man who over six years had done so much to attempt to rationalize the fear and inhibition which is generic in the Italian game. Whatever his players might do – and they had simultaneously fulfilled his highest aspirations and worst fears – he would always be a gentleman. If he was also a pragmatist, like Ramsey, who would not stop short of exploiting Gentile's excesses any more than Ramsey would Stiles's, who could blame him?

Stielike's moaning continued all the way home. Of Derwall's tactics he said:

'How could he take off Dremmler, who gets stuck into the game and does all the hard work, when others fail in midfield? And Rummenigge, he realized because of his thigh strain that he could not produce the performance that was needed, so why didn't he have the courage to take himself off sooner? We played with only ten men for four or five matches, while fit players sat on the bench or in the stands.'

Bearzot had said after the match that the turning point for Italy had been against Argentine, that the final was mainly a question of keeping calm. A pity that so few did.

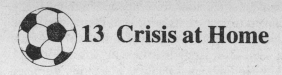 **13 Crisis at Home**

The season prior to the 1982 World Cup finals brought the most alarming crisis in confidence yet as attendance figures for the Football League plunged to an all-time low. The majority of clubs were in dire financial trouble, the receivers hovered at the doors of Bristol City, Hull and in July, Wolves. All the way to the top clubs were cutting back on staff and wages in a desperate bid to remain in business. Not surprisingly, even the mighty such as Manchester United were said to be struggling to meet massive wage bills and interest on overdrafts. A combination of defensive, boring football, too much coverage on television, at times frightening violence in and around football grounds, a huge increase in alternative leisure activities, the increase in the cost of football admissions, and a decline in sympathy for highly-paid stars with whom the public no longer felt an identification when the team was doing badly, all contributed to the accelerating erosion of takings at the turnstiles. This is the statistical story of the post-war decline in League match attendances:

1949–50	40,517,865
1959–60	32,538,611
1969–70	29,600,972
1979–80	24,623,975
1981–82	20,154,963

At last it began to get through to the League chairmen that there might actually be something wrong with the game, that maybe alterations were needed in the way the game was played to restore its appeal to the public in the face of disillusionment and preferably alternatives. At the start of the 1981–2 season, the League President Jack Dunnett, MP, Nottingham solicitor, was still vigorously claiming that football's problems were financial: solve these and all would be well.

Together with many others involved in the game I maintained equally vigorously, in the columns of the *Daily Express*, that even if the multi-million-pound debts of the clubs were removed overnight and they could start afresh with a clean balance sheet, there would still be a crisis. The public was turning its back on football, not least among many factors, quite simply because the game was in many instances no longer worth watching. The spectacle had become corrupted, not only by the downward spiral of financial pressure, negative tactics, and managerial sackings, but by the cynicism of managers and players, who have flagrantly bent the laws with a proliferation of cheating and fouling designed to thwart the skilful player and the skilful team. When week after week the public sees that such corruption is successful, and goes unpunished by both referees and the game's administrators, then it's hardly surprising that they lose faith. Whatever managers and others, including Liverpool chairman John Smith, may claim, football is not just about winning, it is about glory. The strongest motivation at the outset of any player's career, if he is honest, is not the prospect of money or victory, but of becoming, and being thought to be by other players and the public, a good player. The justification of professional sport must always be in entertaining, not in winning, though the two need not be mutually exclusive however much that has tended to become the case. One of the problems of making changes in the game and alterations of the laws, obliging coaches and players to

160

modify their attitudes and restoring the balance in favour of the positive, attacking, skilful player or team, is that because the laws are basically so simple and have been altered so little, there is a huge body of conservative opinion which resists change.

Prominent within this body over the years are some of the game's most respected figures, such as Sir Stanley Rous and Ron Greenwood, who have maintained that there is nothing wrong with the laws, only with people's attitudes. But by the beginning of 1982 the crisis in the motherland of the game had reached such proportions that these claims began to look hollow, and it was with a sense of desperation, mixed with belated realism, that the League chairmen instructed a committee consisting of Sir Matt Busby, Bobby Charlton and Jimmy Hill to investigate, and make recommendations for, alterations to the laws which might simultaneously strike at the cynicism and restore the entertainment.

On the day of the FA Cup final replay between Tottenham Hotspur and Queens Park Rangers, Jimmy Hill announced a set of proposals which adroitly did just that. They identified the problem areas and suggested reforms which, although in only one instance could be said to be really radical, would undoubtedly clean up the game.

1. An indirect free kick for time wasting if the goalkeeper retains the ball for more than four seconds after he has achieved a properly balanced possession [replacing the wildly abused four-step rule].
2. An indirect free kick against a player who intentionally plays the ball back to his goalkeeper from outside the penalty area [the exasperating tactic of countless players when under pressure, anything up to forty yards from their own goal].
3. No off-side against a player who receives the ball direct

from his goalkeeper [thereby eliminating the depressing sight of opposing defences pushing, indeed rushing, towards the half-way line to achieve off-side every time the goalkeeper has the ball].

4. A penalty kick from twelve yards for the deliberate, professional foul committed outside the penalty area if in the opinion of the referee a goal was otherwise likely to have resulted [eliminating, for example, the goalkeeper's rugby tackle on a forward with a clear run at goal two yards outside the area].

5. A throw-in to the other team if a player deliberately throws in from the wrong place [instead of making the player retake the throw].

6. More contact with referees by professionals outside the match environment.

7. Clubs to negotiate a system of fines for dissent in proportion to wages.

Of course, the usual reactionary voices were immediately raised, claiming that FIFA and the International Board would never approve such changes – as indeed proved to be so in June in Madrid. Jimmy Hill, though he may be criticized on many counts for his multiplicity of vested and conflicting interests, had been the most forthright voice in arriving at the recommendations.

The game is ignoring them at its peril.

Yet Hill's fight for the abolition of the maximum wage twenty years before, both admirable and justified, was ironically a cause of the present crisis.

All that the International Board did in Madrid was to restrict goalkeepers to four steps in total – whether or not they put the ball down and dribbled it. I was particularly interested that several weeks before the announcement by Hill, in discussion with Trevor about the problems in the game, he had voiced many opinions which were exactly in line with the committee's thinking.

'I think the four-second rule for goalkeepers would be excellent, better than the new ruling, which still allows delay. They had grossly taken advantage of the old ruling, it was a mockery and very frustrating for forwards. Abolishing the pass-back to the goalkeeper is not a bad idea. From a forward's point of view, if you are pressurizing a defender it's a wretched feeling when he knocks the ball back twenty yards or more, just when you're hoping he'll make a mistake. I'd like to see the idea tested. Eliminating off-side from a goalkeeper's clearance is the best idea of the lot, it's the most infuriating of all present tactics for the spectators, and ruins the game.

On throw-ins, and the deliberate foul outside the area, I would not want the laws to be changed, but for referees to be much more severe with bookings or even sendings-off. If they did this often enough, players would quickly change their ways. Willie Young's foul on young Allen of West Ham in the 1980 FA Cup final was a possible case for sending off. It represents a severe disadvantage for his team. Personally I do not think dirty play is all that serious a factor today. England is bottom of the dirty play league compared with many foreign nations. Certainly we have the reputation for being hard. Yet I don't think there are too many managers today in collusion with kickers. I've known when a player was instructed to kick me, but that sort of thing has decreased in recent years. There was a time when I heard it being shouted from the bench, but the players who kick mostly can't create, and are lucky to be earning a living in the game.

I'm all for a proper system of fines for dissent – and other offences. In fact, directly as a result of a situation involving me last season, and at my suggestion, Manchester City were intending to write such a system into our contracts before the announcement by the League commission. There's too much variation in disciplinary measures from player to player, both within a club and at the FA. Asa Hartford, who was a close friend at Maine Road, was sent off last season and was banned for only one game, with a record as long as your arm. I'd not been booked for nine years, and only booked twice ever, and never sent off, but when I was sent off last season I was banned for two games. Repeated sendings off should get longer suspensions, and all sendings off, whether it is butting somebody or dropping your pants, should carry the same penalty. The same with the totting up of twenty points, some get banned for one game, some for two, some for none. Wages shouldn't be stopped, but a club should have a code of conduct and fines which you sign in your contract, together with your bonuses.

As a player I agree that referees should have discretion as to whether a player off-side is interfering with play, or not, and I am glad to see the League commission's report says referees should have more discretion. I scored one of the best goals of my career last season, and had it disallowed because someone was off-side nowhere near the play. On the other hand you could understand West Ham and John Lyall complaining in the 1981 League Cup final, when Alan Kennedy's goal was allowed with Sammy Lee off-side right in front of the goalkeeper.

The standard of refereeing has dropped in my time, and the commission is right to think that referees and players are growing farther apart. The refs are bringing it on themselves, too many of them trying to be the star of the game. I don't think being full-time professionals would make them any better, but I would like them to train with clubs, so that they were more in touch with players. The slowness of promotion makes it very difficult for ex-players to become referees at the top level, almost impossible if you start at thirty-three. But if we could have people like Martin Peters or Bobby Moore as referees, they would be on the same wave-length as the players. Not all players would make good referees, but who does? Referees should give more of an impression that they like players rather than dislike them, though of course the situation is not made easier when you have some players trying to con the referee. On the other hand, if the referees were better then I think players would not try to con them. Referees should play advantages much more, to wait to see how a move develops, and then not be afraid to bring the game back if the attacking team has eventually lost the advantage because of the original foul. There are far too many bookings, many because of the referees' initial attitude towards players, and I cannot avoid the feeling that some referees appear deliberately not to want to co-operate with players to help the game flow.

Yet I am convinced there are many changes that are needed in the game as important, or more important, than alterations to the laws. For years I've been saying, like many others, that twenty-two clubs were too many for the First Division and should be cut to sixteen. It would be up to the clubs to find other ways of compensating for lost revenue, but the fact is that some of the games now are hardly an attraction for the public. The Second Division should also be reduced to sixteen or eighteen, and the Third and Fourth regionalized, with more chance for non-league clubs to get in.

If we had fewer matches, players could then improve their skills by concentrating more on training. At present there's no time to improve their game because of competition. With fewer matches, we could do fitness training in the morning and come back for skills training in the afternoon. People say that you only acquire skills between the ages of ten and fifteen, but I disagree, I think you are learning all the time. I learned a lot with Clough, with

John Bond at Manchester City and again now in Italy. Maybe there are certain basic skills you are born with, that you can never acquire, but you can always improve on what you have. No one has more skill than Glen Hoddle, but there are aspects of his game he can still improve.

I don't think the game has deteriorated that much, except that there aren't so many outstanding players at the top. There are a great many players of much the same quality, and that's why it's difficult to pick a national team. But at the bottom end of the First Division I think it is now easier to get into a first team than when I started. The standard among the lower clubs has dropped, and we are getting to the point where, for example, Liverpool against Middlesbrough almost guarantees a home victory. That's never been so before, I always felt that whatever the match in the First Division, either team had a chance. The situation has been made worse by three-up and three-down promotion and relegation, which has done nothing for the quality of the game and only increased fear and defensive play. From the start of the season you now have *half* the First Division just playing not to lose. There ought to be only *one* team relegated from the First Division; that would make it much easier to think positively. Three points for a win has only served to make things worse at the bottom.

By reducing the number of league matches we would also give more opportunity for the England manager to do his job properly, we would be able to forget the crazy business before a major international of meeting on Sunday evening, training Monday and Tuesday and then playing Wednesday. Since I started playing for England, there has only been one occasion when Saturday league matches have been cancelled. That ought to be standard practice, as it is in most European countries; there are always one or two people injured on the Saturday.

166

Everybody wants the Football League to be brilliant, *and* for us to do well in the European Cup and World Cup. Frankly, I have always had reservations about the Football League and those claims that it is the best in Europe, or even the world. I think the leagues in West Germany and Italy are now the best, whatever happens in European competitions.

Just look at last season, with our international players finishing league soccer half-way through May, and then having two weeks to prepare for the World Cup. That cannot be right. What do other countries think when they see what we are doing – playing in front of millions for international prestige without any sort of proper preparation? For me the most important challenge deep down has always been international football. Yet after England qualified in November, and people regularly stopped me in the street to say, 'You must be excited!' I had to reply truthfully, 'No, not really, there's no time, there's too much else going on.' Few players were thinking about the World Cup, or they would have had their managers down on them like a ton of bricks. Bob Paisley, with several Scots and English at Liverpool, was quoted as saying, 'I hope they're not distracted.' He was right. Under our system, you just cannot properly combine the two.

There's another area we should be taking a hard look at: What do the public *really* want besides entertaining play? *They* are the people who keep us in business, and a lot of them think they're getting a raw deal. If Sunday football is what they want, let's give it to them. Facilities in England are so poor. Once it was just sport, now it's big business. People today don't want to pay £2 and queue for a Bovril at half-time. We should send someone from every club to America, to see what *they* do for their supporters, to get it right *off* the field, never mind the quality of American football. In America whenever I was there, they used to get the players on the pitch after the match to

167

pose for pictures for supporters using their own cameras, and every so often there used to be a special photo day. At some matches the first thousand through the turnstiles would receive a team photograph, or at another match there would be a rose for every woman, a pennant or badge for every child. All this might sound trivial, but is shows that the club *cares*. I did a commercial on Radio Piccadilly for a Manchester City match against Everton. The crowd was 33,000 and the commercial may well have put 2,000 on the gate. That's something new, but I used to do it a lot in America. The Americans had lots of sales schemes – sometimes with each ticket you could get a voucher for a certain value at a particular restaurant.

Car parking facilities in England are terrible, too, and I think twice about going to a game I'm not playing in. Who wants to walk a mile in the rain? I know the feeling, I've done it myself. Manchester United and Liverpool are two of the best clubs in England, yet they don't have adequate parking facilities.

I think the season should be no more than seven and a half months, at present one season runs into the next. There should be much more of a gap, which would whet people's appetite for the new season. If there was a longer close season, we would be free to postpone more games in bad weather. If there is any doubt, a match should be called off in plenty of time. We, as players, cannot give value for money in bad conditions. Sometimes the weather is fine but the ground is frozen, and I believe it should be complusory, with England's unpredictable weather, for every club to have under-soil heating as they have at Maine Road.

A thought about loyalty, too. It's a word that used to be used a lot in the game, but it no longer applies very much. Not so long ago it was the players who were being branded as disloyal, but things have changed and now some managers and chairmen are as bad. When I signed for

Forest I signed for three years. They wanted me to sign for longer, but I thought three years was about right, and I certainly had no intention of leaving before. Yet after two years, they sold me. If players are on contracts shorter than three years, which people complain about, then that's usually the manager's fault.

Sadly, as a result of all this, I think many players are no longer conscious of the importance of the survival of the club. I think that mainly's the fault of the clubs. When you're not playing well, they mostly don't think of you. But they don't go out of their way on the whole to help plan your future, your coaching, your career. You're just a number in most clubs, a bit like cattle, really. If you're doing well, they'll keep you, if not, they'll get you out. There's no sentiment. So it's not surprising that many players are not too bothered, that they think first of themselves and their families. A lot of clubs are run so badly. Look at Bristol City. I don't think it was up to the players to save the club.

Now, with the evidence of a continuing sharp fall in attendances experienced during the 1982–3 season, the clubs have got to act before the League collapses. Sending off players who deliberately foul to stop a probable goal, which I agree with, is only touching on the crisis in the game. The public is showing an alarming vote of no confidence. I think the League will be failing in their duty if they refuse yet again to implement the recommendations of the latest Chester Report, especially the streamlining of the First Division and the regionalizing of the Third. The 1982–3 season again showed that there is too much football for the better players, that there is not sufficient chance to build an England team, and that serious injuries are on the increase, because of the demands – for example Brooking, Hoddle, Robson, Anderson, Wilkins, Mariner, Thompson, Coppell and Woodcock. And there were many more: the body cannot take it.'

# 14 Send Them Off –
The World Crisis

'I had been worried before the World Cup about
violence, on and off the pitch. With the past experience of
the behaviour of English supporters in Turin, Luxembourg
and Basle, not to mention the trouble with club teams, the
FA was right to have been anxious. Yet all the evidence
suggests that our supporters, and Scotland's, behaved
reasonably well, and the only bit of bother seems to have
been with the Algerians in Gijon. On the field it was
different. I expected there might be trouble with
Argentina, Italy or Spain. I've always found Spanish teams
very hard physically. I was talking to Cruyff recently, and
he admitted he didn't know how he survived the sort of
tackling which went on every week. What happened in the
World Cup was that there were many bookings, an average
of almost two per game, but few sending offs. I expected it
to be more violent than it was, but only the Italy-Argentina
match looked like getting out of control.

Yet the profusion of bad professional fouls prevented the
better players from exhibiting their skills, and stopped the
public from seeing what they really want to see. The awful
truth, the reason why there was not more serious trouble, is
that we, the forwards, the men who are on the receiving
end of the kicking, have come to accept it. Because we are
conditioned to it, we don't lose our tempers and retaliate
like Best or Law might have done twelve years ago. *This* is
what prevents matches getting out of hand – which is a
serious admission, and a terrible reflection on the way the
game is being played.

Everyone will remember that in the 1982 finals Maradona was sent off. Sure, it was a stupid, serious foul, but the guys who had been kicking Maradona, the Belgians and Italians, *they* didn't get sent off. Sammy McIlroy was booked against Spain. He had just been badly injured by Saura. McIlroy didn't kick or hit Saura, he just swung round with an angry gesture. But he was booked and Saura wasn't. So it all came down to the referees. They are the only people who can stop it. And the only way they will do it, is to give more penalties, and to send off more players who commit the fouls. Not just for the isolated bad foul, but for *repeated* fouling. It's there in the laws.

It's absolute nonsense, too, that in fifty-two matches there were only twelve penalties. There should have been one or two in most of the matches played. But inside the penalty area the game turns back to front. *Outside* the area the fouls are mostly against defenders, but as soon as the play is *inside*, suddenly it is the forwards who are committing the fouls, the free-kicks are given in favour of the defenders. Is that honestly likely to be correct? I know the referees have a very hard job but it did not help to have forty-one referees from forty-one different countries, a seemingly political decision.

Defenders set out to stop opponents, *knowing* they will get booked for fouls. So if they keep doing it, get them OFF. The public pays to see Rossi, Boniek, Zico, Maradona, Rummenigge, and some of the exciting new players like Faisal of Kuwait and Madjer of Algeria – to see them going past defenders and crossing the ball or shooting, not to see defenders kicking the stars up in the air. The trouble is that penalties and sending offs make too much of a headline. If only we could reach a situation where it was not a sensation every time, *when the sending off and not the foul was the acceptable action*, then it would rapidly change the picture. Managers could not afford to keep losing players – and probably losing matches. It's so simple, so logical. Defenders will go on doing what they're doing as long as they can get away with it.

If the World Cup final between Italy and Germany had been a rugby match, the referee would have called the two captains together after a quarter of an hour and given them a warning. But the Brazilian referee did almost nothing. I gather that Joao Havelange, the president of FIFA, said that no result of any match had been altered by an incorrect action of a referee. I cannot agree. The penalty for the Czechs against Kuwait was for blatant obstruction, which is not a penalty offence, and anyway was outside the area. Apparently, the instructions which FIFA gave to referees, ordering that *all* obstruction involving physical contact *had* to be a penalty if in the area, were sent to all competing finalists, but England certainly were not aware of the instructions.

There were many instances where it seemed the referee's action affected the game and, potentially, the result. To name just a few occasions: the disallowed France goal against Kuwait; Spain's penalty against Yugoslavia which was outside the area; the penalty Peru should have had against Italy and didn't; the penalty Scotland should have had against Russia when Demianenko pushed Wark off the ball; the penalty France should have had for Schumacher's foul; the penalty Maradona should have had against Brazil. And so on. Passarella should have been sent off for his foul on Zico, he'd already been booked. That would have affected Argentina's next match, if they'd had one. Zoff should have been penalized in every match he played for taking too many paces. I once counted eighteen! And both goalkeepers were moving early in the penalty shoot-out between France and Germany. There were dozens of instances when the referees' decisions raised grave doubts.

What annoyed me as much as anything was the persistent conning that was going on by the players. Most of the blame must rest with the offenders, but the referees have to take some responsibility for not spotting instances of diving and of staying down feigning injury when there was nothing wrong. If I can spot the offenders, why can't the referee? This is one of the aspects the players mean when they talk about referees not understanding the game. The referee *ought* to know as well as I do what is going on. I believe a lot of them do, that they can tell the difference between the player who is genuinely hurt and the cheat, but won't take action. Yet the referee is quite within his rights, if a player stays down more than a minute and then gets up and is clearly not hurt, to book him for ungentlemanly conduct. Germany have always been guilty of this. When we played them, Breitner, Dremmler and Littbarski were continually going down when they were not hurt. It's up to the managers as much as the referees to stop this.

Another grossly unsatisfactory aspect of the finals was the shape of the tournament, the arranging of the second round and semi-finals, the staggering of the kick-offs, the afternoon matches in that heat, and the absurdity of penalties or, worse, drawing lots for a place in the semi-final. If England had reached the semi-final, we should not have had to play France, whom we had already beaten. If I go to a World Cup and beat someone, I want to go on and play other teams, new challenges, not play the same team again, as Italy and Poland did. When you get to the second round, it should be knock-out – a cup is a cup, not a league. Playing a second round where you don't have to *win* to win is like something out of *Alice in Wonderland* – to be able to win a place in the semi-final by *drawing* because of a goal scored against *another* team! The public have to watch the matches with a slide rule in their pocket.

To think about having a lottery to determine who plays

173

in the semi-final is scandalous. At the very least it should be decided on the first-round points and goals, but more fairly there should be a play-off, and the same for the semi-final. I'm sure players would rather play again the next day, however tired they were, than decide on penalties. I know I would. The trouble is the competition is too big and too long, there is no time for a play-off. They should do away with the third/fourth place match for a start. They soon did away with it in the FA Cup. Who wants it? France showed what they thought of it by making seven changes against Poland. I'm convinced like a lot of people that twenty-four teams are too many. They've confirmed it again for 1986, but I cannot see how they will cope in Columbia.

It's quite wrong, also, to have different kick-off times for matches, with some teams playing in the afternoon and others in the evening. It's been going on since 1970, when they played in Mexico at midday for the benefit of television. There were matches in Spain which were decided by the heat rather than by skill. I know from the experience, that chances were missed in the last twenty minutes of matches because of the heat, chances which would normally have produced goals. Do FIFA care about this? It's asking too much to have us playing in temperatures of over 100°F. As for having vital matches in the same group on different days, that is asking for trouble. The Germany-Austria scandal would not have happened if they had kicked-off at the same time as Algeria-Chile.'

It is estimated that a worldwide TV audience of four billion watched the fifty-two matches of the World Cup, with a billion tuned into the final. However, figures in Britain were well down on 1978, with thousands, switching off while the match was in progress, according to ratings analysis. Live spectators found they had even less value for money. The rip-offs in Spain were shameless: hotel rooms were charged at double or treble rate, with many supporters who had booked 'package' trips finding that they were not getting what they had paid for. The claim in advance by the British agency Sportsworld Travel, that it was only possible to obtain tickets by booking a package which included travel, accommodation, and tickets, proved quite false, with tickets available at the gate at most of the matches apart from the final. The trouble stemmed from the setting up of the Spanish company *Mundiespaña* to handle all tickets and hotels – a move which FIFA ultimately admitted to have been a mistake. Even Spanish travel agents and hoteliers agreed that the arrangements were a shambles, and several admitted to me personally that things were far worse than they had ever been in Mexico, Germany or Argentina in previous tournaments. *Mundiespaña* succeeded in pricing their own hotels out of business, achieving only half their target of one million package bookings. The Madrid daily paper *Diario* claimed: 'In this sad World Cup, there are two great winners and one great loser. The winners are FIFA and their publicity company, the loser is Spain.' The publicity company's profits were expected to approach £10 million, with FIFA taking forty per cent.

The competition was out of control, both on and off the pitch. It tended to be said that Italy, be defeating in succession the cup holders, then the favourites and finally the European Champions, had given the tournament a satisfactory conclusion. But had they?

Those who look beyond the noise, colour, emotion and celebration which always accompany the final, find themselves, like Trevor Francis, deeply disturbed about the direction football is taking. The treasured memories are of France and Brazil, not Italy or Germany. Unless the authorities devise ways to allow entertainment to prosper again, football will become as commercially odious as pornography. In 1973, the FA fined Leeds for amassing forty-three first team bookings the previous season – roughly one per match. Yet Italy, the new World Champions, had twelve bookings (the most) in seven games, and it could have been twenty. Gentile and Conti, central figures in the brilliant technical performance in the final, could have been sent off for persistent fouling. There were ninety-one bookings in fifty-two matches.

France and Brazil were the two teams playing the game with a sense of glory – though the Irish, in their modest way, had a go. Brazil turned their backs on the compromise football they had been persuaded to play in 1974 and 1978, and were cruelly punished for it. Would the rest of the world come to the conclusion that, in spite of their charisma, France and Brazil were tactically inferior, that the right way to play was like Germany and Italy? Expediency spread from the top downwards. When I asked Havelange whether matches should not be played simultaneously in the same group he replied: 'Consideration for TV is important, whether we like it or not.' So now we know, officially. The Cup is played not to commemorate Jules Rimet and football, but Adolf Dasler (Adidas) and the hard sell.

One of the most obvious ironies of the finals was the criticism of the man who started it all – Helenio Herrera, former manager of Internazionale of Milan, high priest of defensive football and the philosophy that one goal is enough to win any match. He said:

'This has been the worst World Cup in modern history. If West Germany had won, we would have had champions who had lost to Algeria. With Italy, we had champions who had been a disaster in the first round and could only draw with Cameroon. Argentina came as World Champions and lost three of their five matches. These things are not good for football at this level. No wonder the crowds are down. People criticized me, but when I was manager of Inter, Fachetti scored seventy goals in the championship from left-back. Italy's victory over Brazil was the perfect justification of my concept. That's how catenaccio should be played.'

It was the most poorly attended Cup since the 1962 finals in Chile. Average attendances were 35,700. In 1962 it was 24,250; in 1974 it was 46,685; and in 1978, 42,374.

'Whatever people said about our football in the second round, England did achieve one distinction. Thanks largely to Peter Shilton, we had the best defensive record in the finals: from the time France scored against us after twenty-four minutes, we kept a clean sheet for seven hours six minutes against Czechoslovakia, Kuwait, Germany and Spain. Yet I think *too* much emphasis has been put on our defensive qualities. Against Spain we did go forward more, and we left a few holes for which we could have been punished. We knew we couldn't afford to go behind, and it was no different from any game – when what you hope to do, ideally, is concede none and score at least two.

The problem for England is that we only come up against a sweeper when we play in international football, for either club or national teams. I'm not saying we should change our system at home, I think it's a better, more entertaining game the way we play it, but coming up against a sweeper does create problems for our front players. You have got to make a lot of cross-over runs to shake off the markers, but you are totally dependent on midfield and defence players making runs to support you – which is what the Italians did so well.

In the England team, we tend to knock long balls up to

the front players, and not support them. But the only point of the front men making runs is to open the space for the midfield players. We should not play so many balls direct into front players. We're too static between front and middle, and playing direct balls to target men most of the time obliges them to remain static. There's not enough interchanging between the front and middle players. As Herrera has said, we're not inventive enough, we make too *many* passes, so in the end we rely too much on the front players. Rossi, for example, doesn't get the ball that often played into him when he's static. Instead, he's always running, and getting support from the back four. Look at Italy's second goal in the final: Rossi's run on the right was supported by Scirea, the sweeper, and Bergomi. Tony Woodcock says that at Cologne, he and Fischer and Littbarski played all over the place, with no set positions. You can't say Littbarski's a winger. Breitner plays midfield, but look how many times he gets into the box – again and again. Look at Briegel: he's a back-four marker, but he's everywhere. And Kaltz is always getting forward from his position at full-back.

It was refreshing for us to have Bryan Robson getting into the box so often in the World Cup, but I don't think we're going to see Ray Wilkins or Graham Rix doing the same, or Steve Coppell coming in from the *left* for variation. What England need, and it is the lesson of the 1982 finals, is more mobility, more flexibility, not only physically but in out attitudes. But it's difficult to change because of the way we play at club level. A change would have to come from the grass roots. At the moment we tend to play in little zones, and stick to them. But we won't lose our markers by leaving the front men central, knocking balls up to them and leaving them to get on with it.

The problem for Greenwood, and now for Bobby Robson, will always be the League system – the fact that the clubs will not give any ground for the preparation of the national team, and that the players coming through are conditioned in a particular way. Certainly I thought Ron Greenwood made some errors, just as I did myself on the pitch, but I had a lovely letter from him after it was all over, saying that I must have been delighted to have played in the World Cup after missing the European Championships, and wishing me luck with City and England. It was typical of the man, a really nice gesture and the kind of thing for which all those who played under him would always respect him.

Now Bobby Robson has taken over. I don't know him too well, I never played under him in the B team. He's been with one of the smaller clubs and done a great job. He's not had the success of Clough or Paisley, but when you think his highest transfer fee, in a successful team, has been £250,000 for Callaghan, it suggests his judgement of players must be good. Ipswich have played attractive football, though you never think of them in the group with Arsenal, Forest and Liverpool – difficult to beat. They're more a good *footballing* team. That shows in the fact that Robson's left behind ten players who are internationals.

I think the future is promising, with the new-look side in the European Championship, in which we play Greece, Hungary, Denmark and Luxembourg in the qualifying group. Once players get past thirty, people start writing them off, but Zoff is forty, Pat Jennings is thirty- seven, and I'm sure that at thirty-two Peter Shilton will still be in line for the next World Cup. In my eyes he was the best in Spain, as good as Dasaev was. Watching him in training, one is impressed by his astonishing appetite for the game, and I'm sure he can remain the best in the world for the next four years. There were afternoons in Spain when we were resting after a hard morning, when Peter would ask for another session! He'd go out in that sun and work himself into the ground, until we all felt tired watching him.

Kenny Sansom should be there at left-back for a long time. His nearest challenger is Derek Statham. Kenny is one player who really does like to keep getting forward, and I thought he might have done so more than he did. Perhaps it was the heat. At Arsenal he often ends up as a front player. Bryan Robson is another who looks like being a fixture for a while. He's so aggressive in his play, with a tremendous will to win. He really attacks the ball all the time, and is now getting into so many scoring positions. He's always prepared to take a chance, and unless you do, you will rarely score. He wants to score that badly, he often risks injury, as he did against Czechoslovakia.

But I'm a bit worried about the situation up front. In 1982–3 I've played with Mariner, Woodcock, Withe and Blissett, and it's important that sooner rather than later we have a settled formation for team understanding.

There's one other thing that bothers me, and that's the question of an orthopaedic specialist when we're away for a tournament as long as the World Cup. We had no one besides the team doctor, whose speciality is general medicine. We had several serious injuries, Keegan's back, Coppell's knee, Brooking's groin, Robson's groin, Corrigan's knee, and no specialist of our own to consult on the spot. Keegan had to go to Hamburg, Coppell had to consult a Spaniard, and Corrigan was sent home, only to find there was nothing wrong with him! All that seems far too much of a risk, when you have something as important as the World Cup at stake.'

Bobby Robson, inheriting the problems from Greenwood, said: 'We must have a positive, direct way of playing. I must try to get the ball forward more than we have been doing. There has been too much square passing.' As a former World Cup player, he would know as well as anyone that since the Second World War, England's record *away* from home in cup-ties is far from impressive. In the World Cup they have won only six times against opposition which could be classed among the world's top ten: France and Czechoslovakia (1982), Hungary (1981), Romania and Czechoslovakia (1970) and Argentina (1962). And in the European Championship only four: Spain (1980), Bulgaria (1979), and Spain and Russia (1968).

At forty-nine, Robson is young, and has a track record after more than thirteen years with Ipswich which will command respect among the players. But as one leading critic asked: Can Bobby Robson stand the hammer? Inevitably, he will be subjected to the public scrutiny which assailed Winterbottom, Ramsey, Revie and Greenwood, and he has not always shown himself calm in times of stress.

Bert Millichip, the FA chairman, said after England's elimination: 'I would hope that eventually we can introduce greater skill into the England team. This can only happen if we get it right at school and youth level, and it is about this that we will be having detailed discussions with Bobby Robson. We would be foolish if we did not sit down and look at the whole situation.' This indicated an involvement of Robson in the national coaching arena, as used to be the case with Walter Winterbottom, who was director of coaching as well as England manager. A week after the finals the FA dismissed the present director Allen Wade.

Wade had always disagreed with Charles Hughes, the assistant director, who has been the producer of a recent series of instructional films and its accompanying book, *Soccer Tactics and Skills*. In these, Hughes seeks to expose the myth evolved around systems of play – 4-2-4, 4-3-3 and so on – and to demonstrate that what players do individually, how they are taught and coached, will have much more influence on results than systems of play. And that a preoccupation with systems of play and eleven-a-side football by schoolmasters has seriously limited the development of many boys. The main theory of Hughes, which Wade never accepted, was that of Charles Reep, the man whose research provided the background to the success of Wolves under Stan Cullis in the Fifties. Reep has kept statistics of goal-scoring for over thirty years, at all levels of the game, which show conclusively that the majority of goals, in fact almost eighty per cent, are not scored from collective play, but from moves of three passes or less. Hughes has pursued this theory and kept his own statistics, further demonstrating that almost fifty per cent of goals come from set-pieces or repossessions in the attacking third of the field.

Since these facts are unarguable – and Hughes confirmed them by doing a goal analysis of every match in the finals – it follows that any team manager should be placing a priority on two things: getting the ball down to the opponent's penalty area with the minimum number of passes, and developing a high success rate of scoring from corners and free-kicks. This is precisely what Hughes did with excellent results during his years as manager of the England Amateur XI and Britsh Olympic Team, achieving improbable wins against European opposition with players drawn largely from two or three London senior amateur clubs. It is also what Graham Taylor did when gaining promotion with Watford to the First Division in 1982, with assistance from Reep's records.

Hughes further states that match analysis will tell you not who you think played well, but who *did* play well: measuring the number of possessions per player, the number of accurate passes, the number of shots on target, and so on. This in turn should influence selection. If a forward is not shooting, he will not score goals. All this information was available to Greenwood, but he rejected it, preferring his theory of collective play and systems of play, like ninety-nine per cent of managers. Yet it cannot be coincidence that against both Poland at Wembley in 1973 and against Spain in Madrid in 1982, England failed to capitalize on more than thirty set-pieces around the opposition's penalty area. If the FA really are to try to make a reappraisal of national coaching, and are to involve Robson, then they should start by taking on board the elementary principles already propounded by their own assistant director of coaching. As Hughes says:

'There is a need for a technical revolution right across the board, including countries like Germany. England's six goals in five matches is clearly not championship-winning football. The revolution has got to be based on two things: an acceptance of match- and player-analysis, and then getting these principles across to those teaching the game. Every profession, business or science makes progress by establishing the facts. Soccer does not. It proceeds on unsubstantial opinions. Yet analysis shows us that, contrary to all popular concepts, possession football with multiple passing does *not* produce goals. Only one goal in the World Cup, Brazil's third against Argentina, came from a ten-pass move. People say practice makes perfect, when all it does it make *permanent*. So much of the time we are practising the wrong things. On the basis of match analysis, England's performance could have been improved inside a *week*.'

The FA can hardly afford to ignore such a claim.

'I guess we ought to end this chapter with the time-honoured armchair game of naming our World XI, the team we would wish for a command performance, all playing at the summit of their ability. Each member of my team was, I thought, outstanding in his position in the 1982 World Cup, and it means I've had to leave out some fairly special players such as Tardelli, whom David Miller would include rather than Socrates. The only other player on whom we differed was Peter Shilton, David opting for Dasaev of Russia, on the basis that he had more scope for proving the range of his abilities. So here is my 1982 team of all talents:

Shilton (England); Gerets (Belgium), Passarella (Argentina), Karl Forster (West Germany), Junior (Brazil); Socrates (Brazil), Giresse (France), Falcao (Brazil); Maradona (Argentina), Rossi (Italy), Zico (Brazil).
Substitutes: Dasaev (USSR), Scirea (Italy), Tardelli (Italy), Boniek (Poland), Rummenigge (West Germany).'

 **15 Genoa Adventure**

Trevor's move to Italy was wholly unpremeditated. As we sat in the sun in the south of France putting the finishing touches to this book, shortly after the end of the World Cup, he was slightly depressed at the imminence of the new season in England, of a tiring pre-season tour with Manchester City consisting of seven or eight matches, necessary to help balance their strained finances. He had been given dispensation to arrive back some days late, to join the squad just before it flew abroad. We discussed the stupidity of these tours, further overcrowding an already bulging fixture list, and we talked of whether City had any chance of success in the coming season. We knew there was the possibility that they would want to sell him to balance the books, but we also knew that the only club likely to want him, and to be able to afford him, was Manchester United, and that City would do everything still in their power to prohibit such a move. As we ranged over the possibilities, there was not a mention of moving abroad, and when I returned to England, leaving Trevor with another two and a half weeks' holiday on the continent, it was on the understanding that we would meet to go through the first draft of the book before he went off with City.

'I was just about to go out to dinner in Marbella, when the phone rang with a message to contact my agent, urgently. I was going to leave it till the morning, but Helen suggested I should find out what it was about there and then. It was then I discovered that City had accepted an offer for me from Sampdoria, just promoted to the Italian First Division. I couldn't even remember which city the club came from, and frankly I didn't take the news seriously. It seemed to be just another of those plans which last a day or two and then subside. By the following day I'd made up my mind to stamp on the idea.

It was a Wednesday. The deadline for Italian transfers for the rest of the season was two days later, and on the Sunday I was due to join City on tour. My agent flew to Marbella, and we talked it over. 'You don't want to go, do you?' he said, and I agreed. We let the matter hang over till Thursday, and by then I had begun to wonder: was there really any future for me with City, knowing the state of their finances? Would the team do anything but struggle, as we had done throughout the spring, without the ability to buy new players? I could insist on seeing out my contract if I wanted to, but was there anything to be gained by that? The money in Italy was far better than anything in England but what about the football – all the defensiveness and kicking? What about the upheaval for my young son Matthew, and the fact that we had only just completed the building of a new house in Manchester? All these things jumbled around in my mind as we flew by private jet from Marbella to Monte Carlo to meet Sampdoria's multi-millionaire president, Paolo Mantovani. Yet the more I thought about it, the more it seemed to make sense, and it wasn't just the champagne that was provided all the way when the jet flew us home specially to Manchester!

It was all a bit far fetched: signing for an Italian club, in Monaco, for a president who for tax reasons could not re-enter Italy to see me play for the club which I myself had never seen, other than as a teenager with Birmingham in the Anglo-Italian Cup – an occasion I could not recollect. Mantovani said that he had watched me during the World Cup, and was very impressed. Of course he was flattering me, and he wanted me to sign for three years, but I insisted on two, with the provision that I should be free for all England internationals, including friendlies, if selected. He thought this was a good idea, that it would give prestige to Sampdoria if I were playing for England, and I just hoped it would prove to be that way.

Of course I was apprehensive about the move, even after I'd signed. Other players such as Keegan, Woodcock and Brady had, I knew, made up their minds to go abroad some time before they went. With me it was different, the decision came out of the blue. During the World Cup I had been asked by foreign journalists whether I would ever consider playing on the continent, and had emphatically said no, that I was twenty-eight, happy with Manchester City, and not interested. Yet here I was a few weeks later, following the trail started years before by John Charles, Jimmy Greaves, Joe Baker and Denis Law. It surprised my wife, my parents, my friends, and it surprised *me*.

Yet once I had arrived, I felt it was the right decision. It was all made so much easier by the fact that Liam Brady was there with me, with all his experience of Italian football, having been with Juventus, and I freely admit that I probably might not have signed but for knowing he would be there, too. It must always be a problem for managers with foreign players, the matter of communication, but Liam had already bridged the gap. I think it must have been an important factor for Keith Burkinshaw at Tottenham in deciding to sign *two* Argentinians together, Ossie Ardiles and Ricky Villa. It helped him and them – and the same went for Muhren and Thyssen at Ipswich.

Not only would Liam be a great help off the field, but I reckoned that his style and mine would prove to be a good partnership in the team, that we could work together. Going to play against some of the best defenders in the world, it would be an advantage to have at least one man in the team with whom I could speak the same language and discuss tactics. In fact Liam has been invaluable in creating the link between me and the manager, Renzo Ulivieri, known simply as 'Mister', as at all Italian clubs. The three of us have chats together to sort out the details of what has been discussed at general team talks.

They say that Sampdoria is even richer than Juventus, with the Fiat money from their president Agnelli, though Sampdoria have always up to now been the 'second' club in Genoa, competing in the shadow of FC Genoa, who were formed in the last century by an English doctor as a cricket and football club for English residents only. And Sampdoria still share the same old pre-First-World-War stadium built by FC Genoa. Mantovani obviously intends to make us number one in the city, a situation so similar to the one I came from in Manchester . . . But he is realistic. He said when I signed that Sampdoria had no chance of winning the championship this season and that he wanted to consolidate the team in the First Division.

He knew about my various bad injuries, and said that what impressed him was the way I'd fought my way back, and that this was what he liked about me, and I appreciated that. He had told Liam Brady (when he signed earlier) that he intended to buy other players, and he had kept his word, paying £1.5 million for Roberto Mancini, a seventeen-year-old striker from Bologna, and now almost a million for me.

I found out in no time, however, even playing against Third Division Teams, just how difficult it was going to be to score goals. Italian football is completely different from English football, it's played as though every game was an international. My first home game, a cup tie against Varese was astonishing. Even though I knew what to expect, I found it hard to believe. There were more fouls in that one game than in any I've ever played, but nobody other than me seemed to think anything of it! There could have been two or three players sent off, but no one was surprised, it was all just taken as normal. In England, a lot of the fouls are bad timing, people going for the ball late, but in Italy it's just a blatant 'thou shalt not pass' attitude. Every game is a constant battle. The biggest difference is the referees' interpretation, in Italy they are so lenient. If an attacker is running at the last defender, he will be stopped by whatever means, but without a booking for the defender – in such contrast to the new crackdown in England. The difference is unbelievable.

The marking is as tight as it was against Germany in the World Cup, when Karl Heinz Forster didn't give me an inch, but the difference with Sampdoria is that I'm not as isolated as I am with England: I'm playing closer to midfield. Italian defenders are so good at man-for-man marking that it is very difficult for forwards, so midfield players with an eye for goal are vital and our top scorer was Scanziani from midfield, and Platini was top scorer in the Leauge with Juventus. The biggest problem is trying to get a run at the ball at set pieces. Most of the kicking tends to be in midfield, and of course you expect the shirt pulling and tripping. But at set pieces it's almost impossible to take up a position from which you can attack the ball. An opponent blocks you, holding your shirt, your arm, and standing on your foot with his studs. And that's just when the ball is stationary! You get none of that at home in England. So against these kind of tactics, even if you are a Maradona, you need support from midfield and even defenders if the pressure is going to be taken off you.

We talk of pressure in England, but it is far more intense in Italy, more emotional. I couldn't believe the reception at the airport when I arrived. When the British

Caledonian plane touched down from Gatwick, two stewards on the tarmac kissed the ground. There were so many cars bringing supporters that the route to the airport was blocked for a time. It was almost frightening, the fans were so hysterical, chanting my name. I could just imagine how it would be if I didn't deliver the goods! In the crush leaving the airport and getting to the car, I had a really expensive Yves St Laurent jumper snatched from round my neck. Because of the crowds, a press conference was switched from the airport to the city centre, and all the fans followed by car, still chanting my name. It was great, in a sense, but I knew I had to go out and justify it. It was the same when we had the first day's training in Genoa, after we had been away for a week in a training camp further south. There was a crowd of 5,000 just to watch us train, paying 50p each! It really is like the old Jock Stein joke, that if you hung out the Celtic shirts to dry, the public would turn out to cheer. Imagine, over £2,000 paid to see us training!

I was very nervous going to the training camp. To some extent it's the same wherever you are on the first day back, you want to do well. The warmth shown to me by the other Sampdoria players was really encouraging, they could not have been nicer, and it's continued since on the pitch and during social hours. I remembered the stories of the difficulties Keegan had experienced in Hamburg, of German players ignoring him at first, but now I found the Italians were only too ready to include me if they were going out to dinner. It was strange that although there was a big language barrier, with me speaking no Italian and few of them knowing any English, we could understand each other quite a bit in training and on the pitch.

'Mister' has been impressed with the amount of running I'm prepared to do both in training and in matches, and it is only now, having been in Italy, that I have realized the extent of the running we do in the English game. I think this is one of the reasons why, in spite of inferior technical skills some of the time, we have such good club record in the European Cup. The crowd has also taken quickly to the amount of effort I put in, they recognize someone who is playing for the team and not just himself. I think basically in football if you show you are prepared to work hard you will be accepted anywhere. It's when you don't work for the team that you can have problems.

I was soon impressed with the skills of the Italian players, particularly their finishing ability, the fact that they all – even defenders – have a high ratio of hitting the target, much better than English players. Italian players are very composed and very confident in front of goal. Yet the pre-season period was one of the easiest I have ever experienced. In England we have this fixation that teams have got to come back four or five weeks before the season starts and train themselves into the ground. But is it really necessary? The Italians concentrate much more in training on agility work, and on tactical ideas. Yet, at the time of writing, I've never felt fitter.

I know there was talk in Manchester of me being sold because I was alleged to be injury prone, but it was really because of finance, and I finished top scorer in 1981–2, almost with a goal in every two matches I played. Of course, I accept that I've had more than my fair share of injuries, but the fact that I've three times been sold for a million suggests that there are people who still have confidence in me.

I'm very sensitive to such accusations, even more so after a long injury in 1982–3. I've always been a worrier, and I've never been more anxious than in Italy to do well, to prove myself and to prove that an England striker can succeed abroad. At present the Sampdoria players are great with me, the manager – who was not responsible for signing me – likes me, and the crowd are really with me. Yet in some ways I felt at the start like I did when I was sixteen and at Birmingham, as if I was starting my career all over again.

I know one thing, though, I'll never complain again about the British Press! The Italian Press really is something different, and I can understand how the Italian team came to put a ban on their own Press during the World Cup. In the England camp there were one or two of the usual moans about Press comments. Phil Thompson was upset by something in *The Guardian* which was not all *that* critical, and Greenwood often got angry with Press comment. None of us, I suppose, likes to be criticized, but on the field I accept that you have to take the criticism along with the praise. What I hate is being misquoted. In twelve seasons in England that never happened too much, but out in Italy I can't believe what I'm supposed to have said, almost every day of the week. On my second day, following the press conference, there was a headline saying I had received a cold reception from the other players. In fact it had been very friendly, but the article was based on the fact that I had only shaken hands with everyone, and had not been embraced! Then another day they said I was ill, when I was as fit as a fiddle. I was also quoted as saying I would score twenty goals in the season, when I'd never even discussed the question; and it was said that I thought Mancini, the youngster, was another Kevin Keegan when I had not even mentioned him.

Every day I pick up the papers wondering what on earth there will be in them. But I'm determined to enjoy myself, to settle in with my family and make it a success, to score the goals which will justify the move. And then Liam and I can go out and have a few beers. The Italian players are most surprised when we have a lager, which they don't like, yet they have wine with most of their meals even on match days. There are so many things that are different in Italy, but putting the ball in the net is the same in any language.

After a few weeks I knew just how hard it was going to be. In the early matches, such as against Juventus, I was effectively up against four defenders single-handed – my own marker, another marker, the sweeper and the goal-keeper! But going to Italy has been marvellous experience, with so many brilliant foreign players there in addition to the men who won the World Cup: Boniek and Platini with Juventus, Falcao with Roma, Passarella and Bertoni at Fiorentina, Krol and Diaz at Napoli and Hansi Muller with Inter. I feel at this moment it is the most exciting stage in Europe.

There were dozens of Union Jacks being waved by Sampdoria fans when we played Juventus, with my name written on them. It took me time to win over the fans at Forest. With Manchester City it was immediate, and so it has been with Sampdoria. The start couldn't have been better. The first three games were Juventus, Inter, Roma, three of the top teams in the country, and incredibly we won all three. In the second, away to Inter, I got the first goal. But disaster struck against Roma when I was carried off with a bad injury which took almost five months to get right. It was the same adductor strain I'd had at Manchester City the previous season which had threatened my chances of going to the World Cup. Now I'd actually ruptured the muscle. I've had some bad injuries in the past but this was the most worrying of them all. I was at such a low ebb at times I thought my career was at an end. I eventually returned after an abortive comeback of half a game in November on 27 February against Torino. The club were tremendous in their attitude throughout: so was the president. They put no pressure on me – the president just kept telling the press that I was an honest professional and 'he will decide when he is ready to play'.

There were ten games left when I came back and in those I scored six goals including a hat-trick against Udinese. At the end of the season we'd only just missed out on a place in the UEFA cup, finishing seventh. At the start of the season everyone would have been pleased with that but having got ourselves into position we let it slip a bit in the last three games. Yet our supporters were delighted by the fact that at least we'd finished above our rivals, Genoa FC. The Derby matches against them are unbelievable – without doubt the biggest game I've played in for atmosphere and I'm not excluding the World Cup, the European Cup Final or England v. Scotland. Nothing matched this. The ground was completely full, 55,000, almost three hours before the kick-off. They were arriving from breakfast time. The one I played in ended 2-2. It was a ferocious battle from start to finish. And I hardly got a touch of the ball but plenty of kicks!

I was delighted to finish the season with seven goals in my fourteen league games, only one less than our top scorer Scanziani who had eight in thirty. Being a striker in Italy, I'd learned, was difficult but not impossible. The biggest difference was in the number of chances I got compared to England. In a season at home I would have far more but in Italy you've got to take them when they come. I can't think of one really bad miss I had, whereas in England you regularly feel 'I should have scored there'. You don't get that luxury in Italy.

I had a bit of a difficult time over the business with Gentile and my criticism of him in the first edition of this book which was published soon after I arrived in Italy. I was injured but still making the headlines because of the row that broke out. An inquiry was demanded and I had to appear in front of a committee in Milan but the club supported me up to the hilt and I was completely cleared. I was confident all the way through that even though I was in a foreign country nobody could deny the truth and fairness of what I'd said. I later met Gentile in Turin and though we weren't able to hold a proper conversation, because my Italian wasn't good enough, we shook hands and there was no problem.

All in all I've been so pleased with my experience in Italy that I may consider staying longer than my two year contract if they want me. I've loved it all – the city, the climate, the food, the people – and I know that it's sharpened my game, that I'm now a better player. I think this is reflected in the fact that I have probably played my best football for England in the season 1982–3. People have remarked how much Italy has helped me, that I've been playing for England at last the way I always played for club teams. But I think this is for another reason as well, that I now feel more of a fixture in the side, more important, one of the senior members. So I'm more confident, able perhaps to be a little bit more arrogant towards the opposition. Italy has taught me to shield the ball better, to hold defenders off physically. I've got more awareness. I'm now twenty-nine, but I honestly think I've got a reasonable chance of playing through to the next World Cup Finals in 1986. Because of my light build I think I can retain my sharpness. My two goals against Denmark and one against Hungary took my tally to eleven for England. My immediate ambition is to reach fifty caps and hopefully by the end of 1983–4 I'll be close to that.'

Appendices

APPENDIX I

Results of Previous World Cup Final Competitions

URUGUAY 1930

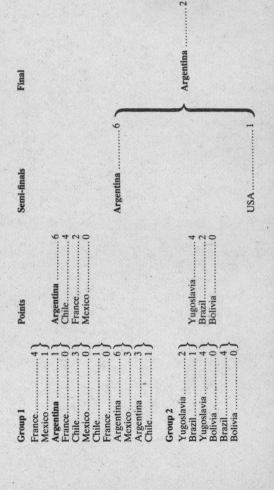

Group 1

France.......4
Mexico.......1

Argentina.......1
France.......0

Chile.......3
Mexico.......0

Chile.......1
France.......0

Argentina.......6
Mexico.......3

Argentina.......3
Chile.......1

Group 2

Yugoslavia.......2
Brazil.......1

Yugoslavia.......4
Bolivia.......0

Brazil.......4
Bolivia.......0

Points

Argentina.......6
Chile.......4
France.......2
Mexico.......0

Yugoslavia.......4
Brazil.......2
Bolivia.......0

Semi-finals

Argentina.......6

USA.......1

Final

Argentina.......2

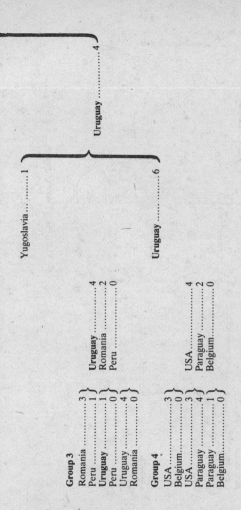

ITALY 1934

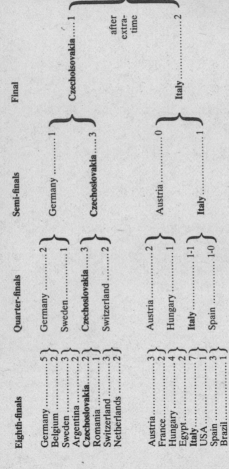

Eighth-finals	Quarter-finals	Semi-finals	Final
Germany 5	Germany 2	Germany 1	Czecholsovakia 1
Belgium 2	Sweden 1		
Sweden 3	Czechoslovakia 3	Czechoslovakia 3	after
Argentina 2	Switzerland 2		extra-
Czechoslovakia 2			time
Romania 1			
Switzerland 3	Austria 2	Austria 0	Italy 2
Netherlands 2	Hungary 1		
	Italy 1-1	Italy 1	
Austria 3	Spain 1-0		
France 2			
Hungary 4			
Egypt 2			
Italy 7			
USA 1			
Spain 3			
Brazil 1			

Third Place Final: Germany 3 Austria 1

200

FRANCE 1938

Eighth-finals	Quarter-finals	Semi-finals	Final
Hungary 6			
Dutch East Indies ... 0	Hungary 2		
Switzerland 1-4	Switzerland 0	Hungary 5	
Germany 1-2			
Cuba 3-2	Cuba 0		Hungary 2
Romania 3-1	Sweden 8	Sweden 1	
Sweden .... Bye			
France 3	France 1		
Belgium 1	Italy 3	Italy 2	
Italy 2			Italy 4
Norway 1			
Czechoslovakia 3	Czechoslovakia 1-1		
Netherlands 0	Brazil 1-2	Brazil 1	
Brazil 6			
Poland 5			

Third Place Final: Brazil 4 Sweden 2

BRAZIL 1950

Group 1

	Points
Brazil	4
Mexico	0
Yugoslavia	3
Switzerland	0
Yugoslavia	4
Mexico	1
Brazil	2
Switzerland	2
Brazil	2
Yugoslavia	0
Switzerland	2
Mexico	1

Points	
Brazil	5
Yugoslavia	4
Switzerland	3
Mexico	0

Group 2

	Points
Spain	3
USA	1
England	2
Chile	0
USA	1
England	0
Spain	2
Chile	0

Points	
Spain	6
England	2
Chile	2
USA	2

Final Pool

Uruguay	2
Spain	2
Brazil	7
Sweden	1
Uruguay	3
Sweden	2
Brazil	6
Spain	1

Points	
Uruguay	5
Brazil	4
Sweden	2
Spain	1

Spain 1
England .... 0 }
Chile 5
USA .... 2 }

Sweden 3
Spain .... 1 }

Group 3
Sweden 3
Italy .... 2 }
Sweden 2
Paraguay .... 2 }
Italy 2
Paraguay .... 0 }

Sweden 3
Italy 2
Paraguay 1

Uruguay 2
Brazil .... 1 }

Group 4
Uruguay 8
Bolivia .... 0 }

Uruguay 2
Bolivia 0

SWITZERLAND 1954

Points	Quarter-finals	Semi-finals	Final

Group 1

Yugoslavia 1
France 0
Brazil 5
Mexico 0
France 3
Mexico 2
Brazil 1
Yugoslavia 1

Brazil 3
Yugoslavia 3
France 2
Mexico 0

W. Germany 2
Yugoslavia 0

W. Germany 6

W. Germany 3

Group 2

Hungary 9
Korea 0
W. Germany 4
Turkey 1
Hungary 8
W. Germany 3
Turkey 7
Korea 0

Hungary 4
W. Germany 2
Turkey 2
Korea 0

Hungary 4
Brazil 2

Austria 1

Play-off match:
W. Germany 7
Turkey 2

204

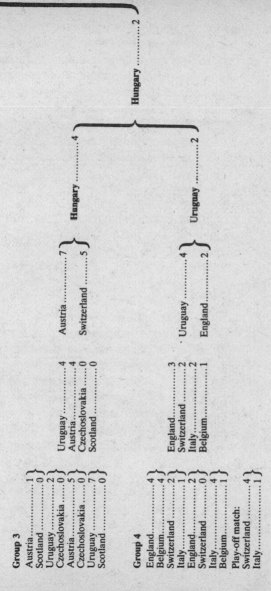

Group 3

Austria	1
Scotland	0
Uruguay	2
Czechoslovakia	0
Austria	5
Czechoslovakia	0
Uruguay	7
Scotland	0

Uruguay	4
Austria	4
Czechoslovakia	0
Scotland	0

Austria	7
Switzerland	5

Group 4

England	4
Belgium	4
Switzerland	2
Italy	1
England	2
Switzerland	0
Italy	4
Belgium	1

Play-off match:

Switzerland	4
Italy	1

England	3
Switzerland	2
Italy	2
Belgium	1

Uruguay	4
England	2

Hungary 4

Uruguay 2

Hungary 2

Third Place Final: Austria 3 Uruguay 1

SWEDEN 1958

Points — **Quarter-finals** — **Semi-finals** — **Final**

Group 1

Argentina 1
W. Germany ......3 }

Czechoslovakia 2
W. Germany ....2 }

Argentina 1
Czechoslovakia ....6 }

Northern Ireland ...1
Czechoslovakia ....0 }

Argentina 3
Northern Ireland ...1 }

W. Germany 2
Northern Ireland ...2 }

W. Germany 4
Northern Ireland ...3
Czechoslovakia 3
Argentina 2

Play-off match:
Northern Ireland ...2
Czechoslovakia ....1 }

Group 2

France 7
Paraguay ....3 }

Yugoslavia 1
Scotland ....1 }

Paraguay 3
Scotland ....2 }

Yugoslavia 3
France ....2 }

Paraguay 3
Yugoslavia ....3 }

France 3
Scotland ....1 }

France 4
Yugoslavia 4
Paraguay 3
Scotland 1

Quarter-finals

Brazil 1
Wales ....0 }

France 4
Northern Ireland ..0 }

Semi-finals

Brazil ....5 }

France ....2 }

Final

Brazil 5

206

Group 3

Sweden	3
Mexico	0
Hungary	1
Wales	1
Mexico	1
Wales	1
Sweden	2
Hungary	1
Hungary	0
Mexico	0
Hungary	4
Sweden	0
Sweden	0
Wales	0

Play-off match:

Wales	2
Hungary	1

Group 4

England	2
USSR	2
Brazil	3
Austria	0
USSR	2
Austria	0
Brazil	0
England	0
Brazil	2
USSR	0
England	2
Austria	2

Play-off match:

USSR	1
England	0

Sweden	5
Wales	3
Hungary	3
Mexico	1

Brazil	5
USSR	3
England	3
Austria	1

W. Germany	1
Yugoslavia	0

USSR	0
Sweden	2

W. Germany 1

Sweden 3

Sweden 2

Third Place Final: France 6 W. Germany 3

CHILE 1962

Group 1	Points	Quarter-finals	Semi-finals	Final

Group 1

Uruguay .... 2 }
Colombia 1

USSR .... 2 }
Yugoslavia 0

Uruguay .... 1 }
Yugoslavia 3

Yugoslavia .... 4 }
Colombia 1

USSR .... 4 }
Uruguay 1

USSR .... 2 }
Colombia 0

Colombia .... 5 }
Yugoslavia 5

Points

USSR 5
Yugoslavia 4
Uruguay 2
Colombia 1

Group 2

Chile .... 3 }
Switzerland 1

W. Germany .... 0 }
Italy 0

Chile .... 2 }
Italy 0

Italy .... 3 }
Switzerland 1

Switzerland .... 1 }
W. Germany 2

W. Germany .... 2 }
Chile 0

Switzerland .... 0 }
Italy 3

Points

W. Germany 5
Chile 4
Italy 3
Switzerland 0

Quarter-finals

Brazil .... 3 }
England 1

USSR .... 1 }
Chile 2

Semi-finals

Brazil .... 4 }
Chile 2

Final

Brazil 3

208

Group 3

Brazil	2	Brazil	3
Mexico	0	Czechoslovakia	3
Czechoslovakia	1	Spain	2
Spain	0	Mexico	2
Brazil	0		
Czechoslovakia	0		
Spain	1		
Mexico	0		
Brazil	2		
Spain	1		
Mexico	3		
Czechoslovakia	1		

Group 4

Argentina	1	Hungary	5
Bulgaria	0	England	3
Hungary	2	Argentina	3
England	1	Bulgaria	1
Argentina	3		
England	6		
Hungary	1		
Bulgaria	0		
Argentina	0		
Hungary	0		
Bulgaria	0		
England	0		

Bracket (quarter-finals → semi-finals → final):

```
W. Germany......0 ─┐
                   ├─ Yugoslavia......1 ─┐
Yugoslavia......1 ─┘                     │
                                         ├─ Czechoslovakia......1
Hungary......0 ─┐                        │
                ├─ Czechoslovakia......3 ┘
Czechoslovakia......1 ─┘
```

Third Place Final: Chile 1 Yugoslavia 0

ENGLAND 1966

Group 1		Points	Quarter-finals	Semi-finals	Final
England........0	Uruguay........0	England........5			
France........1	Mexico........1	Uruguay........4			
Uruguay........2	France........1	Mexico........2			
England........2	Mexico........0	France........1			
Mexico........0	Uruguay........0		England........1	England........2	England........4
England........2	France........0		Argentina........0		

Group 3		Points			
Bulgaria........0	Brazil........2	Portugal........6			
Hungary........1	Portugal........3	Hungary........4			
Brazil........1	Hungary........3	Brazil........2			
Portugal........3	Bulgaria........0	Bulgaria........0			
Portugal........3	Brazil........1		Portugal........5	Portugal........1	
Hungary........3	Bulgaria........1		North Korea........3		

after extra-time

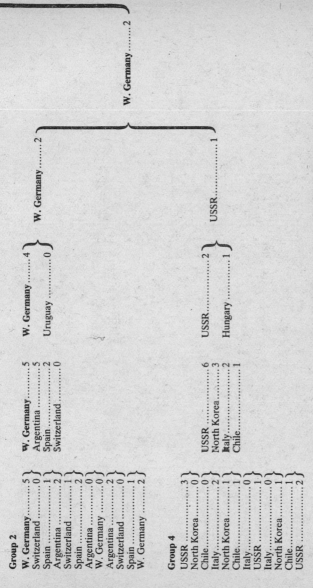

Group 2

W. Germany.........5	W. Germany.........5
Switzerland.........0	Argentina.........5
Spain.........1	Spain.........2
Argentina.........2	Switzerland.........0
Argentina.........2	
Switzerland.........1	
Spain.........2	
Argentina.........0	
W. Germany.........0	
Argentina.........2	
Switzerland.........0	
Spain.........1	
Spain.........1	
W. Germany.........2	

W. Germany.........4
Uruguay.........0

⎱

W. Germany.........2

Group 4

USSR.........3	USSR.........6
North Korea.........0	North Korea.........3
Chile.........0	Italy.........2
Italy.........2	Chile.........1
North Korea.........1	
Chile.........1	
Italy.........0	
USSR.........1	
Italy.........0	
North Korea.........1	
Chile.........1	
USSR.........2	

USSR.........2
Hungary.........1

⎱

USSR.........1

W. Germany.........2

Third Place Final: Portugal 2 USSR 1

MEXICO 1970

	Points	Quarter-finals	Semi-finals	Final

Group 1

Mexico............0	
USSR.............0	
Belgium..........3	
El Salvador......0	USSR.............5
USSR.............4	Mexico...........5
Belgium..........1	Belgium..........2
Mexico...........4	El Salvador......0
El Salvador......2	
USSR.............2	
El Salvador......0	
Mexico...........1	
Belgium..........0	

USSR...............0
Uruguay...........1

Uruguay...........1

Brazil...............4

Brazil...............3

Brazil...............4
Peru................2

Group 4

Peru.............3	
Bulgaria.........2	
Morocco..........1	W. Germany.......6
W. Germany.......2	Peru.............4
Peru.............3	Bulgaria.........1
Morocco..........0	Morocco..........1
Bulgaria.........2	
W. Germany.......5	
Peru.............1	
W. Germany.......3	
Morocco..........1	
Bulgaria.........1	

212

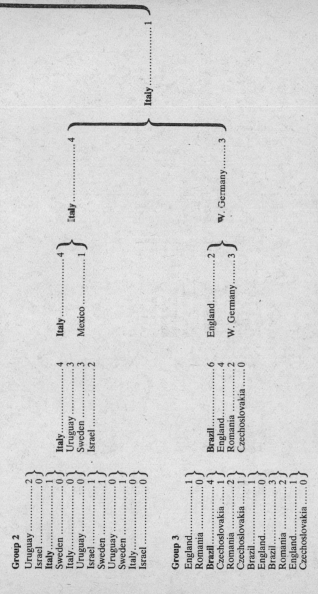

Group 2

Uruguay	2
Israel	0
Italy	1
Sweden	0
Italy	0
Uruguay	0
Israel	1
Sweden	1
Uruguay	0
Sweden	1
Italy	0
Israel	0

Italy 4
Uruguay 3
Sweden 3
Israel 2

Italy 4
Mexico 1

Italy 4

Group 3

England	1
Romania	0
Brazil	4
Czechoslovakia	1
Romania	2
Czechoslovakia	1
Brazil	1
England	0
Brazil	3
Romania	2
England	1
Czechoslovakia	0

Brazil 6
England 4
Romania 2
Czechoslovakia 0

England 2
W. Germany 3

W. Germany 3

Italy 1

213

WEST GERMANY 1974

	Points			Final

Group 1

			Points
W. Germany	1		
Chile	0	GDR	5
GDR	2	W. Germany	4
Australia	0	Chile	2
Chile	1	Australia	1
GDR	1		
W. Germany	3		
Australia	0		
Australia	0		
Chile	0		
W. Germany	0		
GDR	1		

Group 2

			Points
Brazil	0		
Yugoslavia	0	Yugoslavia	4
Zaire	0	Brazil	4
Scotland	2	Scotland	4
Yugoslavia	9	Zaire	0
Zaire	0		
Scotland	0		
Brazil	0		
Zaire	0		
Brazil	3		
Scotland	1		
Yugoslavia	1		

Group A

			Points
Netherlands	4		
Argentina	0	Netherlands	6
Brazil	1	Brazil	4
GDR	0	GDR	1
GDR	0	Argentina	1
Netherlands	2		
Argentina	1		
Brazil	2		
Netherlands	2		
Brazil	0		
Argentina	1		
GDR	1		

Final

Netherlands 1

Group 3

Uruguay	0
Netherlands	2
Sweden	0
Bulgaria	0
Netherlands	0
Sweden	0
Bulgaria	1
Uruguay	1
Bulgaria	1
Netherlands	4
Sweden	3
Uruguay	0

Netherlands	5
Sweden	4
Bulgaria	2
Uruguay	1

Group B

Yugoslavia	0
W. Germany	2
Sweden	0
Poland	1
W. Germany	4
Sweden	2
Poland	2
Yugoslavia	1
Sweden	2
Yugoslavia	1
Poland	0
W. Germany	1

W. Germany	6
Poland	4
Sweden	2
Yugoslavia	0

Group 4

Italy	3
Haiti	1
Poland	3
Argentina	2
Haiti	0
Poland	7
Argentina	1
Italy	1
Argentina	4
Haiti	1
Poland	2
Italy	1

Poland	6
Argentina	3
Italy	3
Haiti	0

W. Germany 2

Third Place Final: Poland 1 Brazil 0

ARGENTINA 1978

Group 1

	Points
Italy......2	Italy......6
France......1	Argentina......4
Argentina......2	France......2
Hungary......1	Hungary......0
Italy......3	
Hungary......1	
Argentina......2	
France......1	
France......3	
Hungary......1	
Italy......1	
Argentina......0	

Group 2

	Points
W. Germany......0	Poland......5
Poland......0	W. Germany......4
Tunisia......3	Tunisia......3
Mexico......1	Mexico......0
W. Germany......6	
Mexico......0	
Poland......1	
Tunisia......0	
W. Germany......0	
Tunisia......0	
Poland......3	
Mexico......1	

Group A

	Points
Italy......0	Netherlands......5
W. Germany......0	Italy......3
Netherlands......5	W. Germany......2
Austria......1	Austria......2
Italy......1	
Austria......0	
Netherland......2	
W. Germany......2	
Netherlands......2	
Italy......1	
Austria......3	
W. Germany......2	

Final

Netherlands......1

after
extra-
time

Group 3

Austria	2 }	Austria	4
Spain	1 }	Brazil	4
Brazil	1 }	Spain	3
Sweden	0 }	Sweden	1
Brazil	0 }		
Spain	0 }		
Austria	1 }		
Sweden	0 }		
Spain	1 }		
Sweden	0 }		
Brazil	1 }		
Austria	0 }		

Group B

Brazil	3 }	Argentina	5
Peru	0 }	Brazil	5
Argentina	2 }	Poland	2
Poland	0 }	Peru	0
Poland	1 }		
Peru	0 }		
Argentina	0 }		
Brazil	0 }		
Poland	3 }		
Peru	1 }		
Argentina	6 }		
Peru	0 }		

Group 4

Peru	3 }	Peru	5
Scotland	1 }	Netherlands	3
Netherlands	3 }	Scotland	3
Iran	0 }	Iran	1
Scotland	1 }		
Iran	1 }		
Netherlands	0 }		
Peru	0 }		
Scotland	3 }		
Netherlands	2 }		
Peru	4 }		
Iran	1 }		

Argentina 3

Third Place Final: Brazil 2 Italy 1

217

Preliminary Competition for 1982 World Cup

Entries, Dates, Venues, Matches, Results, Referees and Final Classifications
Entries – 109
(Africa 29, Asia/Oceania 22, Europe 33, South America 10, Concacaf 15)

EUROPE
Entries: 33 (including Spain as 1982 Organizing Country)
Albania, Austria, Belgium, Bulgaria, Cyprus, Czechoslovakia, Denmark, England, Finland, France, German Democratic Republic, W. Germany, Greece, Hungary, Ireland Republic, Northern Ireland, Italy, Luxembourg, Malta, Netherlands, Norway, Poland, Portugal, Romania, Scotland, Sweden. Switzerland, Turkey, USSR, Wales, Yugoslavia
(Top 2 teams in each group qualify for Finals)

Group 1 (West Germany, Austria, Bulgaria, Finland, Albania)

4. 6.80	Helsinki	Finland v. Bulgaria	0:2(0:1)	B. McGinlay, Scotland
3. 9.80	Tirana	Albania v. Finland	2:0(2:0)	E. Platopoulos, Greece
24. 9.80	Helsinki	Finland v. Austria	0:2(0:1)	C. Thomas, Wales
19.10.80	Sofia	Bulgaria v. Austria	2:1(1:0)	T. Tokat, Turkey
15.11.80	Vienna	Austria v. Albania	5:0(3:0)	R. Renggli, Switzerland
3.12.80	Sofia	Bulgaria v. West Germany	1:3(0:2)	R. Lattanzi, Italy
6.12.80	Tirana	Albania v. Austria	0:1(0:1)	L. Padar, Hungary
1. 4.81	Tirana	Albania v. West Germany	0:2(0:1)	A. Wencl, Czechoslovakia
29. 4.81	Hamburg	West Germany v. Austria	2:0(2:0)	C. Corver, Netherlands
13. 5.81	Sofia	Bulgaria v. Finland	4:0(1:0)	E. Sostaric, Yugoslavia
24. 5.81	Lahti	Finland v. West Germany	0:4(0:3)	J. Carpenter, Ireland Rep.
28. 5.81	Vienna	Austria v. Bulgaria	2:0(1:0)	P. Partridge, England
17. 6.81	Linz	Austria v. Finland	5:1(2:0)	A. Jarguz, Poland
2. 9.81	Kotka	Finland v. Albania	2:1(0:0)	I. Nielsen, Denmark
23. 9.81	Bochum	West Germany v. Finland	7:1(2:1)	N. Rolles, Luxembourg
14.10.81	Vienna	Austria v. West Germany	1:3(1:2)	A. Ponnet, Belgium
14.10.81	Tirana	Albania v. Bulgaria	0:2(0:0)	A. Prokop, GDR
11.11.81	Sofia	Bulgaria v. Austria	0:0(0:0)	M. Vautrot, France
18.11.81	Dortmund	West Germany v. Albania	8:0(5:0)	R. Björnestad, Norway
22.11.81	Düsseldorf	West Germany v. Bulgaria	4:0(1:0)	E. Fredriksson, Sweden

Final Classification:

1. West Germany	8	8	0	0	33:3	16
2. Austria	8	5	1	2	16:6	11
3. Bulgaria	8	4	1	3	11:10	9
4. Albania	8	1	0	7	4:22	2
5. Finland	8	1	0	7	4:27	2
	40	19	2	19	68:68	40

Group 2 (Netherlands, France, Belgium, Ireland Rep., Cyprus)

Date	City	Match	Score	Referee
26. 3.80	Nicosia	Cyprus v. Ireland Rep.	2:3(1:3)	Zvi Sharir, Israel
10. 9.80	Dublin	Ireland Rep. v. Netherlands	2:1(0:0)	H. Lund-Sørensen, Denmark
15.10.80	Limassol	Cyprus v. France	0:7(0:4)	B. Galler, Switzerland
15.10.80	Dublin	Ireland Rep. v. Belgium	1:1(1:1)	N. Rolles, Luxembourg
28.10.80	Paris	France v. Ireland Rep.	2:0(1:0)	A. Lamo Castillo, Spain
19.11.80	Brussels	Belgium v. Netherlands	1:0(0:0)	E. Azim-Zade, USSR
19.11.80	Dublin	Ireland Rep. v. Cyprus	6:0(4:0)	E. Gudmundsson, Iceland
21.12.80	Nicosia	Cyprus v. Belgium	0:2(0:1)	R. Valentine, Scotland
18. 2.81	Brussels	Belgium v. Cyprus	3:2(2:1)	A. Ravander, Finland
22. 2.81	Groningen	Netherlands v. Cyprus	3:0(1:0)	H. W. King, Wales
25. 3.81	Rotterdam	Netherlands v. France	1:0(0:0)	L. Agnolin, Italy
25. 3.81	Brussels	Belgium v. Ireland Rep.	1:0(0:0)	R. J. Nazare, Portugal
29. 4.81	Paris	France v. Belgium	3:2(3:1)	V. Sanchez Arminio, Spain
29. 4.81	Nicosia	Cyprus v. Netherlands	0:1(0:1)	I. Yossifov, Bulgaria
9. 9.81	Rotterdam	Netherlands v. Ireland Rep.	2:2(1:1)	V. Christov, Czechoslovakia
9. 9.81	Brussels	Belgium v. France	2:0(1:0)	K. Palotai, Hungary
14.10.81	Rotterdam	Netherlands v. Belgium	3:0(2:0)	B. McGinlay, Scotland
14.10.81	Dublin	Ireland Rep. v. France	3:2(3:1)	B. Ericsson, Sweden
18.11.81	Paris	France v. Netherlands	2:0(0:0)	A. da Silva Garrido, Portugal
5.12.81	Paris	France v. Cyprus	4:0(2:0)	E. Borg, Malta

Final Classification:

1.	Belgium	8	5	1	2	12:9	11
2.	France	8	5	0	3	20:8	10
3.	Ireland Rep.	8	4	2	2	17:11	10
4.	Netherlands	8	4	1	3	11:7	9
5.	Cyprus	8	0	0	8	4:29	0
		40	18	4	18	64:64	40

Group 3 (Czechoslovakia, USSR, Wales, Turkey, Iceland)

2. 6.80	Reykjavik	Iceland v. Wales	0:4(0:1)		R. Nyhus, Norway
3. 9.80	Reykjavik	Iceland v. USSR	1:2(0:1)		O. Donnelly, N. Ireland
24. 9.80	Izmir	Turkey v. Iceland	1:3(0:1)		I. Igna, Romania
15.10.80	Cardiff	Wales v. Turkey	4:0(2:0)		T. Mansson, Denmark
15.10.80	Moscow	USSR v. Iceland	5:0(2:0)		A. Suchanek, Poland
19.11.80	Cardiff	Wales v. Czechoslovakia	1:0(1:0)		W. Eschweiler, W. Germany
3.12.80	Prague	Czechoslovakia v. Turkey	2:0(2:0)		E. Fredriksson, Sweden
25. 3.81	Ankara	Turkey v. Wales	0:1(0:0)		S. Kuti, Hungary
15. 4.81	Istanbul	Turkey v. Czechoslovakia	0:3(0:0)		R. Schoeters, Belgium
27. 5.81	Bratislava	Czechoslovakia v. Iceland	6:1(2:0)		N. Zlatanos, Greece
30. 5.81	Wrexham	Wales v. USSR	0:0(0:0)		B. Galler, Switzerland
9. 9.81	Reykjavik	Iceland v. Turkey	2:0(1:0)		K. O'Sullivan, Ireland Rep.
9. 9.81	Prague	Czechoslovakia v. Wales	2:0(1:0)		F. Wöhrer, Austria
23. 9.81	Reykjavik	Iceland v. Czechoslovakia	1:1(1:0)		K. H. Hope, Scotland
23. 9.81	Moscow	USSR v. Turkey	4:0(3:0)		D. Matovinovic, Yugoslavia
7.10.81	Izmir	Turkey v. USSR	0:3(0:2)		E. Eschweiler, W. Germany
14.10.81	Swansea	Wales v. Iceland	2:2(1:0)		A. Ravander, Finland
28.10.81	Tbilisi	USSR v. Czechoslovakia	2:0(1:0)		M. Vautrot, France
18.11.81	Tbilisi	USSR v. Wales	3:0(2:0)		J. Keizer, Netherlands
29.11.81	Bratislava	Czechoslovakia v. USSR	1:1(1:1)		C. White, England

Final Classification

1. USSR	8	6	2	0	20:2	14
2. Czechoslovakia	8	4	2	2	15:6	10
3. Wales	8	4	2	2	12:7	10
4. Iceland	8	2	2	4	10:21	6
5. Turkey	8	0	0	8	1:22	0
	40	16	8	16	58:58	40

Group 4 (England, Hungary, Switzerland, Romania, Norway)

Date	City	Match	Score	Referee
10. 9.80	London	England v. Norway	4:0(1:0)	M. v. Langenhove, Belgium
24. 9.80	Oslo	Norway v. Romania	1:1(1:1)	S. Kirschen, GDR
15.10.80	Bucharest	Romania v. England	2:1(1:0)	U. Ericsson, Sweden
29.10.80	Berne	Switzerland v. Norway	1:2(0:1)	D. Krchnak, Czechoslovakia
19.11.80	London	England v. Switzerland	2:1(2:0)	J. Keizer, Netherlands
28. 4.81	Lucerne	Switzerland v. Hungary	2:2(1:1)	I. Foote, Scotland
29. 4.81	London	England v. Romania	0:0(0:0)	H. Aldinger, W. Germany
13. 5.81	Budapest	Hungary v. Romania	1:0(1:0)	A. Ponnet, Belgium
20. 5.81	Oslo	Norway v. Hungary	1:2(0:0)	M. Moffatt, Northern Ireland
30. 5.81	Basle	Switzerland v. England	2:1(2:0)	A. Prokop, GDR
3. 6.81	Bucharest	Romania v. Norway	1:0(0:0)	E. Göksel, Turkey
6. 6.81	Budapest	Hungary v. England	1:3(1:1)	P. Casarin, Italy
17. 6.81	Oslo	Norway v. Switzerland	1:1(0:0)	E. Shklovski, USSR
9. 9.81	Oslo	Norway v. England	2:1(2:1)	J. Kacprzak, Poland
23. 9.81	Bucharest	Romania v. Hungary	0:0(0:0)	E. Linemayr, Austria
10.10.81	Bucharest	Romania v. Switzerland	1:2(0:0)	E. Barbaresco, Italy
14.10.81	Budapest	Hungary v. Switzerland	3:0(1:0)	T. Tokat, Turkey
31.10.81	Budapest	Hungary v. Norway	4:1(1:1)	E. Sostaric, Yugoslavia
11.11.81	Berne	Switzerland v. Romania	0:0(0:0)	C. Correia Dias, Portugal
18.11.81	London	England v. Hungary	1:0(1:0)	G. Konrath, France

Final Classification:

1. Hungary	8	4	2	2	13:8	10
2. England	8	4	1	3	13:8	9
3. Romania	8	2	4	2	5:5	8
4. Switzerland	8	2	3	3	9:12	7
5. Norway	8	2	2	4	8:15	6
	40	14	12	14	48:48	40

Group 5 (Italy, Yugoslavia, Greece, Denmark, Luxembourg)

Date	Venue	Fixture	Score	Referee
10. 9.80	Luxembourg	Luxembourg v. Yugoslavia	0:5(0:0)	F. Latzin, Austria
27. 9.80	Ljubljana	Yugoslavia v. Denmark	2:1(2:1)	A. Garrido, Portugal
11.10.80	Luxembourg	Luxembourg v. Italy	0:2(0:1)	H. Weerink, Netherlands
15.10.80	Copenhagen	Denmark v. Greece	0:1(0:0)	E. Farrel, Ireland Rep.
1.11.80	Rome	Italy v. Denmark	2:0(1:0)	B. Lacarne, Algeria
15.11.80	Turin	Italy v. Yugoslavia	2:0(1:0)	A. Klein, Israel
19.11.80	Copenhagen	Denmark v. Luxembourg	4:0(2:0)	C. White, England
6.12.80	Athens	Greece v. Italy	0:2(0:1)	M. Vautrot, France
28. 1.81	Thessalonika	Greece v. Luxembourg	2:0(2:0)	N. Doudine, Bulgaria
11. 3.81	Luxembourg	Luxembourg v. Greece	0:2(0:1)	P. Scherz, Switzerland
29. 4.81	Split	Yugoslavia v. Greece	5:1(3:0)	V. Butenko, USSR
1. 5.81	Luxembourg	Luxembourg v. Denmark	1:2(1:0)	L. Delsemme, Belgium
3. 6.81	Copenhagen	Denmark v. Italy	3:1(0:0)	F. Wöhrer, Austria
9. 9.81	Copenhagen	Denmark v. Yugoslavia	1:2(0:0)	S. Kirschen, GDR
24.10.81	Thessalonika	Greece v. Denmark	2:3(0:2)	J. Bucek, Austria
17.10.81	Belgrade	Yugoslavia v. Italy	1:1(1:1)	E. Eschweiler, W. Germany
14.11.81	Turin	Italy v. Greece	1:1(0:0)	N. Rainea, Romania
21.11.81	Novi Sad	Yugoslavia v. Luxembourg	5:0(2:0)	C. Scerri, Malta
29.11.81	Athens	Greece v. Yugoslavia	1:2(1:2)	G. Courtney, England
5.12.81	Naples	Italy v. Luxembourg	1:0(1:0)	W. Tzontschev, Bulgaria

Final Classification:

1.	Yugoslavia	8	6	1	1	22:7	13
2.	Italy	8	5	2	1	12:5	12
3.	Denmark	8	4	0	4	14:11	8
4.	Greece	8	3	1	4	10:13	7
5.	Luxembourg	8	0	0	8	1:23	0
		40	18	4	18	59:59	40

Group 6 (Scotland, Sweden, Portugal, Northern Ireland + Israel from Asia/Oceania)

Date	Venue	Match	Score	Referee
26. 3.80	Tel-Aviv	Israel v. Northern Ireland	0:0(0:0)	S. Glavina, Yugoslavia
18. 6.80	Solna	Sweden v. Israel	1:1(1:0)	M. Hirviniemi, Finland
10. 9.80	Solna	Sweden v. Scotland	0:1(0:0)	F. Wöhrer, Austria
15.10.80	Belfast	Northern Ireland v. Sweden	3:0(3:0)	A. Ponnet, Belgium
15.10.80	Glasgow	Scotland v. Portugal	0:0(0:0)	J. Redelfs, W. Germany
12.11.80	Tel-Aviv	Israel v. Sweden	0:0(0:0)	G. Courtney, England
19.11.80	Lisbon	Portugal v. Northern Ireland	1:0(0:0)	G. Konrath, France
17.12.80	Lisbon	Portugal v. Israel	3:0(2:0)	E. Barbaresco, Italy
25. 2.81	Tel-Aviv	Israel v. Scotland	0:1(0:0)	O. Anderco, Romania
25. 3.81	Glasgow	Scotland v. Northern Ireland	1:0(0:0)	K. Scheurell, GDR
28. 4.81	Glasgow	Scotland v. Israel	3:1(2:0)	G. Heraldsson, Iceland
29. 4.81	Belfast	Northern Ireland v. Portugal	1:0(0:0)	S. Thime, Norway
3. 6.81	Solna	Sweden v. Northern Ireland	1:0(0:0)	P. Bergamo, Italy
24. 6.81	Solna	Sweden v. Portugal	3:0(1:0)	A. Milchenko, USSR
9. 9.81	Glasgow	Scotland v. Sweden	2:0(1:0)	A. Daina, Switzerland
14.10.81	Lisbon	Portugal v. Sweden	1:2(0:1)	R. Bridges, Wales
14.10.81	Belfast	Northern Ireland v. Scotland	0:0(0:0)	V. Butenko, USSR
28.10.81	Tel-Aviv	Israel v. Portugal	4:1(4:1)	S. Afxentiou, Cyprus
18.11.81	Belfast	Northern Ireland v. Israel	1:0(1:0)	E. Guruceta, Spain
18.11.81	Lisbon	Portugal v. Scotland	2:1(1:1)	C. Corver, Netherlands

Final Classification

1. Scotland	8	4	3	1	9:4	11
2. Northern Ireland	8	3	3	2	6:3	9
3. Sweden	8	3	2	3	7:8	8
4. Portugal	8	3	1	4	8:11	7
5. Israel	8	1	3	4	6:10	5
	40	14	12	14	36:36	40

Group 7 (Poland, German Democratic Republic, Malta)
(Top group only qualifies for Finals)

7.12.80	La Valletta	Malta v. Poland*	0:2(0:0)			D. Maksimovic, Yugoslavia
		*match abandoned at 82nd minute				
4. 4.81	La Valletta	Malta v. GDR	1:2(1:2)			P. Reeves, England
2. 5.81	Warsaw	Poland v. GDR	1:0(0:0)			V. Christov, Czechoslovakia
10.10.81	Leipzig	GDR v. Poland	2:3(0:2)			A. Lamo Castillo, Spain
11.11.81	Jena	GDR v. Malta	5:1(2:1)			F. McKnight, N. Ireland
15.11.81	Wroclaw	Poland v. Malta	6:0(1:0)			B. Helen, Sweden

Final Classification

1. Poland	4	4	0	0	12:2	8
2. GDR	4	2	0	2	9:6	4
3. Malta	4	0	0	4	2:15	0
	12	6	0	6	23:23	12

SOUTH AMERICA (CONMEBOL)

Entries: 10 (including Argentina, 1978 World Champions)
Bolivia, Brazil, Chile, Colombia, Ecuador, Paraguay, Peru, Uruguay, Venezuela
(Top team in each group qualifies for Finals)

Group 1 (Brazil, Bolivia, Venezuela)

Date	Venue	Match	Result	Referee
8.2.81	Caracas	Venezuela v. Brazil	0:1(0:0)	R. Barreto, Uruguay
15.2.81	La Paz	Bolivia v. Venezuela	3:0(1:0)	F. Valdez, Paraguay
22.2.81	La Paz	Bolivia v. Brazil	1:2(1:1)	E. Labó, Peru
15.3.81	Caracas	Venezuela v. Bolivia	1:0(1:0)	E. Iacome, Ecuador
22.3.81	Rio de Jan.	Brazil v. Bolivia	3:1(1:0)	G. Castro, Chile
29.3.81	Goiania	Brazil v. Venezuela	5:0(1:0)	J. Romero, Argentina

Final Classification					
1. Brazil	4	4	0	0	11:2	8
2. Bolivia	4	1	0	3	5:6	2
3. Venezuela	4	1	0	3	1:9	2
	12	6	0	6	17:17	12

Group 2 (Colombia, Peru, Uruguay)

26.7.81	Bogotá	Colombia v. Peru	1:1(0:0)	A. Ithurralde, Argentina
9.8.81	Montevideo	Uruguay v. Colombia	3:2(1:1)	O. Scolfaro, Brazil
16.8.81	Lima	Peru v. Colombia	2:0(1:0)	V. Llobregat, Venezuela
23.8.81	Montevideo	Uruguay v. Peru	1:2(0:2)	J. Silvagno, Chile
6.9.81	Lima	Peru v. Uruguay	0:0(0:0)	C. Coelho, Brazil
13.9.81	Bogotá	Colombia v. Uruguay	1:1(1:1)	J. Wright, Brazil

Final Classification

1. Peru	4	2	2	0	5:2	6
2. Uruguay	4	1	2	1	5:5	4
3. Colombia	4	0	2	2	4:7	2
	12	3	6	3	14:14	12

Group 3 (Chile, Ecuador, Paraguay)

17.5.81	Guayaquil	Ecuador v. Paraguay	1:0(0:0)	L. Barrancos, Bolivia
24.5.81	Guayaquil	Ecuador v. Chile	0:0(0:0)	J. Cardellino, Uruguay
31.5.81	Asunción	Paraguay v. Ecuador	3:1(0:0)	R. Cerullo, Uruguay
7.6.81	Asunción	Paraguay v. Chile	0:1(0:0)	C. Esposito, Argentina
14.6.81	Santiago	Chile v. Ecuador	2:0(1:0)	G. Aristizabal, Colombia
21.6.81	Santiago	Chile v. Paraguay	3:0(3:0)	R. Arppi, Brazil

Final Classification

1. Chile	4	3	1	0	6:0	7
2. Ecuador	4	1	1	2	2:5	3
3. Paraguay	4	1	0	3	3:6	2
	12	5	2	5	11:11	12

AFRICA

Entries: 29

Algeria, Cameroon, Central Africa*, Egypt, Ethiopia, Gambia, Ghana, Guinea, Kenya, Lesotho, Liberia, Libya, Madagascar, Malawi, Morocco, Mozambique, Niger, Nigeria, Senegal, Sierra Leone, Somalia, Sudan, Tanzania, Togo, Tunisia, Uganda, Zaire, Zambia, Zimbabwe

*excluded as entry fee not paid
(Teams in italics qualify for next round)

1st Round

(Qualified by draw for 2nd Round: *Zimbabwe, Sudan, Liberia, Togo*)

22.6.80	Dakar	Senegal v. Morocco	0:1(0:1)	A. Boudabbous, Tunisia
6.7.80	Casablanca	*Morocco* v. Senegal	0:0(0:0)	P. Koudou, Ivory Coast
13.7.80	Kinshasa	Zaire v. Mozambique	5:2(1:1)	S. Kamdem, Cameroon
27.7.80	Maputo	Mozambique v. *Zaire*	1:2(0:2)	D. Ralibenia, Madagascar
29.6.80	Yaoundé	Cameroon v. Malawi	3:0(1:0)	F. Okubule, Nigeria
20.7.80	Kamusu	Malawi v. *Cameroon*	1:1(0:0)	N. Hoohlo, Lesotho
22.6.80	Conakry	Guinea v. Lesotho	3:1(1:1)	Doudou N'Jie, Gambia
6.7.80	Maseru	Lesotho v. *Guinea*	1:1(0:1)	Z. Bundalla, Tanzania
29.6.80	Tunis	Tunisia v. Nigeria	2:0(1:0)	E. Dörflinger, Switzerland
12.7.80	Lagos	*Nigeria* v. Tunisia*	2:0(1:0)	J. Hunting, England

*after penalty kicks 4:3 – no extra-time

228

8.5.80	Tripoli	Libya v. Gambia	2:1(1:0)	G. Tesfaye, Ethiopia
6.7.80	Banjul	Gambia v. *Libya*	0:0(0:0)	M. N'Diaye, Mali
18.5.80	Addis Ababa	Ethiopia v. Zambia	0:0(0:0)	Bahig Fahmy, Egypt
1.6.80	N'Dola	*Zambia* v. Ethiopia	4:0(2:0)	Z. Bundalla, Tanzania
16.7.80	Niamey	Niger v. Somalia	0:0(0:0)	T. Lawson-Hetcheli, Togo
27.7.80	Mogadishu	Somalia v. *Niger**	1:1(0:1)	Demeke Abate, Ethiopia

*qualified by 'away' goal

| 31.5.80 | Freetown | Sierra Leone v. Algeria | 2:2(0:0) | T. Lawson-Hetcheli, Togo |
| 13.6.80 | Oran | *Algeria* v. Sierra Leone | 3:1(1:0) | Y. El-Ghoul, Libya |

Ghana v. Egypt — withdrawal Ghana, 11.6.80: qualified for 2nd round: *Egypt*
Egypt v. Ghana

| 5.7.80 | Nairobi | Kenya v. Tanzania | 3:1(1:1) | B. El-Bedawi, Sudan |
| 19.7.80 | Dar-es-Sal. | *Tanzania* v. Kenya | 5:0(1:0) | W. Gumboh, Zambia |

Uganda v. Madagascar — withdrawal Uganda, 26.6.80: qualified for 2nd round: *Madagascar*
Madagascar v. Uganda

2nd Round

| 12.12.80 | Constantine | Libya v. Egypt | | |
| 28.12.80 | Khartoum | Egypt v. *Libya* | | |

withdrawal Libya, 22.12.80
cualified for 3rd round: *Egypt*

12.12.80	Constantine	Algeria v. Sudan	2:0(2:0)	A. Boudabbous, Tunisia
28.12.80	Khartoum	Sudan v. *Algeria*	1:1(0:0)	Y. El-Ghoul, Libya
14.12.80	Niamey	Niger v. Togo	C:1(0:0)	M. N'Diaye, Mali
28.12.80	Lomé	Togo v. *Niger*	1:2(0:0)	Y. Thiombiano, U. Volta
7.12.80	Monrovia	Liberia v. Guinea	0:0(0:0)	T. Lawson-Hetcheli, Togo
21.12.80	Conakry	*Guinea* v. Liberia	1:0(1:0)	B. Dwomoh, Ghana
12.10.80	Douala	Cameroon v. Zimbabwe	2:0(0:0)	F. Okubule, Nigeria
16.11.80	Salisbury	Zimbabwe v. *Cameroon*	1:0(1:0)	K. Chayu, Zambia

Date	Venue	Match	Score	Referee
16.11.80	Fez	Morocco v. Zambia	2:0(2:0)	A. Ben Naceur, Tunisia
30.11.80	Lusaka	Zambia v. *Morocco**	2:0(0:0)	C. Testaye, Ethiopia

*after penalty kicks 4:5 – no extra-time

Date	Venue	Match	Score	Referee
6.12.80	Lagos	Nigeria v. Tanzania	1:1(1:0)	M. Larache, Morocco
20.12.80	Dar-es-Sal.	Tanzania v. *Nigeria*	0:2(0:1)	Bahig Fahmy, Egypt
16.11.80	Tananarive	Madagascar v. Zaire	1:1(1:0)	J.C. Monty, Mauritius
21.12.80	Kinshasa	*Zaire* v. Madagascar	3:2(2:2)	J.B. Angaud, Congo

3rd Round

Date	Venue	Match	Score	Referee
1.5.81	Constantine	Algeria v. Niger	4:0(1:0)	D. N'Jie, Gambia
31.5.81	Niamey	Niger v. *Algeria*	1:0(0:0)	B. Dwomoh, Ghana
12.4.81	Conakry	Guinea v. Nigeria	1:1(0:1)	E. Bukenya, Uganda
25.4.81	Lagos	*Nigeria* v. Guinea	1:0(0:0)	G. Tesfaye, Ethiopia
26.4.81	Casablanca	Morocco v. Egypt	1:0(1:0)	L.N. Chayu, Zambia
8.5.81	Cairo	Egypt v. *Morocco*	0:0(0:0)	Ch. D. Mbaye, Senegal
12.4.81	Kinshasa	Zaire v. Cameroon	1:0(1:0)	S. El-Naim, Sudan
26.4.81	Yaoundé	*Cameroon* v. Zaire	6:1(3:0)	A. Boudabbous, Tunisia

Final Round

Date	Venue	Match	Score	Referee
10.10.81	Lagos	Nigeria v. Algeria	0:2(0:2)	L. Agnolin, Italy
30.10.81	Constantine	*Algeria* v. Nigeria	2:1(1:1)	A. Daina, Switzerland
15.11.81	Kenitra	Morocco v. Cameroon	0:2(0:2)	Cheikh Mbaye, Senegal
29.11.81	Yaoundé	*Cameroon* v. Morocco	2:1(1:1)	Hussein Fahmy, Egypt

ASIA/OCEANIA

Entries: 22

Australia, Bahrain, People's Republic of China, Chinese Taipei, Fiji, Hong Kong, Indonesia, Iran, Iraq, Israel*, Japan, DPR Korea, Korea Rep., Kuwait, Macao, Malaysia, New Zealand, Qatar, Saudi Arabia, Singapore, Syria, Thailand
*playing in a European group

Group 1 (Indonesia, Australia, Fiji, New Zealand, Taipei)

Date	Venue	Match	Score	Referee
25.4.81	Auckland	New Zealand v. Australia	3:3(2:3)	G. Menegali, Italy
3.5.81	Suva	Fiji v. New Zealand	0:4(0:3)	Othman Bin Omar, Malaysia
7.5.81	Taipei	Taipei v. New Zealand	0:0(0:0)	Toshio Asami, Japan
11.5.81	Djakarta	Indonesia v. New Zealand	0:2(0:1)	N. Ausukont, Thailand
16.5.81	Sydney	Australia v. New Zealand	0:2(0:1)	G. Courtney, England
20.5.81	Melbourne	Australia v. Indonesia	2:0(2:0)	V. Graca Oliva, Portugal
23.5.81	Auckland	New Zealand v. Indonesia	5:0(2:0)	V. Graca Oliva, Portugal
30.5.81	Auckland	New Zealand v. Taipei	2:0(1:0)	T. Boskovic, Australia
31.5.81	Suva	Fiji v. Indonesia	0:0(0:0)	Lee Kok Leong, Singapore
6.6.81	Suva	Fiji v. Taipei	2:1(1:0)	H. Dhillon, Singapore
10.6.81	Adelaide	Australia v. Taipei	3:2(1:0)	V. Getkaew, Thailand
15.6.81	Djakarta	Indonesia v. Taipei	1:0(0:0)	V. Charupunt, Thailand
28.6.81	Taipei	Taipei v. Indonesia	2:0(2:0)	Nishi Jun-Ichi, Japan
26.7.81	Suva	Fiji v. Australia	1:4(0:4)	H. Sudarso, Indonesia
4.8.81	Taipei	Taipei v. Fiji	0:0(0:0)	C. Brillantes, Philippines
10.8.81	Djakarta	Indonesia v. Fiji	3:3(3:1)	T. Gurkan, Philippines
14.8.81	Melbourne	Australia v. Fiji	10:0(3:0)	A. Nobnom, Thailand
16.8.81	Auckland	New Zealand v. Fiji	13:0(7:0)	V. Getkaew, Thailand

| 30.8.81 | Djakarta | Indonesia v. Australia | 1:0(0:0) | R. Reyes, Philippines |
| 6.9.81 | Taipei | Taipei v. Australia | 0:0(0:0) | T. Gurkan, Philippines |

Classification

1. New Zealand	8	6	2	0	31:3	14
2. Australia	8	4	2	2	22:9	10
3. Indonesia	8	2	2	4	5:14	6
4. Taipei	8	1	3	4	5:8	5
5. Fiji	8	1	3	4	6:35	5
	40	14	12	14	69:69	40

New Zealand qualified to take part in the Final Round

Group II (Iraq, Syria, Bahrain, Qatar, Saudi Arabia)

18.3.81	Riyadh	Qatar v. Iraq	0:1(0:0)	T. Boskovic, Australia
19.3.81		Syria v. Bahrain	0:1(0:0)	T. Sano, Japan
21.3.81		Iraq v. Saudi Arabia	0:1(0:0)	M. Rubio, Mexico
22.3.81		Qatar v. Bahrain	3:0(2:0)	Lee Kok Leong, Singapore
24.3.81		Syria v. Saudi Arabia	0:2(0:0)	Nishi Jun-Ichi, Japan
25.3.81		Iraq v. Bahrain	2:0(1:0)	H. Dhillon, Singapore
27.3.81		Qatar v. Syria	2:1(1:1)	P. Rampley, Australia
28.3.81		Bahrain v. Saudi Arabia	0:1(0:0)	S. Toshikazu, Japan
30.3.81		Iraq v. Syria	2:1(1:0)	P. Rampley, Australia
31.3.81		Qatar v. Saudi Arabia	0:1(0:0)	T. Boskovic, Australia

Classification

1. Saudi Arabia	4	4	0	0	5:0	8
2. Iraq	4	3	0	1	5:2	6
3. Qatar	4	2	0	2	5:3	4
4. Bahrain	4	1	0	3	1:6	2
5. Syria	4	0	0	4	2:7	0
	20	10	0	10	18:18	20

Saudi Arabia qualified to take part in the Final Round

Group III (Kuwait, Thailand, Malaysia, Korea Rep.)
Iran withdrew 17.3.81

21.4.81	Kuwait	Malaysia v. Korea Rep.	1:2(1:1)		Chan Tam Sun, Hong Kong
22.4.81		Kuwait v. Thailand	6:0(4:0)		M. D'Souza, India
24.4.81		Korea Rep. v. Thailand	5:1(2:1)		H. Sudarso, Indonesia
25.4.81		Kuwait v. Malaysia	4:0(2:0)		Cheung Kwok Kui, Hong Kong
27.4.81		Malaysia v. Thailand	2:2(0:0)		R. Valentine, Scotland
29.4.81		Kuwait v. Korea Rep.	2:0(0:0)		G. Aristizabal, Colombia

Classification

1. Kuwait	3	3	0	0	12:0	6
2. Korea Rep.	3	2	0	1	7:4	4
3. Malaysia	3	0	1	2	3:8	1
4. Thailand	3	0	1	2	3:13	1
	12	5	2	5	25:25	12

Kuwait qualified to take part in the Final Round

Group IV (Hong Kong, Macao, PR China, DPR Korea, Japan, Singapore)

Play-off matches

21.12.80	Hong Kong	Hong Kong v. PR China	0:1(0:0)		A.R. Al-Marzan, S. Arabia
22.12.80		DPR Korea v. Macao	3:0(2:0)		D. Sarkis, Lebanon
22.12.80		Singapore v. Japan	0:1(0:1)		N. Ausukont, Thailand

Group matches

Group A (PR China, Macao, Japan)

24.12.80	PR China v. Macao	3:0(2:0)	V. Getkaew, Thailand
26.12.80	PR China v. Japan	1:0(1:0)	A. Albanni, Kuwait
28.12.80	Japan v. Macao	3:0(0:0)	M. Arafat, Syria

Classification

1. PR China	2	2	0	0	4:0	4
2. Japan	2	1	0	1	3:1	2
3. Macao	2	0	0	2	0:6	0
	6	3	0	3	7:7	6

Group B (Hong Kong, DPR Korea, Singapore)

24.12.80	Hong Kong	Hong Kong v. Singapore	1:1(0:0)	M. Arafat, Syria
26.12.80		Singapore v. DPR Korea	0:1(0:1)	E. Al-Doy, Bahrain
28.12.80		Hong Kong v. DPR Korea	2:2(1:2)	D. Sarkis, Lebanon

Classification

1. DPR Korea	2	1	1	0	3:2	3
2. Hong Kong	2	0	2	0	3:3	2
3. Singapore	2	0	1	1	1:2	1
	6	1	4	1	7:7	6

Semi-Finals

30.12.80	DPR Korea v. Japan	1:0(0:0)	A. Albanni, Kuwait
31.12.80	PR China* v. Hong Kong	0:0(0:0)	V. Getkaew, Thailand

*by penalty kicks: 5:4

Final

4.1.81	DPR Korea v. PR China	2:2(1:1)	E. Al-Doy, Bahrain

after extra-time: 2:4

PR China qualified to take part in the Final Round

Final Round
(Top 2 teams qualify for Finals)

Date	Venue	Match	Score	Referee
24. 9.81	Peking	PR China v. New Zealand	0:0(0:0)	T. Sano, Japan
3.10.81	Auckland	New Zealand v. PR China	1:0(1:0)	V. Getkaew, Thailand
10.10.81	Auckland	New Zealand v. Kuwait	1:2(1:0)	H. Sudarso, Indonesia
18.10.81	Peking	PR China v. Kuwait	3:0(2:0)	T. Boskovic, Australia
4.11.81	Riyadh	Saudi Arabia v. Kuwait	0:1(0:0)	A.W. Grey, England
12.11.81	K. Lumpur	Saudi Arabia v. PR China	2:4(2:0)	A. Ponnet, Belgium
19.11.81	K. Lumpur	PR China v. Saudi Arabia	2:0(2:0)	J.R. Wright, Brazil
28.11.81	Auckland	New Zealand v. Saudi Arabia	2:2(2:1)	A. Ithurralde, Argentina
30.11.81	Kuwait	Kuwait v. PR China	1:0(1:0)	Lee Kok Leong, Singapore
7.12.81	Kuwait	Kuwait v. Saudi Arabia	2:0(1:0)	J. Redelfs, Germany FR
14.12.81	Kuwait	Kuwait v. New Zealand	2:2(1:0)	H. Lund-Sørensen, Denmark
19.12.81	Riyadh	Saudi Arabia v. New Zealand	0:5(0:5)	C. Corver, Netherlands

Final Classification

1.	Kuwait	6	4	1	1	8:6	9
2-3.	PR China	6	3	1	2	9:4	7
	New Zealand	6	2	3	1	11:6	7
4.	Saudi Arabia	6	0	1	5	4:16	1
		24	9	6	9	32:32	24

Deciding match for second place:

10.1.82	Singapore	PR China v. New Zealand	1:2(0:1)	R. Arppi Filho, Brazil

CONCACAF

Entries: 15

Canada, Costa Rica, Cuba, Grenada, Guatemala, Guyana, Haiti, Honduras, Mexico, Netherlands Antilles, Panama, El Salvador, Surinam, Trinidad and Tobago, USA

Northern Zone (Canada, USA, Mexico)

18.10.80	Toronto	Canada v. Mexico	1:1(1:0)	L. Siles, Costa Rica
25.10.80	F. Lauderd.	USA v. Canada	0:0(0:0)	T. Herrera, El Salvador
1.11.80	Vancouver	Canada v. USA	2:1(2:0)	R. Mendez, Guatemala
9.11.80	Mexico City	Mexico v. USA	5:1(4:0)	J. Valverde, Costa Rica
16.11.80	Mexico City	Mexico v. Canada	1:1(0:0)	C.M. Torres, Honduras
23.11.80	F. Lauderd.	USA v. Mexico	2:1(1:1)	M.G. Regalado, Guatemala

Classification

1. Canada	4	1	3	0	4:3	5
2. Mexico	4	1	2	1	8:5	4
3. USA	4	1	1	2	4:8	3
	12	3	6	3	16:16	12

Canada and *Mexico* qualified to take part in the Final Tournament in Honduras

Central Zone (Panama, Costa Rica, El Salvador, Guatemala, Honduras)

2. 7.80	Panama City	Panama v. Guatemala	0:2(0:1)	R. Evans, USA
30. 7.80	Panama City	Panama v. Honduras	0:2(0:1)	H. Tromp, Neth. Antilles
10. 8.80	Panama City	Panama v. Costa Rica	1:1(1:0)	J. Goede, Surinam
24. 8.80	Panama City	Panama v. El Salvador	1:3(0:1)	F. Hoyte, Barbados
1.10.80	San José	Costa Rica v. Honduras	2:3(0:2)	C. Soupliotis, Canada

5.10.80	San Salvador	El Salvador v. Panama	4:1(2:1)	W. Winsemann, Canada
12.10.80	Guatem. C.	Guatemala v. Costa Rica	0:0(0:0)	J. Narvaez, Mexico
26.10.80	Tegucigalpa	Honduras v. Guatemala	0:0(0:0)	M. Dorantes, Mexico
26.10.80	San Salvador*	El Salvador v. Costa Rica		D. de la Mora, Mexico

Match not played – Result by forfeit: 2:0

5.11.80	San José	Costa Rica v. Panama	2:0(1:0)	D. Maglio, Canada
9.11.80	Guatem. C.	Guatemala v. El Salvador	0:0(0:0)	D. Socha, USA
16.11.80	Guatem. C.	Guatemala v. Panama	5:0(2:0)	P. Johnson, Canada
16.11.80	Tegucigalpa	Honduras v. Costa Rica	1:1(0:1)	D. Socha, USA
23.11.80	San Salvador	El Salvador v. Honduras	2:1(1:0)	R. Fusco, Canada
26.11.80	San José	Costa Rica v. Guatemala	0:3(0:1)	I. Matos, Canada
30.11.80	Tegucigalpa	Honduras v. El Salvador	2:0(1:0)	A. Evangelista, Canada
7.12.80	Guatem. C.	Guatemala v. Honduras	0:1(0:0)	T. Kibritjian, USA
10.12.80	San José	Costa Rica v. El Salvador	0:0(0:0)	M. Rubio, Mexico
14.12.80	Tegucigalpa	Honduras v. Panama	5:0(3:0)	E. Mendoza, Mexico
21.12.80	San Salvador	El Salvador v. Guatemala	1:0(0:0)	G. d'Ippolito, USA

Classification

1. Honduras	8	5	2	1	15:5	12
2. El Salvador	8	5	2	1	12:5	12
3. Guatemala	8	3	3	2	10:2	9
4. Costa Rica	8	1	4	3	6:10	6
5. Panama	8	0	1	7	3:24	1
	40	14	12	14	46:46	40

Honduras and *El Salvador* qualified to take part in the Final Tournament in Honduras

Caribbean Zone (Grenada, Guyana, Cuba, Surinam, Haiti, Trinidad and Tobago, Netherlands Antilles)

Extra Preliminary Round – (Grenada, Guyana)

| 30.3.80 | Georgetown | Guyana v. Grenada | 5:2(2:2) | J. Rogel Rivera, El Salvador |
| 13.4.80 | Grenada | Grenada v. Guyana | 2:3(0:2) | R. Mollinedo, Guatemala |

Group A (*Cuba, Surinam, Guyana*)

17. 8.80	Havana	Cuba v. Surinam	3:0(0:0)	A. Marquez, Mexico
7. 9.80	Paramaribo	Surinam v. Cuba	0:0(0:0)	H. Tromp, Neth. Antilles
28. 9.80	Georgetown	Guyana v. Surinam	0:1(0:1)	R. Wooding, Trinidad-Tobago
12.10.80	Paramaribo	Surinam v. Guyana	4:0(2:0)	L. de Boer, Neth. Antilles
9.11.80	Havana	Cuba v. Guyana	1:0(1:0)	W. Taylor, Jamaica
30.11.80	Lynden	Guyana v. Cuba	0:3(0:3)	R. Goede, Surinam

Classification

1. Cuba	4	3	1	0	7:0	7
2. Surinam	4	2	1	1	5:3	5
3. Guyana	4	0	0	4	0:9	0
	12	5	2	5	12:12	12

Group B (*Haiti, Trinidad and Tobago, Netherlands Antilles*)

1. 8.80	P.-au-Prince	Haiti v. Trinidad-Tobago	2:0(0:0)	M. Pérez, Mexico
17. 8.80	S. Fernando	Trinidad-Tobago v. Haiti	1:0(0:0)	C. Monge Solano, C. Rica
12. 9.80	P.-au-Prince	Haiti v. Neth. Antilles	1:0(0:0)	W.D. Taylor, Jamaica
9.11.80	P. of Spain	Trinidad-Tobago v. Neth. Antilles	0:0(0:0)	F. Hoyte, Barbados
29.11.80	Curaçao	Neth. Antilles v. Trinidad-Tobago	0:0(0:0)	G. Kranenburg, Surinam
12.12.80	Curaçao	Neth. Antilles v. Haiti	1:1(0:1)	D. de la Mora, Mexico

Classification:

1. Haiti	4	2	1	1	4:2	5
2. Trinidad-Tobago	4	1	2	1	1:2	4
3. Neth. Antilles	4	0	3	1	1:2	3
	12	3	6	3	6:6	12

Cuba and *Haiti* qualified to take part in the Final Tournament in Honduras

Final Round
(Top 2 teams qualify for Finals)

1.11.81	Tegucigalpa	Mexico v. Cuba	4:0(2:0)	R. Mendez M., Guatemala
2.11.81		Canada v. El Salvador	:0(0:0)	C. Pagano, Peru
3.11.81		Honduras v. Haiti	4:0(2:0)	J. de Assis Aragáo, Brazil
6.11.81		Haiti v. Canada	1:1(1:0)	M. Gracias R., Guatemala
6.11.81		Mexico v. El Salvador	0:1(0:0)	J. de Assis Aragáo, Brazil
8.11.81		Honduras v. Cuba	2:0(1:0)	L. Siles C., Costa Rica
11.11.81		El Salvador v. Cuba	0:0(0:0)	D. Socha, USA
11.11.81		Mexico v. Haiti	1:1(0:0)	C. Pagano, Peru
12.11.81		Honduras v. Canada	2:1(2:1)	R. Mendez M., Guatemala
15.11.81		Haiti v. Cuba	C:2(0:0)	O. E. Bijlhout, Surinam
15.11.81		Mexico v. Canada	1:1(0:1)	D. Socha, USA
16.11.81		Honduras v. El Salvador	C:0(0:0)	P. Siles C., Costa Rica
19.11.81		Haiti v. El Salvador	C:1(0:1)	O. Downer, Trinidad-Tobago
21.11.81		Cuba v. Canada	2:2(1:0)	C. Pagano, Peru
22.11.81		Honduras v. Mexico	0:0(0:0)	D. Socha, USA

Final Classification:

1.	Honduras	5	3	2	0	8:1	8
2.	El Salvador	5	2	2	1	2:1	6
3.	Mexico	5	1	3	1	6:3	5
4.	Canada	5	1	3	1	6:6	5
5.	Cuba	5	1	2	2	4:8	4
6.	Haiti	5	0	2	3	2:9	2
		30	8	14	8	28:28	30

239

Results of the the 1982 World Cup Finals

FIRST ROUND

Group One

Vigo – 14 June
Italy 0
Poland 0
Att: 35,000. **Ref:** Vautrot (France).

Italy: Zoff – Gentile, Scirea, Collovati, Cabrini – Marini, Tardelli, Antognoni – Conti, Rossi, Graziani.

Poland: Mlynarczyk – Majewski, Zmuda, Janas, Jalocha – Lato, Matysik, Boniek – Buncol, Iwan (Kusto 71), Smolarek.

La Coruña – 15 June
Cameroon 0
Peru 0
Att: 18,000. **Ref:** Wöhrer (Aus).

Cameroon: Nkono – Kaham, Kunde, Onana, Ndjeya – Mbom, Abega, Mbida – Aoudou, Nguea (Bahoken 72), Milla (Tokoto 89).

Peru: Quiroga – Duarte, Diaz, Salguero, Olaechea – Leguia (La Rosa 56), Cueto, Velasquez – Oblitas, Uribe, Cubillas (Barbadillo 56).

Vigo – 18 June
Italy 1 (Conti 18)
Peru 1 (Diaz 83)
HT: 1-0. **Att:** 25,000. **Ref:** Eschweiler (WG)

Italy: Zoff – Gentile, Scirea, Collovati, Cabrini – Tardelli, Antognoni, Marini – Rossi (Causio 46), Graziani, Conti.

Peru: Quiroga – Duarte, Diaz, Salguero, Olaechea – Cueto, Velasquez (La Rosa 64), Cubillas – Barbadillo (Leguia 51), Uribe, Oblitas.

La Coruña – 19 June
Cameroon 0
Poland 0
Att: 20,000. **Ref:** Ponnet (Bel).

Cameroon: Nkono – Kaham, Kunde, Onana, Ndjeya – Mbom, Abega, Mbida – Aoudou, Nguea (Tokoto 46), Milla.

Poland: Mlynarczyk – Majewski, Janas, Zmuda, Jalocha – Lato, Palasz (Kusto 66), Boniek, Buncol – Iwan (Szarmach 25), Smolarek.

La Coruña – 22 June
Peru 1 (La Rosa 82)
Poland 5 (Smolarek 55, Lato 58, Boniek 61, Buncol 67, Ciolek 76).
HT: 0-0. **Att:** 26,000. **Ref:** Rubio (Mex).

Peru: Quiroga – Duarte, Diaz, Salguero, Olaechea – Leguia, Cueto, Velasquez, Cubillas (Barbadillo 49) – La Rosa, Oblitas.

Poland: Mlynarczyk – Majewzki, Zmuda, Janas, Jalocha (Dziuba 26) – Matysik, kupcewicz, Buncol, Lato – Boniek, Smolarek (Ciolek 73).

Vigo – 23 June
Cameroon 1 (Mbida 61)
Italy 1 (Graziani 60)
HT: 0-0. **Att:** 20,000. **Ref:** Dotschev (Bul).

Cameroon: Nkono – Kaham, Kunde, Onana, Ndjeya – Mbom, Tokoto, Abega – Mbida, Aoudou, Milla.

Italy: Zoff – Gentile, Scirea, Collovati, Cabrini – Oriali, Tardelli, Antognoni – Conti, Graziani, Rossi.

	P	W	D	L	F	A	Pts
1. Poland	3	1	2	0	5	1	4
2. Italy	3	0	3	0	2	2	3
3. Cameroon	3	0	3	0	1	1	3
4. Peru	3	0	2	1	2	6	2

Group Two

Gijon – 16 June
West Germany 1 (Rummenigge 67)
Algeria 2 (Madjer 52, Belloumi 68)
HT: 0-0. **Att:** 42,500. **Ref:** Labo (Peru).

  West Germany: Schumacher – Kaltz, Kh. Förster, Stielike, Briegel – Dremmler, Breitner, Magath (Fischer 82) – Littbarski, Hrubesch, Rummenigge.

  Algeria: Cerbah – Merzekane, Kourichi, Guendouz, Mansouri – Dahleb, Fergani, Belloumi – Madjer (Bensaoula 63), Zidane (Larbes 88), Assad.

Oviedo – 17 June
Austria 1 (Schachner 21)
Chile 0
HT: 1-0. **Att:** 19,000. **Ref:** Cardeñlino (Uru).

  Austria: Koncilia – Krauss, Obermayer, Pezzey, Degeorgi (Baumeister 77) – Prohaska, Hattenberger, Weber (Jurtin 77), Hintermaier – Schachner, Krankl.

  Chile: Osben – Garrido, Figueroa, Valenzuela, Bigorra – Neira (MRojas 71), Dubo, Bonvallet, Moscoso (Gamboa 66) – Caszely, Yanez.

Gijon – 20 June
West Germany 4 Rummenigge 9, 57, 66, Reinders 81)
Chile 1 (Moscoso 89)
HT: 1-0. **Att:** 42,000. **Ref:** Galler (Swz).

  W. Germany Schumacher – Kaltz, Stielike, Kh. Förster, Briegel – Dremmler, Breitner (Matthaus 61), Magath – Littbarski (Reinders 79), Hrubesch, Rummenigge.

  Chile: Osben – Garrido, Valenzuela, Figueroa, Bigorra – Dubo, Bonvallet, Soto (Letelier 46) – Yanez, Gamboa (Neira 66), Moscoso.

Oviedo – 21 June
Austria 2 (Schachner 56, Krankl 67)
Algeria 0
HT: 0-0. **Att:** 22,000. **Ref:** Boskovic (Australia).
   Austria: Koncilia – Krauss, Obermayer, Pezzey, Degeorgi –
Hattenberger, Prohaska (Weber 80), Hintermaier, Baumeister
(Welzl 46) – Schachner, Krankl.
   Algeria: Cerbah – Merzekane, Mansouri, Kourichi, Guendouz
– Fergani, Dahleb (Tlemcani 76), Belloumi (Bensaoula 65) –
Assad, Zidane, Madjer.

Oviedo – 24 June
Chile 2 (Neira 61 pen, Letelier 73)
Algeria 3 (Assad 7, 31, Bensaoula 35)
HT: 0-3. **Att:** 18,500. **Ref:** Mendez (Guat).
   Chile: Osben – Galindo, Valenzuela, Figueroa, Bigorra –
Bonvallet (Soto 37), Dubo, Neira – Yanez, Caszely (Letelier
58), Moscoso.
   Algeria: Cerbah – Merzekane, Guendouz, Kourichi, Larbes –
Fergani, Mansouri (Dahleb 73), Bensaoula, Bourebbou (Yahi
31) – Assad, Madjer.

Gijon – 25 June
West Germany 1 (Hrubesch 10)
Austria 0
HT: 1-0. **Att:** 41,000. **Ref:** Valentine (Scotland).
   W. Germany: Schumacher – Kaltz, Stielike, Kh. Förster,
Briegel – Dremmler, Breitner, Magath – Littbarski, Hrubesch
(Fischer 68), Rummenigge (Matthaus 65).
   Austria: Koncilia – Krauss, Obermayer, Pezzey, Degeorgi –
Hattenberger, Hintermaier, Prohaska, Weber – Krankl,
Schachner.

	P	W	D	L	F	A	Pts
1. West Germany	3	2	0	1	6	3	4
2. Austria	3	2	0	1	3	1	4
3. Algeria	3	2	0	1	5	5	4
4. Chile	3	0	0	3	3	8	0

Group Three

Barcelona – 13 June
Argentina 0
Belgium 1 (Vandenbergh 62)
HT: 0-0. **Att:** 95,000. **Ref:** Christov (Czech)
    Argentina: Fillol – Olguin, Galvan, Passarella, Tarantini – Ardiles, Gallego, Maradona – Bertoni, Diaz (Valdano 63), Kempes.
    Belgium: Pfaff – Gerets, Millecamps, De Schrijver, Baecke – Vandersmissen, Coeck, Ceulemans, Vercauteren – Czerniatynski, Vandenbergh.

Elche – 15 June
Hungary 10 (Nyilasi 3, 82, Poloskei 10, Fazekas 23, 55, Toth 51, Kiss 69, 73, 78, Szentes 71)
El Salvador 1 (Ramirez 65)
HT: 3-0. **Att:** 19,750. **Ref:** Al-Doy (Bahrain).
    Hungary: Meszaros – Martos, Balint, Garaba, Toth – Muller (Szentes 69), Nyilasi, Sallai – Fazekas, Torocsik (Kiss 56), Poloskei.
    El Salvador: Mora – Castillo, Jovel, Recinos, Ventura (Fagoga 75) – Rugamas (Ramirez 28), F. Hernandez, Huezo – Rivas, Rodriguez, Gonzalez.

Alicante – 18 June
Argentina 4 (Bertoni 27, Maradona, 29, 57, Ardiles 61)
Hungary 1 (Poloskei 76)
HT: 2-0. **Att:** 30,000. **Ref:** Lacarne (Algeria).
    Argentina: Fillol – Olguin, Galvan, Passarella, Tarantini (Barbas 51) – Ardiles, Gallego, Kempes – Valdano (Calderon 25), Maradona, Bertoni.
    Hungary: Meszaros – Martos (Fazekas 46), Balint, Toth, Varga – Garaba, Nyilasi, Sallai, Rab – Kiss (Szentes 61), Poloskei.

Elche – 19 June
Belgium 1 (Coeck 18)
El Salvador 0
HT: 1-0. **Att:** 18,000. **Ref:** Moffat (N. Ireland).
  Belgium: Pfaff – Gerets, Millecamps, Meeuws, Baecke – Vandersmissen (Van Der Elst 45), Coeck, Vercauteren – Ceulemans (Van Moer 80), Czerniatynski, Vandenbergh.
  El Salvador: Mora – Osorto (Diaz 45), Jovel, Rodriguez, Recinos – Fagoga, Ventura, Huezo – Ramirez, Gonzalez, Rivas.

Elche – 22 June
Belgium 1 (Czerniatynski 76)
Hungary 1 (Varga 27)
HT: 0-1. **Att:** 37,000. **Ref:** White (England).
  Belgium: Pfaff – Gerets (Plessers 62), Millecamps L., Meeuws, Baecke – Coeck, Vercauteren, Vandersmissen (Van Moer 46) – Czerniatynski, Vandenbergh, Ceulemans.
  Hungary: Meszaros – Martos, Kerekes (Sallai), Garaba, Varga – Nyilasi, Muller, Fazekas – Torocsik, Kiss (Csongradi 70), Poloskei.

Alicante – 23 June
Argentina 2 (Passarella pen 22, Bertoni 52)
El Salvador 0
HT: 1-0. **Att:** 28,000 **Ref:** Barrancos (Bol).
  Argentina: Fillol – Olguin, Galvan, Passarella, Tarantini – Ardiles, Gallego – Kempes, Bertoni (Diaz 68), Maradona, Calderon (Santamaria 68).
  El Salvador: Mora – Osorto (Arevalo 34), Jovel, Rodriguez, Ortiz – Recinos, Ventura (Alfaro 79), Heuzo – Zapata, Gonzalez, Rivas.

	P	W	D	L	F	A	Pts
1. Belgium	3	2	1	0	3	1	5
2. Argentina	3	2	0	1	6	2	4
3. Hungary	3	1	1	1	12	6	3
4. El Salvador	3	0	0	3	1	13	0

Group Four

Bilbao – 16 June
England 3 (Robson 27 sec, 66, Mariner 82)
France 1 (Soler 25)
HT: 1-1. **Att:** 44,000. **Ref:** Garrido (Port).

England: Shilton – Mills, Thompson, Butcher, Sansom (Neal 90) – Coppell, Robson, Wilkins, Rix – Francis, Mariner.

France: Ettori – Battiston, Tresor, Lopez, Bossis – Larios (Tigana 73), Girard, Giresse – Rocheteau (Six 71), Platini, Soler.

Vallodolid – 17 June
Czechoslovakia 1 (Panenka 20 pen)
Kuwait 1 (Al-Dakhil 58)
HT: 1-0. **Att:** 25,000. **Ref** Dwomoh (Ghana).

Czechoslovakia: Hruska – Barmos, Jurkemik, Fiala, Kukucka – Panenka, Berger, Kriz (Bicovsky 63) – Janecka (Petrzela 69), Nehoda, Vizek.

Kuwait: Al-Tarabulsi – Mubarrak, Mahoub, Mayoof, Waleed Jasem – Al-Bouloushi, Al-Houti, Karam (Marzouq 57) – Al-Dakhil, Yacoub, Al-Anbari.

Bilbao – 20 June
England 2 (Francis 63, Barmos o.g. 66)
Czechoslovakia 0
HT: 0-0. **Att:** 41,000. **Ref:** Corver (Hol).

England: Shilton – Mills, Thompson, Butcher, Sansom – Coppell, Wilkins, Robson (Hoddle 46), Rix – Mariner, Francis.

Czechoslovakia: Seman (Stromsik 75) – Barmos, Vojacek, Radimac, Fiala – Berger, Chaloupka, Jurkemik – Vizek, Janecka (Masny 77), Nehoda.

Valladolid – 21 June
France 4 (Genghini 31, Platini 43, Six 48, Bossis 96)
Kuwait 1 (Al-Bouloushi 74)
HT: 2-0. **Att:** 30,000. **Ref:** Stupar (USSR).
The game was held up for nine minutes in the second half because of Kuwait protests over a French 'goal'.
  France: Ettori – Amoros, Janvion (Lopez 60), Tresor, Bossis – Giresse, Platini (Girard 89), Genghini – Soler, Lacombe, Six.
  Kuwait: Al-Tarabulsi – Naem Mubarak, Mayoof, Mahoub, Al-Mubartak (Al-Shemmari 78) – Al-Bouloushi, Al-Houti, Karam Ahmed (Fahti Kamel 46) – Al-Dakhil, Jasem Sultan, Al-Anbari.

Valladolid – 24 June
France 1 (Six 66)
Czechoslovakia 1 (Panenka 85 pen)
HT: 0-0. **Att:** 29,000. **Ref:** Casarin (Italy).
  France: Ettori – Amoros, Janvion, Tresor, Bossis – Giresse, Platini, Genghini – Soler (Girard 89), Lacombe (Couriol 70), Six.
  Czechoslovakia: Stromsik – Barmos, Vojacek, Radimac, Fiala – Nehoda, Bicovsky, Stambacher – Janecka (Panenka 70), Vizek, Kriz (Masny 30).

Bilbao – 25 June
England 1 (Francis 26)
Kuwait 0
HT: 0-0. **Att:** 39,700. **Ref:** Aristizabal (Col).
  England: Shilton – Neal, Thompson, Foster, Mills – Coppell, Hoddle, Wilkins, Rix – Francis, Mariner.
  Kuwait: Al-Tarabulsi – Naem Mubarek, Mahboud, Al-Mubartak (Al-Shemmari 6), Mayoof – Al-Houti, Al-Bouloushi, Al-Suwaayed, Marzouq – Al-Dakhil, Al-Anbari.

		P	W	D	L	F	A	Pts
1.	England	3	3	0	0	6	1	6
2.	France	3	1	1	1	6	5	3
3.	Czechoslovakia	3	0	2	1	2	4	2
4.	Kuwait	3	0	1	2	2	6	1

Group Five

Valencia – 16 June
Spain 1 (Ufarte pen 66)
Honduras 1 (Zelaya 7)
   Spain: Arconada – Camacho, Tendillo, Alesanco, Gordillo –
Alonso, Joaquin (Sanchez 45), Zamora – Juanito (Saura 45),
Satrustegui, Ufarte.
   Honduras: Arzu – Gutierez, Villegas, Bulnes, Costly – Mara-
diaga, Zelaya, Gilberto – Betancourt, Norales (Caballero 69),
Figueroa.

Zaragoza – 17 June
Yugoslavia 0
Northern Ireland 0
Att: 25,000. Ref: Fredriksson (Sweden).
   Yugoslavia: Pantelic – Jovanovic, Hrstic, Zajec, Stojkovic –
Petrovic, Gudelj, Slijvo, Vujovic – Susic, Surjak.
   Northern Ireland: Jennings – J. Nicholl, C. Nicholl, McClel-
land, Donaghy – O'Neill, McCreery, McIlroy – Armstrong,
Hamilton, Whiteside.

Valencia – 20 June
Spain 2 (Juanito pen 14, Saura 66)
Yugoslavia 1 (Gudelj 10)
HT: 1-1. Att: 48,000. Ref: S. Lund (Denmark).
   Spain: Arconada – Camacho, Tendillo, Alesanco, Gordillo –
Sanchez (Saura 63), Alonso, Zamora – Juanito, Satrustegui
(Quini 63), Ufarte.
   Yugoslavia: Pantelic – Krmpotic, Jovanovic (Halilhodzic 74),
Zajec, Stojkovic – Petrovic, Slijvo, Gudelj – Surjak, Vujovic
(Sestic 83), Susic.

Zaragoza – 21 June
Honduras 1 (Laing 60)
Northern Ireland 1 (Armstrong)
HT: 0-1. **Att:** 15,000. **Ref:** Chan Tam Sun (Hong Kong).
   Honduras: Arzu – Gutierez, Costly, Villegas, Cruz – Gilberto, Zelaya, Maradiaga – Norales (Laing 58), Betancourt, Figueroa.
   Northern Ireland: Jennings – J. Nicholl, C. Nicholl, McClelland, Donaghy – O'Neill (Healy 77), McCreery, McIlroy – Armstrong, Hamilton, Whiteside (Brotherston 65).

Zaragoza – 24 June
Honduras 0
Yugoslavia 1 (Patrovic pen 88)
HT: 0-0. **Att:** 25,000. **Ref:** Castro (Chile).
   Honduras: Arzu – Drummond, Villegas, Costly, Bulnes – Zelaya, Gilberto, Maradiaga – Cruz (Laing 65), Betancourt, Figueroa.
   Yugoslavia: Pantelic – Krmpotic, Stojkovic, Zajec, Jovanovic (Halilhodzic 46) – Slijvo, Gudelj, Surjak – Vujovic (Sestic 62), Susic, Petrovic.

Valencia – 25 June
Spain 0
Northern Ireland 1 (Armstrong 47)
HT: 0-0. **Att:** 48,000. **Ref:** Ortiz (Paraguay).
   Spain: Arconada – Camacho, Tendillo, Alesanco, Gordillo – Saura, Alonso, Sanchez – Juanito, Satrustegui (Quini 45), Ufarte (Gallego 77).
   Northern Ireland: Jennings – J. Nicholl, C. Nicholl, McClelland, Donaghy – O'Neill, McCreery, McIlroy (Cassidy 50) – Armstrong, Hamilton, Whiteside (Nelson 73).

	P	W	D	L	F	A	Pts
1. Northern Ireland	3	1	2	0	2	1	4
2. Spain	3	1	1	1	3	3	3
3. Yugoslavia	3	1	1	1	2	2	3
4. Honduras	3	0	2	1	2	3	2

Group Six

Seville – 14 June
Brazil 2 (Socrates 75, Eder 87)
USSR 1 (Bal 34)
HT: 0-1. **Att:** 68,000 **Ref:** Lamo Castillo (Spain).
  Brazil: Waldir Peres – Leandro, Oscar, Luizinho, Junior – Dirceu (Paolo Isidoro 45), Socrates, Falcao – Serginho, Zico, Eder.
  USSR: Dasaev – Sulakvelidze, Chivadze, Baltacha, Demianenko – Shengelia (Andreev 88), Bessonov, Gavrilov (Sousloparov 73), Blokhin – Bal, Daraselia.

Malaga – 15 June
Scotland 5 (Daglish 18, Wark 30, 32, Robertson 74, Archibald 80)
New Zealand 2 (Summer 55, Wooddin 65)
HT: 3-0. **Att:** 35,000. **Ref:** David Socha (USA).
  Scotland: Rough – McGrain, Hansen, Evans, Gray – Souness, Strachan (Narey 84), Wark, Robertson – Dalglish, Brazil (Archibald 54).
  New Zealand: Van Hattum – Elrick, Hill, Malcolmson (Cole 78), Almond (Herbert 66) – Summer, McKay, Cresswell – Boath, Rufer, Wooddin.

Seville – 18 June
Brazil 4 (Zico 33, Oscar 48, Eder 63, Falcao 85)
Scotland 1 (Narey 18)
HT: 1-1. **Att:** 45,000. **Ref:** Siles (Costa Rica).
  Brazil: Waldir Peres – Leandro, Oscar, Luizinho, Junior – Socrates, Falcao, Cerezo – Eder, Zico, Serginho (Paolo Isidoro 81).
  Scotland: Rough – Narey, Miller (McLeish 66), Hansen, Gray – Strachan, Wark, Souness, Hartford (Dalglish 67), Robertson – Archibald.

Malaga – 19 June
USSR 3 (Gavrilov 24, Blokhin 48, Baltacha 69)
New Zealand 0
HT: 1-0. Att: 19,000. Ref: El-Ghoul (Libya).
　USSR: Dasaev – Sulakvelidze, Chivadze, Baltacha, Demianenko – Shengelia, Bessonov, Gavrilov (Rodianov 78) – Bal, Daraselia (Oganesian 45), Blokhin.
　New Zealand: Van Hattem – Dods, Herbert, Elrick, Boath – Cole, Summer, McKay – Cresswell, Rufer, Woodin.

Malaga – 22 June
Scotland 2 (Jordan 15, Souness 86)
USSR 2 Chivadze 59, Shengelia 84)
HT: 1-0. Att: 45,000. Ref: Rainea (Rom).
　Scotland: Rough – Narey, Hansen, Miller, Gray – Strachan (McGrain 70), Souness, Wark, Archibald, Jordan (Brazil 70), Robertson.
　USSR: Daseav – Sulakvelidze, Chivadze, Baltacha, Demianenko – Borovski, Shengelia (Andreev), Bessonov, Gavrilov, Bal, Blokhin.

Seville – 23 June
Brazil 4 (Zico 28, 31, Falcao 55, Serginho 70)
New Zealand 0
HT: 2-0. Att: 43,000. Ref: Matovinovic (Yug).
　Brazil: Waldir Peres – Leandro, Oscar (Edinho 73), Luizinho, Junior – Falcao, Cerezo, Socrates – Zico, Serginho (Paulo Isidoro 73), Eder.
　New Zealand: Van Hattum – Dods, Herbert, Elrick, Boath – Summer, McKay, Cresswell (Cole 77), Almond – Rufer (B. Turner 77), Wooddin.

	P	W	D	L	F	A	Pts
1. Brazil	3	3	0	0	10	2	6
2. USSR	3	1	1	1	6	4	3
3. Scotland	3	1	1	1	8	8	3
4. New Zealand	3	0	0	3	2	12	0

SECOND ROUND

Group A

Barcelona (Nou Camp) – 28 June
Poland 3 (Boniek, 4, 26, 53)
Belgium 0
HT: 2-0. **Att:** 65,000. **Ref:** Siles (Costa Rica).

Poland: Mlynarczyk – Dziuba, Janas, Zmuda, Majewski – Matysik, Buncol, Kupcewicz (Ciolek 82) – Lato, Boniek, Smolarek.

Belgium: Custers – Renquin, Millecamps, Meeuws, Plessers (Baecke 87) – Ceulemans, Van Moer (Van Der Elst 45), Coeck, Vercauteren – Vandenbergh, Czerniatynski.

Barcelona (Nou Camp) – 1 July
Belgium 0
USSR 1 (Oganesian 48)
HT: 0-0. **Att:** 45,000. **Ref:** Vautrot (Fr).

Belgium: Munaron – Renquin, Millecamps, Meeuws, De Schrijver (M. Millecamps 65) – Vandersmissen (Czerniatynski 67), Verheyen, Coeck, Vercauteren – Ceulemans, Vandenbergh.

USSR: Dasaev – Borovski, Chivadze, Baltacha, Demianenko – Bal (Daraselia 87), Oganesian, Bessonov, Gavrilov – Shengelia (Rodianov 89), Blokhin.

Barcelona (Nou Camp) – 4 July
USSR 0
Poland 0
Att: 35,000. **Ref:** Valentine (Scot).

USSR: Dasaev – Sulakvelidze, Chivadze, Borovsky, Demianenko – Baltacha, Gavrilov (Daraselia 78), Bessonov, Oganesian – Shengelia (Andreev 57), Blokhin.

Poland: Mlynarczyk – Dziuba, Zmuda, Janas, Majewski – Lato, Matysik, Buncol – Kupcewicz (Ciolek 51), Boniek, Smolarek.

	P	W	D	L	F	A	Pts
1. Poland	2	1	1	0	3	0	3
2. USSR	2	1	1	0	1	0	3
3. Belgium	2	0	0	2	0	4	0

Group B

Madrid (Bernabeu) – 29 June
England 0
West Germany 0
Att: 70,000. **Ref:** Coelho (Brz).

England: Shilton – Mills, Thompson, Butcher, Sansom – Wilkins, Robson, Rix – Coppell, Francis (Woodcock 77), Mariner.

W. Germany: Schumacher – Kaltz, Kh. Förster, Stielike, B. Förster – Breitner, Briegel, Dremmler, H. Müller (Fischer 73) – Rummenigge, Reinders (Littbarski 62).

Madrid (Bernabeu) – 2 July
West Germany 2 (Littbarski 49, Fischer 75)
Spain 1 (Zamora 81)
HT: 0-0. **Att:** 90,000. **Ref:** Casarin (It).

W. Germany: Schumacher – Kaltz, Kh. Förster, Stielike, Briegel – Dremmler, Breitner, B. Förster – Rummenigge (Reinders 46), Fischer, Littbarski.

Spain: Arconada – Urquiaga, Tendillo, Alesanco, Gordillo – Alonso, Zamora, Camacho – Juanito (Ufarte 46), Santillana, Quini (Saura 65).

Madrid (Bernabeu) – 5 July
Spain 0
England 0
Att: 75,000. **Ref:** Ponnet (Bel).

Spain: Arconada – Urquiaga, Tendillo (Maceda 72) Alesanco, Gordillo – Saura (Uralde 67), Camacho, Alonso, Zamora – Santillana, Satrustegui.

England: Shilton – Mills, Thompson, Butcher, Sansom – Robson, Wilkins, Rix (Brooking 63) – Francis, Mariner, Woodcock (Keegan 63).

	P	W	D	L	F	A	Pts
1. West Germany	2	1	1	0	2	1	3
2. England	2	0	2	0	0	0	2
3. Spain	2	0	1	1	1	2	1

Group C

Barcelona (Sarria) – 29 June
Italy 2 (Tardelli 56, Cabrini 68)
Argentina 1 Passarella 83)
HT: 0-0. **Att:** 43,000. **Ref:** Rainea (Romania).

Italy: Zoff – Gentile, Collovati, Scirea, Cabrini – Tardelli, Antognoni, Oriali, (Marini 75) – Conti, Rossi (Altobelli 81), Graziani.

Argentina: Fillol – Olguin, Galvan, Passarella, Tarantini – Ardiles, Gallego, Kempes (Valencia 58) – Diaz (Calderon 58), Maradona, Bertoni.

Barcelona (Sarria) – 2 July
Argentina 1 (Diaz 89)
Brazil 3 (Zico 11, Serginho 67, Junior 74)
HT: 0-1. **Att:** 45,000. **Ref:** Rubio Vazquez (Mex.).

Argentina: Fillol – Olguin, Galvan, Passarella, Tarantini, Barbas, Ardiles, Kempes (Diaz 45) – Bertoni (Santamaria 63), Maradona, Calderon.

Brazil: Waldir Peres – Leandro (Edevaldo 81), Oscar, Cerezo, Junior – Zico (Batista 84), Luizinho, Socrates, Falcao – Serginho, Eder.

Barcelona (Sarria) – 5 July
Italy 3 (Rossi 5, 25, 74)
Brazil 2 (Socrates 12, Falcao 68)
HT: 2-1. **Att:** 44,000. **Ref:** Klein (Israel).

Italy: Zoff – Gentile, Collovati (Bergomi 33), Scirea, Cabrini – Oriali, Antognoni, Tardelli (Marini 74) – Conti, Rossi, Graziani.

Brazil: Waldir Peres – Leandro, Oscar, Luizinho, Junior – Socrates, Cerezo, Falcao – Zico, Serginho (Paulo Isidoro 68), Eder.

		P	W	D	L	F	A	Pts
1.	Italy	2	2	0	0	5	3	4
2.	Brazil	2	1	0	1	5	4	2
3.	Argentina	2	0	0	2	2	5	0

Group D

Madrid (Calderon) – 28 June
France 1 (Genghini 39)
Austria
HT: 1-0. Att: 37,000. Ref: Palotai (Hungary).
   France: Ettori – Battiston, Tresor, Janvion, Bossis – Giresse, Tigana, Genghini (Girard 85) – Soler, Lacombe (Rocheteau 14), Six.
   Austria: Koncilia – Krauss, Pezzey, Obermayer, Degeorgi (Baumeister 46) – Hintermaier, Hattenberger, Prohaska, Jara (Welzl 46) – Krankl, Schachner.

Madrid (Calderon) – 1 July
Austria 2 (Pezzey 50, Hintermaier 67)
N. Ireland 2 (Hamilton 27, 74)
HT: 0-1. Att: 25,000. Ref: Prokop (EG).
   Austria: Koncilia – Krauss, Pezzey, Obermayer, Pichler – Hagemayr (Welzl 46), Pregesbauer (Hintermaier 46), Prohaska, Baumeister – Schachner, Jurtin.
   N. Ireland: Platt – J. Nicholl, C. Nicholl, McClelland, Nelson – McCreery, M. O'Neill, McIlroy – Armstrong, Whiteside (Brotherston 66), Hamilton.

Madrid (Calderon) – 4 July
France 4 (Giresse 33, 80, Rocheteau 46,67)
N. Ireland 1 (Armstrong 74)
HT: 1-0. Att: 40,000. Ref: Jarguz (Pol).
   France: Ettori – Amoros, Janvion, Tresor, Bossis – Genghini, Giresse, Tigana – Rocheteau (Couriol 82), Platini, Soler (Six 62).
   N. Ireland: Jennings – J. Nicholl, C. Nicholl, McClelland, Donaghy – McCreery (J. O'Neill 84), M. O'Neill, McIlroy – Hamilton, Armstrong, Whiteside.

	P	W	D	L	F	A	Pts
1. France	2	2	0	0	5	1	4
2. Austria	2	0	1	1	2	3	1
3. Northern Ireland	2	0	1	1	3	6	1

Semi Finals

Barcelona (Nou Camp) – 8 July
Italy 2 (Rossi 22 and 73)
Poland 0
HT: 1-0. **Att:** 50,000. **Ref:** Cardellino (Uru).

Italy: Zoff – Bergomi, Collavati, Scirea, Cabrini – Oriali, Antognoni (Marini 29), Tardelli – Conti, Rossi, Graziani (Altobelli 70).

Poland: Mlynarcyzk – Dziuba, Zmuda, Janas, Majewski – Kupcewicz, Buncol, Matysik – Lato, Ciolek (Palasz 46), Smolarek (Kusto 77).

Seville (Sanchez Pizjuan) – 8 July
West Germany 3 (Littbarski 17, Rummenigge 102, Fischer 107)
France 3 (Platini 27 pen, Tresor 92, Giresse 98)
HT: 1-1. **90 min:** 1-1. **Att:** 70,000. **Ref:** Corver (Hol).

West Germany won 5-4 on penalties, after extra-time.
Penalty sequence (France first):
Giresse scores, Kaltaz scores 1-1; Amoros scores, Breitner scores 2-2; Rocheteau scores, Stielike shot saved by Ettori 3-2; Six shot saved by Schumacher, Littbarski scores 3-3; Platini scores, Rummenigge scores 4-4; Bossis shot saved by Schumacher, Hrubesch scores 4-5.

W. Germany: Schumacher – Kaltz, Stielike, Kh. Förster, Briegel (Rummenigge 95) – Dremmler, Breitner, B. Förster, Magath (Hrubesch 72) – Littbarski, Fischer.

France: Ettori – Amoros, Janvion, Tresor, Bossis – Genghini (Battiston 50, Lopez 59), Tigana, Giresse, Platini – Rocheteau, Six.

Third Place Play-off

Alicante – 10 July
France 2 (Girard 12, Couriol 73)
Poland 3 (Szarmach 40, Majewski 45, Kupcewicz 47)
HT: 1-2. **Att:** 30,000. **Ref:** Garrido (Portugal).

France: Castaneda – Amoros, Mahut, Tresor, Janvion (Lopez 64) – Tigana (Six 82), Girard, Larios – Couriol, Soler, Bellone.

Poland: Mlynarczyk – Dziuba, Janas, Zmuda, Majewski – Lato, Kupcewicz, Matysik (Wojcicki 45), Bucol – Boniek, Szarmach.

Final

Madrid (Bernabeu) – 11 July
Italy 3 (Rossi 56, Tardelli 68, Altobelli 80)
West Germany 1 (Breitner 82)
HT: 0-0. **Att:** 90,089. **Ref:** Arnaldo Cesar Coelho (Brz); **linesmen:** Abraham Klein (Is) and Vojtech Christov (Cz).

Italy: Zoff – Gentile, Bergomi, Collovati, Scirea, Cabrini – Tardelli, Oriali – Conti, Rossi, Graziani (Altobelli 7, Causio 88). Subs not used: Dossena, Marini, Bordon. Manager: Enzo Bearzot.

W. Germany: Schumacher – Kaltz, Kh. Förster, B. Förster, Stielike, Briegel – Dremmler (Hrubesch 62), Breitner – Rummenigge (Müller 70), Fischer, Littbarski. Subs not used: Hannes, Magath, Franke. Manager: Jupp Derwall.

APPENDIX IV

The Twenty-four Squads of the 1982 World Cup Finals

Group One

CAMEROON

Goalkeepers
 1 Nkono (Canon)
12 Bell (Africa Sports)
22 Tchobang (Dynamo Douala)

Defenders
 2 Kaham (Quimper)
 7 Mbom (Canon)
 5 Onana (Fédéral Foubam)
11 Toubé (Tonnerre)
 4 Ndjeya (Union Douala)
16 Aoudou (Cannes)
15 Doumbe Lea (Union Douala)
 3 Enoka (Dynamo Douala)

Midfields
 6 Kunde (Canon)
14 Abega (Canon)
17 Kamga (Union Douala)
10 Tokoto (Jacksonville)
19 Enanga (Union Douala)
 8 Mbida (Canon)

Attackers
 9 Milla (Bastia)
13 Bahoken (Cannes)
21 Ebongue (Tonnerre)
18 Nguea (Canon)
20 Eyobo (Dynamo Douala)

ITALY

Goalkeepers
 1 Zoff (Juventus)
12 Bordon (Inter)
22 Galli (Fiorentina)

Defenders
 2 Baresi (Milan AC)
 3 Bergomi (Inter)
 4 Cabrini (Juventus)
 5 Collovti (Milan AC)
 6 Gentile (Juventus)
 7 Scirea (Juventus)
 8 Vierchowod (Fiorentina)

Midfields
 9 Antognoni (Fiorentina)
10 Dossena (Torino)
11 Marini (Inter)
13 Oriali (Inter)
14 Tardelli (Juventus)
17 Massaro (Fiorentina)

Attackers
15 Causio (Udine)
16 Conti (AS Roma)
18 Altobelli (Inter)
19 Graziani (Fiorentina)
20 Rossi (Juventus)
21 Selvaggi (Cagliari)

PERU

Goalkeepers
21 Quiroga (Sporting Cristal)
 1 Ganoza Acasuzo (Universitario)
12 Gonzales (Alianza Lima)

Defenders
 2 Duarte (Alianza Lima)
15 Diaz (Sporting Cristal)
16 Olaechea (Alianza Lima)
14 Gutierrez (Sporting Cristal)
13 Arizaga (Chalaco)
20 Rojas (Canal)

4 Gastulo (Universitario)
3 Salguero (Alianza Lima)
Midfields
8 Cueto (Canal)
9 Uribe (Sporting Cristal)
10 Cubillas (Fort Lauderdale)
5 Leguia (Universitario)
6 Velasquez (Canal)
21 Reyna (Sporting Cristal)
Attackers
19 La Rosa (Canal)
7 Barbadillo (Universidad Leon)
11 Oblitas (Seraing)
18 Malasquez (Municipal)
17 Navarro (Municipal)

POLAND
Goalkeepers
1 Mlynarczyk (Widzew Lodz)
21 Kazimierski (Legia Warsaw)
22 Mowlik (Lech Poznan)
Defenders
5 Janas (Legia Warsaw)
10 Majewski (Legia Warsaw)
9 Zmuda (Widzew Lodz)
4 Dolny (Gornik Zabrze)
7 Jalocha (Wisla Cracov)
6 Skrobowski (Wisla Cracov)
2 Dziuba (KS Lodz)
12 Wojcicki (Slask Wroclaw)
Midfields
20 Boniek (Widzew Lodz)
8 Matysik (Gornik Zabrze)
13 Buncol (Legia Warsaw)
15 Ciolek (Stal Mielec)
3 Kupcewicz (Arka Gdynia)
16 Lato (Lokeren, Belgium)
Attackers
11 Smolarek (Widzew Lodz)
19 Iwan (Wisla Cracov)

18 Kusto (Legia Warsaw)
17 Szarmach (Auxerre, France)
14 Palasz (Gornik Zabrze)

Group Two

ALGERIA
1 Cerbah (RS Kouba)
21 Amara (JE Tizi-Ouzou)
22 Ben-Taala (MA Hussein-Dey)
Defenders
4 Kourichi (Bordeaux)
2 Guendouz (MA Hussein-Dey)
5 Merzekane (MA Hussein-Dey)
3 Kouici (CM Belcourt)
12 Larbes (JE Tizi-Ouzou)
16 Mansouri (Montpellier)
17 Horr (DNC Alger)
Midfields
18 Maroc (Tours)
15 Dahleb (Paris-SG)
6 Ben-Cheikh (MP Alger)
10 Belloumi (GCR Mascara)
8 Fergani (JE Tizi-Ouzou)
13 Yahi (CM Belcourt)
Attackers
20 Bourebbou (Laval)
19 Tlemcani (Reims)
11 Madjer (MA Hussein Dey)
7 Assad (RS Kouba)
14 Zidane (Courtrai)
9 Bensaouala (MP Oran)

WEST GERMANY
Goalkeepers
1 Schumacher (FC Cologne)
22 Immel (Borussia Dortmund)
21 Franke (Eintracht Brunswick)

Defenders
2 Briegel (Kaiserslautern)
5 B. Forster (Stuttgart)
4 K.-H. Forster (Stuttgart)
12 Hannes (Mönchengladbach)
20 Kaltz (Hamburg)
15 Stielike (Real Madrid)
19 Hieronymus (Hamburg)
Midfields
3 Breitner (Bayern Munich)
6 Dremmler (Bayern Munich)
14 Magath (Hamburg)
18 Matthaus (Mönchengladbach)
10 Müller (Stuttgart)
17 Engels (FC Cologne)
Attackers
8 Fischer (FC Cologne)
7 Littbarski (FC Cologne)
9 Hrubesch (Hamburg)
11 Rummenigge (Bayern Munich)
13 Reinders (Werder Bremer)
16 Allofs (Fortuna Düsseldorf)

AUSTRIA
Goalkeepers
1 Koncilia (Austria Vienna)
21 Feurer (Rapid Vienna)
22 Lindenberger (Linz ASK)
Defenders
2 Krauss (Rapid Vienna)
19 Weber (Rapid Vienna)
17 Pregesbauer (Rapid Vienna)
15 Dihanich (Austria Vienna)
3 Obermayer (Austria Vienna)
4 Degeorgi (Admira Wacker)
16 Messlender (Admira Wacker)
5 Pezzey (Eintracht Frankfurt)

Midfields
14 Baumeister (Austria Vienna)
8 Prohaska (Inter Milan)
11 Jara (Grasshopper Zurich)
10 Hintermaier (Nuremberg)
6 Hattenberger (Innsbruck)
12 Pichler (Sturm Graz)
Attackers
7 Schachner (Cesena)
9 Krankl (Rapid Vienna)
20 Welzl (Valence)
18 Jurtin (Sturm Graz)

CHILE
Goalkeepers
22 Osben (Colo-Colo)
1 Wirth (Cobreloa)
12 Cornez (Palestino)
Defenders
18 Galindo (Colo-Colo)
2 Garrido (Colo-Colo)
3 Valenzuela (Université Catholique)
10 Soto (Cobreloa)
5 Figueroa (Colo-Colo)
4 Bigorra (Université du Chili)
19 Escobar (Cobreloa)
17 Rojas (Colo-Colo)
Midfields
16 Rojas (Université Catholique)
20 Neira (Université Catholique)
7 Bonvallet (Université Catholique)
6 Dubo (Palestino)
8 Rivas (Colo-Colo)
Attackers
15 Yanez (San Luis)
13 Caszely (Colo-Colo)

9 Letelier (Cobreloa)
21 Gamboa (Université du
   Chili)
11 Moscoso (Université
   Catholique)

Group Three

ARGENTINA
Goalkeepers
 2 Bailey (Talleres)
 7 Fillol (River Plate)
16 Pumpido (Velez Sarsfield)
Defenders
 8 Galvan (Talleres)
13 Olarticoechea (River Plate)
14 Olguin (Independiente)
15 Passarella (River Plate)
18 Tarantini (River Plate)
19 Trossero (Independiente)
20 Valdano (Real Zaragoza)
22 Van Tuyne (Racing Club)
Midfields
 1 Ardiles (Tottenham)
 3 Barbas (Racing Club)
 9 Gallego (River Plate)
10 Maradona (Boca Juniors)
12 Hernandez (Estudiantes)
Attackers
 4 Bertoni (Fiorentina)
 5 Calderon (Independiente)
 6 Diaz (River Plate)
11 Kempes (River Plate)
17 Santamaria (Newel's Old
   Boys)
21 Valencia (Talleres)

BELGIUM
Goalkeepers
 1 Pfaff (Beveren)
12 Custers (Espanol Barcelona)

22 Munaron (Anderiecht)
Defenders
 2 Gerets (Standard Liège)
 3 Millecamps (Waregem)
 4 Meeuws (Standard Liège)
 5 Renquin (Anderlecht)
14 Baecke (Beveren)
15 De Schrijver (Lokeren)
16 Plessers (Standard Liège)
Midfields
 6 Vercauteren (Anderlecht)
 7 Van Der Eycken (Gênes)
 8 Van Moer (Beveren)
10 Coeck (Anderlecht)
17 Verheyen (Lokeren)
18 Mommens (Lokeren)
19 Millecamps (Waregem)
20 Vandersmissen (Standard
   Liège)
Attackers
 9 Vandenbergh (Lierse)
11 Ceulemans (Bruges)
13 Van Der Elst (West Ham)
21 Czerniatynski (Antwerp)

HUNGARY
Goalkeepers
 1 Meszaros (Sporting
   Lisbonne)
21 Katzirz (Pesci MSC)
22 Kiss (Tatabanyaï)
Defenders
 2 Martos (Waterschei)
 3 Balint (Toulouse)
 4 Toth (Ujpest Dosza)
 6 Garaba (Honved)
13 Rab (Ferencvaros)
19 Varga (Honved)
20 Csuhay (Videoton)
Midfields
 5 Muller (Herc. Alicante)

8 Nyilasi (Ferencvaros)
12 Szentes (Raba Eto)
14 Sallai (Debrecen)
16 Csongradi (Videoton)
17 Csapo (Tatabanyaï)
Attackers
 7 Fazekas (FC Antwerp)
 9 Torocsik (Ujpest Dozsa)
10 Kiss (Vasas)
11 Poloskei (Ferencvaros)
15 Bodonyi (Honved)
18 Kerekes (Bakescaba)

EL SALVADOR
Goalkeepers
 1 Mora (Platense)
19 Fuentes (Santigueno)
Defenders
 2 Castillo (Santigueno)
 3 Cruz (Aguila)
 4 Ortiz (Fas)
 5 Fagoga (Atletico Marte)
12 Osorto (Santigueno)
18 Arevalo (Chalatenango)
Midfields
 6 Ventura (Santigueno)
 8 Portillo (Atletico Marte)
10 Huezo Montoya (Atletico
   Marte)
15 Rodriguez (Bayer
   Uergingen)
20 Munguia (Fas)
Attackers
 7 Aquino (Alianza)
 9 Hernandez (Santigueno)
11 Barillas (Fas)
13 Martinez (Independiente)
14 Zapata (Aguila)
16 Valladares (Alianza)
17 Ragazzone (Atletico Marte)

Group Four

ENGLAND
Goalkeepers
 1 Clemence (Tottenham)
13 Corrigan (Manchester City)
22 Shilton (Nottingham)
Defenders
 2 Anderson (Nottingham)
 4 Butcher (Ipswich)
 6 Foster (Brighton)
12 Mills (Ipswich)
14 Neal (Liverpool)
17 Sansom (Arsenal)
18 Thompson (Liverpool)
Midfields
 3 Brooking (West Ham)
 9 Hoddle (Tottenham)
10 McDermott (Liverpool)
16 Robson (Manchester
   United)
19 Wilkins (Manchester
   United)
Attackers
 5 Coppell (Manchester
   United)
 7 Keegan (Southampton)
 8 Francis (Manchester City)
11 Mariner (Ipswich)
15 Rix (Arsenal)
20 Withe (Aston Villa)
21 Woodcock (Cologne)

FRANCE
Goalkeepers
 1 Baratelli (Paris-SG)
21 Castaneda (Saint-Etienne)
22 Ettori (Monaco)
Defenders
 2 Amoros (Monaco)
 3 Battiston (Saint-Etienne)

4 Bossis (Nantes)
 5 Janvion (Saint-Etienne)
 6 Lopez (Saint-Etienne)
 7 Mahut (Metz)
 8 Tresor (Bordeaux)
Midfields
 9 Genghini (Sochaux)
10 Platini (Saint-Etienne)
11 Girard (Bordeaux)
12 Giresse (Bordeaux)
13 Larios (Saint-Etienne)
14 Tigana (Bordeaux)
Attackers
15 Bellone (Monaco)
16 Couriol (Monaco)
17 Lacombe (Bordeaux)
18 Rocheteau (Paris-SG)
19 Six (Stuttgart)
20 Soler (Bordeaux)

KUWAIT
Goalkeepers
 1 Al-Tarabulsi (Kuwait)
21 Ahbmad (Kazma)
22 Bahman (Qadisiyya)
Defenders
 2 Mubarrak (Tadamon)
 3 Mubarak (Salimiyya)
 4 Al-Qabendi (Kazma)
 5 Al-Mubartak (Kuwait)
13 Marzouq Al-Issa (Tadamon)
14 Ma'Yoof (Kazma)
15 Al-Hashash (Al-Arabi)
17 Al-Shemmari (Kazma)
Midfields
18 Ahmed Karan (Al-Arabi)
12 Al-Suwaayed (Kazma)
 8 Al-Buloushi (Al-Arabi)
11 Al-Ghanem (Kazma)
 6 Al-Houti (Kuwait)

Attackers
16 Al-Dakhil (Qadisiyya)
10 Aziz Al-Anbari (Kuwait)
20 Aziz (Khitan)
 9 Yacoub Sultan (Qadisiyya)
 7 Kameel Marzouq
   (Tadamon)
19 Rehayyem (Khitan)

CZECHOSLOVAKIA
Goalkeepers
 1 Seman (Lokomotiv Kosice)
21 Hruska (Bohemians Prague)
22 Stromsik (Dukla Prague)
Defenders
 2 Jakubec (Bohemians
   Prague)
 3 Fiala (Dukla Prague)
 4 Jurkemik (Inter Bratislava)
 5 Barmos (Inter Bratislava)
 6 Vojacek (Banik Ostrava)
12 Bicovsky (Bohemians
   Prague)
14 Radimac (Banik Ostrava)
15 Kukucka (Plastika Nitra)
Midfields
 7 Kozak (Dukla Prague)
 8 Panenka (Rapid Vienne)
13 Berger (Sparta Prague)
17 Stambacher (Dukla Prague)
Attackers
 9 Vizek (Dukla Prague)
10 Kriz (Dukla Prague)
11 Nehoda (Dukla Prague)
16 Chaloupka (Bohemians
   Prague)
18 Janecka (Zbrojovka Brno)
19 Masny (Slovan Bratislava)
20 Petrzela (Slavia Prague)

Group Five

SPAIN
Goalkeepers
1 Arconada (Real Sociedad)
21 Urruti (Barcelona)
22 Angel (Real Madrid)
Defenders
2 Camacho (Real Madrid)
3 Gordillo (Bétis Séville)
5 Tendillo (Valencia)
6 Alesanco (Barcelona)
12 Urquiaga (Atletico Bilbao)
13 Enrique Jimenez (Gijon)
14 Maceda (Gijon)
Midfields
4 Alonso (Real Sociedad)
8 Joaquin (Gijon)
10 Zamora (Real Sociedad)
15 Saura (Valencia)
16 Vicente Sanchez (Barcelona)
17 Gallego (Real Madrid)
Attackers
7 Gomez dit Juanito (Real Madrid)
9 Satrustegui (Real Sociedad)
18 Uralde (Real Sociedad)
19 Alonso dit Santillana (Real Madrid)
20 Castro dit Quini (Barcelona)
11 Ufarte (Real Sociedad)

HONDURAS
Goalkeepers
2 Ordonnez (Motaga)
7 Arzu (Real Espana)
Defenders
4 Nunez (Marathon)
9 Bulnes (Universidad)
10 Cruz (Atletico Morazan)
12 Gutierez (Broncos)
15 Costly (Real Espana)
17 Zelaya (Motaga)
20 Yearwood (Real Valladolid)
Midfields
3 Toledo (Marathon)
1 Chavez (Motaga)
6 Figueroa (Voda)
11 Murillo (Universidad)
13 Villegas (Real Espana)
Attackers
5 Laing (Platense)
8 Guerrero (Motaga)
14 Drummond (Platense)
16 Norales (Olimpia)
18 Betancourt (Libre)
19 Bailey (Marathon)
21 Steward (Real Espana)
22 Caballero (Real Espana)

NORTHERN IRELAND
Goalkeepers
1 Jennings (Asenal)
17 Platt (Middlesborough)
22 Dunlop (Linfield)
Defenders
2 Nicholl (Toronto)
3 Donaghy (Luton)
5 Nicholl (Southampton)
6 J.P. O'Neill (Leicester City)
12 McClelland (Glasgow Rangers)
13 Nelson (Brighton)
Midfields
4 McCreery (Tulsa)
8 H.M.M. O'Neill (Norwich City)
10 McIlroy (Stoke)
14 Cassidy (Burnley)
15 Finney (Cambridge)
19 Healy (Coleraine)
20 Clearly (Glentoran)

Attackers
7 Brotherston (Blackburn)
9 Armstrong (Watford)
11 Hamilton (Burnley)
16 Whiteside (Manchester United)
18 Jameson (Glentoran)
21 Campbell (Bradford)

YUGOSLAVIA
Goalkeepers
1 Pantelic (Bordeaux)
12 Pudar (Hajduk Split)
22 Svilar (Antwerp)
Defenders
4 Zajec (Dynamo Zagreb)
5 Stojkovic (Partizan)
6 Krmpotic (Red Star)
9 Vujovic (Hajduk Split)
14 Jovanovic (Buducnost)
15 Hrstic (Rijeka)
Midfields
2 Jerolinov (Rijeka)
3 Gudelj (Hajduk Split)
8 Slijvo (Nice)
10 Zikovic (Partizan)
16 Sestic (Red Star)
Attackers
7 Petrovic (Red Star)
17 Jerkovic (FC Zurich)
18 Deveric (Dynamo Zagreb)
11 Vujovic (Hajduk Split)
13 Susic (Sarajevo)
19 Halilhodzic (Nantes)
20 Surjak (Paris-SG)
21 Pasic (Sarajevo)

Group Six

BRAZIL
Goalkeepers
1 Peres (Sao Paulo)
12 Sergio (Botafogo)
22 Carlos (Ponte Preta)
Defenders
2 Leandro (Flamengo)
3 Oscar (Sao Paulo)
4 Luizinho (Atletico Mineiro)
6 Junior (Flamengo)
13 Edevaldo (Fluminense)
14 Juninho (Ponte Preta)
16 Edinho (Fluminense)
17 Pedrinho (Palmeriras)
Midfields
5 Cerezo (Atletico Mineiro)
8 Socrates (Corinthians)
10 Zico (Flamengo)
15 Falcao (AS Rome)
18 Batista (Porto Alegre)
19 Renato (Sao Paulo)
Attackers
7 Isidoro (Porto Alegre)
9 Serginho (Sao Paulo)
11 Eder (Atletico Mineiro)
20 Careca (Guarani)
21 Dirceu (Atletico Madrid)

SCOTLAND
Goalkeepers
1 Rough (Partick Thistle)
12 Wood (Arsenal)
22 Leighton (Aberdeen)
Defenders
2 McGrain (Celtic Glasgow)
3 Gray (Leeds)
5 Hansen (Liverpool)
6 Miller (Aberdeen)
13 McLeish (Aberdeen)

14 Narey (Dundee United)
17 Evans (Aston Villa)
21 Burley (Ipswich)
Midfields
  4 Souness (Liverpool)
  7 Strachan (Aberdeen)
10 Wark (Ipswich)
16 Hartford (Manchester City)
20 Provan (Celtic Glasgow)
Attackers
  8 Dalglish (Liverpool)
  9 Brazil (Ipswich)
11 Robertson (Nottingham
    Forest)
15 Jordan (Milan AC)
18 Archibald (Tottenham)
19 Sturrock (Dundee)

NEW ZEALAND
Goalkeepers
  1 Wilson (Preston United)
21 Pickering (Miramar)
22 Van Hattum (Manurewa)
Defenders
  2 Dods (Adelaide)
  3 Herbert (Mt Wellington)
  5 Bright (Manurewa)
  6 Almond (Invercargill)
11 Malcolmson (Kenwood)
14 Elrick (North Shore)
15 Hill (Gisborne)
16 Adams (Mt Wellington)
Midfields
  4 Turner (Gisborne)
  8 Cole (North Shore)
10 Summer (West Adelaide)
12 McKay (Gisborne)
13 Cresswell (Gisborne)

17 Boath (West Adelaide)
18 Simonsen (Manuwera)
19 McClure (Mt Wellington)
Attackers
  7 Rufer (Miramar)
  9 Wooddin (South
    Melbourne)
20 Turner (Gisborne)

USSR
Goalkeepers
  1 Dasaev (S. Moscow)
21 Tchanov (Dynamo Kiev)
22 Vr. Tchanov (T. Moscow)
Defenders
  2 Sulakvelidze (Dynamo
    Tbilisi)
  3 Chivadze (D. Tbilisi)
  4 Khidiatouline (CSKA
    Moscow)
  5 Baltacha (D. Kiev)
  6 Demianenko (D. Kiev)
14 Borovski (D. Tbilisi)
18 Sousolparov (T. Moscow)
20 Romantsev (S. Moscow)
Midfields
  8 Bessonov (Dynamo Kiev)
  9 Gavrilov (S. Moscow)
10 Oganesian (Ararat Erevan)
12 Bal (Dynamo Kiev)
13 Daraselia (D. Tbilisi)
17 Burjak (Dynamo Kiev)
Attackers
  7 Chenguelia (D. Tbilisi)
11 Blokhin (Dynamo Kiev)
15 Andreev (SKA Rostov)
16 Rodianov (S. Moscow)
19 Evtouchenko (D. Kiev)

APPENDIX V

Leading Goalscorers During World Cup Finals 1982

		Goals
Rossi	Italy	6
Rummenigge	West Germany	5
Zico	Brazil	4
Boniek	Poland	4
L. Kiss	Hungary	3
Armstrong	Northern Ireland	3
Falcao	Brazil	3
Giresse	France	3
Panenka	Czechoslovakia	2
Assad	Algeria	2
Wark	Scotland	2
Nyilasi	Hungary	2
Fazekas	Hungary	2
Poloskei	Hungary	2
Hamilton	Northern Ireland	2
Rocheteau	France	2
Schachner	Austria	2
Francis	England	2
Robson	England	2
Passarella	Argentina	2
Bertoni	Argentina	2
Maradona	Argentina	2

England's Results during Ron Greenwood's Management 1977–82

*denotes captain and small figures are goals scored   †one of England's goals was an own-goal by Czechoslovakia

Versus	Result	1	2	3	4	5	6
1977–78							
Switzerland	0-0	Clemence	Neal	Cherry	McDermott	Watson	Hughes, E.*
Luxembourg	2-0	Clemence	Cherry	Hughes, E.*	Watson	Kennedy, R.[1]	Callaghan
Italy	2-0	Clemence	Neal	Cherry	Wilkins, R.	Watson	Hughes, E.*
West Germany	1-2	Clemence	Neal	Mills, M.	Wilkins, R.	Watson	Hughes, E.*
Brazil	1-1	Corrigan	Mills, M.	Cherry	Greenhoff, B.	Watson	Currie
Wales	3-1	Shilton	Mills, M.*	Cherry	Greenhoff, B.	Watson	Wilkins
N. Ireland	1-0	Clemence	Neal	Mills, M.	Greenhoff, B.	Watson	Hughes, E.*
Scotland	1-0	Clemence	Neal	Mills, M.	Wilkins	Watson	Hughes, E.*
Hungary	4-1	Shilton	Neal[1]	Mills, M.	Wilkins	Watson	Hughes, E.*
1978-79							
Denmark	4-3	Clemence	Neal[1]	Mills, M.	Wilkins, R.	Watson	Hughes, E.*
Rep. of Ireland	1-1	Clemence	Neal	Mills, M.	Wilkins, R.	Watson	Hughes, E.*
Czechoslovakia	1-0	Shilton	Anderson	Cherry	Thompson, P.	Watson	Wilkins
N. Ireland	4-0	Clemence	Neal	Mills, M.	Currie	Watson[1]	Hughes, E.*
N. Ireland	2-0	Clemence	Neal	Mills, M.*	Thompson, P.	Watson[1]	Currie
Wales	0-0	Corrigan	Cherry	Sansom	Currie	Watson	Hughes, E.*
Scotland	3-1	Clemence	Neal	Mills, M.	Thompson, P.	Watson	Wilkins
Bulgaria	3-0	Clemence	Neal	Mills, M.	Thompson, P.	Watson[1]	Wilkins
Sweden	0-0	Shilton	Anderson	Cherry	McDermott	Watson	Hughes, E.*
Austria	3-4	Shilton	Neal	Mills, M.	Thompson, P.	Watson	Wilkins[1]
1979-80							
Denmark	1-0	Clemence	Neal	Mills, M.	Thompson, P.	Watson	Wilkins
N. Ireland	5-1	Shilton	Neal	Mills, M.	Thompson, P.	Watson	Wilkins
Bulgaria	2-0	Clemence	Anderson	Sansom	Thompson, P.*	Watson[1]	Wilkins
Rep. of Ireland	2-0	Clemence	Cherry	Sansom	Thompson, P.	Watson	Robson
Spain	2-0	Shilton	Neal	Mills, M.	Thompson, P.	Watson	Wilkins
Argentina	3-1	Clemence	Neal	Sansom	Thompson, P.	Watson	Wilkins
Wales	1-4	Clemence	Neal	Cherry	Thompson, P.*	Lloyd	Kennedy, R.
N. Ireland	1-1	Corrigan	Cherry	Sansom	Brooking	Watson	Hughes*
Scotland	2-0	Clemence	Cherry	Sansom	Thompson, P.*	Watson	Wilkins
Australia	2-1	Corrigan	Cherry*	Lampard	Talbot	Osman	Butcher
Belgium	1-1	Clemence	Neal	Sansom	Thompson, P.	Watson	Wilkins[1]
Italy	0-1	Shilton	Neal	Sansom	Thompson, P.	Watson	Wilkins
Spain	2-1	Clemence	Anderson	Mills, M.	Thompson, P.	Watson	Wilkins

7	8	9	10	11	Substitutes
Keegan	Channon	Francis, T.	Kennedy, R.	Callaghan	Hill, G.(8) Wilkins, R.(11)
McDermott	Wilkins	Mariner[1]	Francis, T.	Hill, G.	Whymark(7) Beattie(4);
Keegan[1]	Coppell	Latchford, R.	Brooking[1]	Barnes	Pearson, S.(9) Francis, T.(7)
Keegan	Coppell	Pearson, S.[1]	Brooking	Barnes	Francis, T.(7)
Keegan*[1]	Coppell	Latchford, R.	Francis, T.	Barnes	
Coppell	Francis, T.	Latchford, R.[1]	Brooking	Barnes[1]	Currie(3)[1] Mariner(9)
Coppell	Wilkins	Pearson, S.	Currie	Woodcock	
Coppell[1]	Currie	Mariner	Francis, T.	Barnes	Greenhoff, B.(6) Brooking(9)
Keegan	Coppell	Francis, T.[1]	Brooking	Barnes[1]	Greenhoff, B.(5) Currie(8)
Keegan[2]	Coppell	Latchford, R.[1]	Brooking	Barnes	
Keegan	Coppell	Latchford, R.[1]	Brooking	Barnes	Thompson, P.(5) Woodcock(11)
Keegan*	Coppell[1]	Woodcock	Currie	Barnes	Latchford, R.(9)
Keegan[1]	Coppell	Latchford, R.[2]	Brooking	Barnes	
Coppell[1]	Wilkins	Latchford, R.	McDermott	Barnes	
Keegan	Wilkins	Latchford, R.	McDermott	Cunningham	Coppell(9) Brooking(4)
Keegan*[1]	Coppell[1]	Latchford, R.	Brooking	Barnes[1]	
Keegan*[1]	Coppell	Latchford, R.	Brooking	Barnes[1]	Francis, T.(9) Woodcock(11)
Keegan	Francis, T.	Woodcock	Currie	Cunningham	Wilkins, R.(4) Thompson, P.(5) Brooking(10)
Keegan*[1]	Coppell[1]	Latchford, R.	Brooking	Barnes	Clemence(1) Francis, T.(9) Cunningham(11)
Keegan*[1]	Coppell	McDermott	Brooking	Barnes	
Keegan*	Coppell	Francis[2]	Brooking	Woodcock[2]	McDermott(10)
Reeves	Hoddle[1]	Francis	Kennedy, R.	Woodcock	
Keegan*[2]	McDermott	Johnson	Woodcock	Cunningham	Coppell(9)
Keegan*	Coppell	Francis[1]	Kennedy, R.	Woodcock[1]	Hughes(2) Cunningham(9)
Keegan*[1]	Coppell	Johnson[2]	Woodcock	Kennedy, R.	Cherry(2) Birtles(9)
Coppell	Hoddle	Mariner[1]	Brooking	Barnes	Sansom(2) Wilkins(5)
McDermott	Wilkins	Johnson[1]	Reeves	Devonshire	Mariner(10)
Coppell[1]	McDermott	Johnson	Mariner	Brooking[1]	Hughes(10)
Robson	Hoddle[1]	Mariner[1]	Sunderland	Armstrong	Greenhoff(7) Ward(10) Devonshire(11)
Keegan*	Coppell	Johnson	Brooking	Woodcock	McDermott(8) Kennedy, R.(9)
Keegan*	Coppell	Birtles	Kennedy, R.	Woodcock	Mariner(9)
Keegan*	Hoddle	McDermott	Brooking[1]	Woodcock[1]	Cherry(2) Mariner(8)

Versus	Result	1	2	3	4	5	6
1980–1							
Norway	4-0	Shilton	Anderson	Sansom	Thompson*	Watson	Robson
Romania	1-2	Clemence	Neal	Sansom	Thompson*	Watson	Robson
Switzerland	2-1	Shilton	Neal	Sansom	Robson	Watson	Mills*
Spain	1-2	Clemence	Neal	Sansom	Robson	Osman	Butcher
Romania	0-0	Shilton	Anderson	Sansom	Robson	Watson*	Osman
Brazil	0-1	Clemence*	Neal	Sansom	Robson	Martin	Wilkins
Wales	0-0	Corrigan	Anderson	Sansom	Robson	Watson*	Wilkins
Scotland	0-1	Corrigan	Anderson	Sansom	Wilkins	Watson*	Robson
Switzerland	1-2	Clemence	Mills	Sansom	Wilkins	Watson	Osman
Hungary	3-1	Clemence	Neal	Mills	Thompson	Watson	Robson
1981–2							
Norway	1-2	Clemence	Neal	Mills	Thompson	Osman	Robson[1]
Hungary	1-0	Shilton	Neal	Mills	Thompson	Martin	Robson
N. Ireland	4-0	Clemence	Anderson	Sansom	Wilkins[1]	Watson	Foster
Wales	1-0	Corrigan	Neal	Sansom	Thompson*	Butcher	Robson
Holland	2-0	Shilton*	Neal	Sansom	Thompson	Foster	Robson
Scotland	1-0	Shilton	Mills	Sansom	Thompson	Butcher	Robson
Iceland	1-1	Corrigan	Anderson	Neal*	Watson	Osman	McDermott
Finland	4-1	Clemence	Mills	Sansom	Thompson	Martin	Robson[2]
France	3-1	Shilton	Mills*	Sansom	Thompson	Butcher	Robson[2]
Czechoslovakia	2-0+	Shilton	Mills*	Sansom	Thompson	Butcher	Robson
Kuwait	1-0	Shilton	Neal	Mills*	Thompson	Foster	Hoddle
West Germany	0-0	Shilton	Mills*	Sansom	Thompson	Butcher	Robson
Spain	0-0	Shilton	Mills*	Sansom	Thompson	Butcher	Robson